Pro Django

Second Edition

Marty Alchin

Apress®

Pro Django

ISBN-13 (pbk): 978-1-4302-5809-4

ISBN-13 (electronic): 978-1-4302-5810-0

President and Publisher: Paul Manning
Lead Editor: Michelle Lowman
Development Editor: Tom Welsh
Technical Reviewers: Justin Abrahms, Gavin McQuillan
Editorial Board: Steve Anglin, Mark Beckner, Ewan Buckingham, Gary Cornell, Louise Corrigan, Morgan Ertel, Jonathan Gennick, Jonathan Hassell, Robert Hutchinson, Michelle Lowman, James Markham, Matthew Moodie, Jeff Olson, Jeffrey Pepper, Douglas Pundick, Ben Renow-Clarke, Dominic Shakeshaft, Gwenan Spearing, Matt Wade, Tom Welsh
Coordinating Editor: Anamika Panchoo
Copy Editor: Kim Burton-Weismann
Compositor: SPi Global
Indexer: SPi Global
Artist: SPi Global
Cover Designer: Anna Ishchenko

Distributed to the book trade worldwide by Springer Science+Business Media New York, 233 Spring Street, 6th Floor, New York, NY 10013. Phone 1-800-SPRINGER, fax (201) 348-4505, e-mail orders-ny@springer-sbm.com, or visit www.springeronline.com. Apress Media, LLC is a California LLC and the sole member (owner) is Springer Science + Business Media Finance Inc (SSBM Finance Inc). SSBM Finance Inc is a Delaware corporation.

For information on translations, please e-mail rights@apress.com, or visit www.apress.com.

Apress and friends of ED books may be purchased in bulk for academic, corporate, or promotional use. eBook versions and licenses are also available for most titles. For more information, reference our Special Bulk Sales–eBook Licensing web page at www.apress.com/bulk-sales.

Any source code or other supplementary materials referenced by the author in this text is available to readers at www.apress.com. For detailed information about how to locate your book's source code, go to www.apress.com/source-code/.

Dedicated to the memory and legacy of my friend and mentor

Malcolm Tredinnick, 1970–2013

Contents at a Glance

Contents

About the Author

Marty Alchin has been working with the Web for 18 years, since Prodigy first launched its own browser. A veteran of the browser wars, he found a comfortable home on the server side of things, working with a number of languages and tools before finding Django in 2006. Since then, he's released several Django applications and a significant improvement to Django's own file storage.

By day, he works as a senior software engineer with Walt Disney Animation Studios, and after that, he codes for fun and community. His blog can be found at `http://martyalchin.com/` and he has profiles on many other services under the name Gulopine. In particular, his code can be found on GitHub and his random thoughts are on Twitter. He also accepts tips for his open source work at `https://gittip.com/gulopine`.

Lately, he's been working to keep some of the complexity of OAuth out your hair with `https://foauth.org/`. With over 60 different services supported, it's a convenient way to access your own data at your favorite services.

About the Technical Reviewers

Justin Abrahms is an engineer living in Portland, OR, who enjoys rock climbing, clean code and other assorted topics. You may reach him at justin@abrah.ms for any inquiries.

Gavin McQuillan is a longtime Python enthusiast, specializing in building infrastructure for automating myriad services, distributed systems, and scaling and securing web applications. He's shipped Python code for a variety of organizations, including Google, Urban Airship, and Glider. Gavin also enjoys bicycling, rock climbing, and beekeeping with his family in Portland, OR.

Acknowledgments

I can't imagine anyone taking on a project like this alone. In the six years since I first considered putting my thoughts on paper, no one has been more supportive than my beautiful wife, Angel. Without her, I'd be lost and confused, mumbling incoherently about declarative metaclass implementations. She didn't even flinch when I considered moving us from Michigan to California to work for Disney. There are no words to express how much help she's been throughout this process. I'd also like to thank all my tech reviewers: Jacob Kaplan-Moss, George Vilches, Justin Abrahms and Gavin McQuillan. I've had four tech reviewers in just two editions of a single book, and their feedback and advice has been invaluable. I stake the quality of all the code in this book on the quality of their reviews, and I've had no qualms putting my success in their capable hands.

Most of all, I'd like to thank the Django community for their unending support over the years. Django itself originated at the *Lawrence Journal-World*, but once it was released to the world, thousands have stepped up and helped mold it into something remarkably better. It's because of people like you that I decided to take on this challenge, in hopes of giving back in some small way to the community that's given me so much already.

I'd like to call out one community member in particular, as one of my earliest mentors and greatest friends. Malcolm Tredinnick is responsible for more of the code used in this book than anyone else, and I owe my understanding of it to his patience and never-ending willingness to teach everyone who asked for his help. I can only hope to someday be the kind of man he was every day.

Preface

Programming has always been equal parts art and science. It's easy to see the science in teaching computers how to do things, but once that's out of the way, we often try to embrace the artistic side. We spend our first few years learning to make code functional and the rest of our careers trying to make it beautiful.

Django started its life in much the same way, serving the day-to-day needs of a local news organization. In the years since its first public release, Django itself has grown more elegant and has helped its adopters to write more elegant code for their own applications.

This focus on beauty isn't unique to Django. Most Python applications strive for a notion of being "Pythonic"—an unwritten ideal that embodies the nature and spirit of the Python language itself. Having a vague goal like that may seem problematic; after all, how do you know when you've succeeded? Ironically, that's the point: there is no finish line. There's not even a measuring stick to tell you how close you are to achieving your goal.

The true goal is the journey itself, the lessons learned along the way, the discoveries that open your eyes to new ideas. Python includes a number of tools that make this process quite interesting, especially for those programmers coming from other languages. Django builds on that toolset, adding its own techniques for easing the burden on other programmers, making it easy to produce more beautiful code all around.

I first got started with Django shortly after it completed its "magic removal" phase, which was a long process of making the framework more Pythonic overall. I was new to Python at the time, and reading about the process and the ideals that encouraged it caused me to dig deeper into what made Django work. I was fascinated by the richness of the toolset at my disposal and quickly began my own journey of discovery.

What fascinated me most was how few people knew about some of the tricks that can be used to encourage Pythonic code for programmers using the framework. Every time I showed a new trick to someone, I joked that I could write a book about what I've learned so far. After several months of doing so—and several people encouraging me to drop the joke and do it for real—I finally took the plunge and contacted Apress. A second edition has been a natural step, following the progression of Django in the four and a half years since the first edition was published.

I'm not interested in making a fortune with this book. My goal has always been to help more people understand the many tools available with Python and Django, in hopes that they too can have enriching journeys of their own. I hope this book will help bring Django to new people and new places, where it might have been previously considered inappropriate.

Those of us working with Django are often called Djangonauts with good reason. The "-naut" suffix has been used historically to represent sailors and is the same concept as in the word "nautical." More generally, it often refers to those who sail into the unknown, such as astronauts and cosmonauts. It represents explorers and adventurers, those people brave enough to challenge what they knew before and dare to discover new things and new places.

I am a Djangonaut. What follows is my journey thus far.

Introduction

Pro Django represents seven years of accumulated knowledge in Python and Django, designed to educate readers who are already familiar with both topics and would like to take them further than they had previously done. You will learn a wide range of advanced techniques available in both Python and Django, along with tips on how to use them to achieve advanced functionality.

This book is designed to be both a narrative to be read from start to finish and a general reference to be searched for specific information. Since you may not know what to look for or where to find it yet, feel free to read through the book first, then keep it handy for refreshing your memory as necessary.

What This Book Is Not

There are plenty of resources available for learning Python and Django, so this book does not strive to teach the basics. For readers new to Python, I highly recommend *Dive Into Python 3* by Mark Pilgrim (Apress, 2009). For learning Django, I'd recommend *The Definitive Guide to Django: Web Development Done Right* by Adrian Holovaty and Jacob Kaplan-Moss (Second Edition, Apress, 2009). Additionally, *Practical Django Projects* by James Bennett (Second Edition, Apress, 2009) is an excellent resource for general application development.

Who This Book Is For

Because *Pro Django* doesn't dwell on introductory details, readers will be expected to have experience with both Python and Django. If you're new to either subject, please consider one of the books mentioned in the previous section before trying to tackle this book.

Even if you've only experimented on your own without launching a full site yet, a basic familiarity should be sufficient. You don't need to be an expert to start reading *Pro Django*, but you might be by the time you finish.

Interpreting Code Samples

Pro Django uses a simple format, interleaving explanations of Python's and Django's available features with code that demonstrates their use in the real world. There are two types of code samples used, which differ in how they should be executed.

Python's interactive interpreter is a great way to test out small pieces of code and see how it works in a variety of situations. Lines of code intended for use in that environment will always be prefixed with three characters: three greater-than signs (>>>) or three periods (. . .). Lines with greater-than signs are the outermost block of code, while the period-prefixed lines are indented at least one level. The three initial characters are also followed by a space. These first four characters are not typed into the interactive interpreter directly; they simply mimic what the interpreter itself looks like by reproducing its output.

A line started with three periods but containing no other text indicates that you should simply press Enter on a blank line in the interpreter. This completes any open code blocks, bringing you back to the >>> prompt. Any lines that don't begin with either >>> or . . . represent the output of the code or the result of the previous expression.

```
>>> import django
>>> django.get_version()
'1.5.1'
```

The first line of an interactive example will always begin with >>>; everything else is code that should be written in a file and executed as part of a running Django application. The surrounding text will indicate what file the code should be placed in and how it will execute.

Prerequisites

Pro Django is written for Django 1.5, which was released on February 26, 2013. That release or a more recent clone of the Django code repository is required for the code samples to work properly. Since Django in turn relies on Python, these examples also assume a working Python environment of version 2.7 or higher. Most of the code examples are written with Python 3.3 in mind, but there are capability notes available where older versions diverge from the examples shown.

CHAPTER 1

■ ■ ■

Understanding Django

Code alone isn't enough. Sure, it's what the computer runs, but code has to come from somewhere. A programmer has to sit down and decide what features to include, how they should be implemented, what other software to utilize, and how to provide hooks for future enhancements to be added. It's easy to skip straight to code, ignoring the cognitive process that produces it, but great programmers always have reasons for the decisions they make.

With a framework, like Django, many such decisions have already been made, and the tools provided are shaped by these decisions, and by the programmers who made them. By adopting these philosophies in your own code, not only will you be consistent with Django and other applications, but you may even be amazed at what you're able to accomplish.

Beneath even the simplest code is the thought process that went into its creation. Decisions were made about what it should do and how it should do it. This thought process is a step often overlooked in books and manuals, leading to an army of technicians slaving away, writing code that manages to accomplish the task at hand but without a vision for its future.

While the rest of this book will explain in detail the many basic building blocks Django provides for even the most complicated of projects, this chapter will focus on even more fundamental aspects of the framework. For those readers coming from other backgrounds, the ideas presented in this chapter may seem considerably foreign, but that doesn't make them any less important. All programmers working with Python and Django would do well to have a solid understanding of the reasons Django works the way it does, and how those principles can be applied to other projects.

You may want to read this chapter more than once, and perhaps refer to it often as you work with Django. Many of the topics are common knowledge in the Django community, so reading this chapter carefully is essential if you plan to interact with other programmers.

Philosophy

Django relies heavily on philosophy, both in how its code is written and how decisions are made about what goes into the framework. This isn't unique in programming, but it's something newcomers often have trouble with. It is essential to maintain both consistency and quality, and having a set of common principles to refer to when making decisions helps maintain both. Since these concepts are also important to individual applications, and even collections of applications, a firm grasp on these philosophies will yield similar benefits.

Perhaps the best-known and most-quoted passage of Python philosophy comes from Tim Peters, a longtime Python guru who wrote down many of the principles that guide Python's own development process. The 19 lines he came up with, called the Zen of Python, have been so influential to Python programmers over time that they are immortalized as Python Enhancement Proposal (PEP) 20[1] and in the Python distribution itself, as an "Easter egg" module called this.

---

[1]http://prodjango.com/pep-20/

```
>>> import this
Beautiful is better than ugly.
Explicit is better than implicit.
Simple is better than complex.
Complex is better than complicated.
Flat is better than nested.
Sparse is better than dense.
Readability counts.
Special cases aren't special enough to break the rules.
Although practicality beats purity.
Errors should never pass silently.
Unless explicitly silenced.
In the face of ambiguity, refuse the temptation to guess.
There should be one-- and preferably only one --obvious way to do it.
Although that way may not be obvious at first unless you're Dutch.
Now is better than never.
Although never is often better than *right* now.
If the implementation is hard to explain, it's a bad idea.
If the implementation is easy to explain, it may be a good idea.
Namespaces are one honking great idea -- let's do more of those!
```

While some of this is clearly intended for humor, it sums up common Python attitudes pretty well. The remainder of this chapter highlights some specific principles that are often cited within the Django community, but all professional Python programmers should keep this text in mind and reference it often.

One important thing to keep in mind is that many of the lines in the Zen of Python are subjective. For example, "beautiful" may be better than "ugly," but definitions of "beautiful" are plentiful and can vary as much as the people who provide them. Similarly, consider notions of simplicity and complexity, practicality and purity; each developer will have a different opinion on which side of the line a particular piece of code should be placed.

Django's Interpretation of the MVC Pattern

One of the most common application architectures—adopted by hobbyists and corporations alike—is the Model-View-Controller (MVC) pattern, as it provides clean separation of tasks and responsibilities between the prominent aspects of an application. Django only loosely follows this approach. A proper discussion should kick off with a quick overview of its components.

- The model is generally responsible for managing data and core business logic.

- The view displays that data to the user.

The controller accepts user input and performs logic specific to the application. Although this pattern has proven very effective in many domains, Django's authors weren't looking to conform to any kind of pattern at the outset. They were simply interested in finding the most effective way to develop software for the Web. After all, Django was built for the daily needs of a working newspaper, where things have to happen very quickly if they're to happen at all. Ultimately, the separation of tasks into discrete groups serves a few different purposes.

- Code that is designed for a specific set of tasks is much more maintainable because it doesn't need to make assumptions about completely unrelated parts of the application. In general, this concept is called *separation of concerns* and is applicable throughout software development.

- Application development becomes more flexible, as multiple distinctly different view and controller layers may connect to a single model layer. This enables a variety of applications to share the same business logic and data, presenting it and interacting with it in different ways, for different audiences.

- Developers are able to learn just those parts of the system that are pertinent to the work being performed. This specialization helps to curb frustration and fatigue, while fostering creativity and excellence within each developer's domain of specialty.

There are certainly other smaller benefits, but these are generally the main goals achieved with the use of MVC. It's interesting to note, however, that the only part of those benefits that applies to any specific division in the MVC pattern is the ability to plug multiple applications into a single model layer. The rest is just an arbitrary division based on common development plans.

Django's developers sought these same benefits, but with an emphasis on rapid development, and after getting a set of tools that made sense for their workflow, they ended up with what some have called a Model-Template-View (MTV) pattern. However, there are really four primary code divisions in a Django application, which are outlined next.

Model

Given the benefit of keeping models apart from the rest of the application, Django follows that part of MVC to the letter. Django models provide easy access to an underlying data storage mechanism, and can also encapsulate any core business logic, which must always remain in effect, regardless of which application is using it.

Models exist independent of the rest of the system, and are designed to be used by any application that has access to them. In fact, the database manipulation methods that are available on model instances can be utilized even from the interactive interpreter, without loading a Web server or any application-specific logic.

Chapter 3 covers Django models in more detail, including how they're defined and utilized, how to include your own business logic, and much more.

ViewThough they share a name with the original MVC definition, Django views have little else in common with the traditional paradigm. Instead, they combine some of the traditional view's responsibility with the entirety of the controller's tasks. A view accepts user input (including simple requests for information), behaves according to the application's interaction logic, and returns a display that is suitable for users to access the data represented by models.

Views are normally defined as standard Python functions that are called when a user requests a specific URL. In terms of the Web, even a simple request for information is considered an action, so views are intended to handle that alongside data modifications and other submissions. Views can access the models, retrieving and updating information as necessary to accomplish the task requested by the user.

Since views are simply called as functions, without requiring any specific structure, they can be specified in a number of ways. As well as a simple function, a view could take the form of any Python callable, including classes, instance methods, callable objects, and curried or decorated functions.

Template

While views are technically responsible for presenting data to the user, the task of *how* that data is presented is generally delegated to templates, which are an important enough part of Django development to be considered a separate layer entirely. Many have drawn a parallel between Django templates and the traditional view layer, since templates handle all the presentational details the user will see.

Django provides a simple template language for this purpose, so that template designers don't need to learn Python just to work with templates. Django's template language is not dependent on any particular presentation language. It's primarily used for HTML but can be used to generate any text-based format.

Keep in mind, however, that this template engine is just one tool that views can use to render a display for a user. Many views may use HTTP redirects to other URLs, third-party Portable Document Format (PDF) libraries, or anything else to generate their output.

URL Configuration

As a framework for the Web, Django provides a separate layer of glue to make views available to the outside world at specific URLs. By supplying a regular expression as the URL component, a single declaration can accommodate a wide variety of specific URLs, in a highly readable and highly maintainable manner.

This configuration is defined separately from views themselves to allow a view to be configured at more than one URL, possibly with different options at each location. In fact, one of the core features of Django is the concept of generic views. These are views intended for common needs, with configuration options that allow them to be used in any application, requiring only a URL configuration to enable them.

Perhaps most important of all, having URLs as a separate part of the process encourages developers to think of URLs as part of an application's overall design. Since they must be used in bookmarks, blog posts and marketing campaigns, URLs are sometimes more visible than your application. After all, users who are paying attention while browsing the Web will see your URL before they even decide to visit your site. URLs get still more important when using print media for advertising campaigns.

Chapter 4 covers URL configurations in more detail, including some guidelines on proper URL design.

Loose Coupling

One key feature of the MVC architecture, and of Django's slightly modified form, is the notion that sections of code that perform significantly different functions shouldn't rely on how the others operate. This is called *loose coupling*. Contrast this with tight coupling, where modules often rely heavily on the internal details of other modules' implementations.

Tight coupling causes a whole host of problems with long-term code maintenance, as significant changes to one section will invariably affect others. This creates a mountain of extra work for the programmer, having to change code that has little—if anything—to do with the work that needs to be done. This extra work doesn't only affect the programmer; it's often quite costly for the employers as well. Tight coupling also makes testing more difficult because it's harder to isolate individual behaviors.

It may seem that loose coupling advocates that no code should ever know anything about any other code, but that's hardly the case, as a program written like that couldn't do anything at all. Some sections of code will always need to reference others; that's unavoidable. The key is to rely on implementation details as little as possible.

In Python, loose coupling is typically provided in a number of ways, some of which are shown in the following list. There are countless others, which could fill a book on their own, but the techniques shown here are described in detail in Chapter 2.

- Duck typing
- Operator overloading
- Signals and dispatching
- Plugins

Don't Repeat Yourself (DRY)

If you've been around the block a few times, you know all too well how easy it is to write "boilerplate" code. You code once for one purpose, then again for another, and again, and again, and again. After a while, you realize how much code has been duplicated, and if you're lucky, you have the time, energy and presence of mind to look at what's common and move those pieces into a common location.

This process is one of the primary reasons for a framework to exist. Frameworks provide much of this common code, while attempting to make it easier to avoid duplicating your own code in the future. This combines to represent a common programming practice: Don't Repeat Yourself.

Often abbreviated DRY, this term comes up quite often in conversations and can be used as

- A noun—"This code violates DRY."

- An adjective—"I like that approach, it's very DRY."

- A verb—"Let's try to DRY this up a bit."

The basic idea is that you should only write something once. That reduces the risk of accidentally introducing inconsistency between two pieces of code that should match. It should also be as reusable as possible, and if other code needs to know something about what you've already written, you should be able to get the necessary information automatically using Python, without requiring the programmer to repeat any of that information.

To facilitate this, Python provides a wealth of resources for peeking inside your code, a process called *introspection*. Many of these resources, covered in Chapter 2, are incredibly useful when supporting DRY in your code.

A Focus on Readability

"Readability counts." It's mentioned specifically in the Zen of Python, as noted earlier, and is perhaps one of the most important features of Python. Indeed, many Python programmers take pride in the readability of both the language and the code they write. The idea is that code is read far more often than it's written, especially in the world of open source.

To this end, Python provides a number of features designed to improve readability. For instance, its minimal use of punctuation and forced indentation allow the language itself to help maintain the readability of your code. When you're working with code in the real world, however, there's far more to consider.

For real life, the Python community has developed a set of guidelines for writing code, intended to improve readability. Set forth in PEP-8,[2] these guidelines are designed to maintain not only readability of an individual program, but also consistency across multiple programs. Once you get the feel for one well-written program, you'll be able to understand others easily.

The exact details of PEP-8 are too numerous to list here, so be sure to read it thoroughly to get a good idea of how to write good code. Also, note that if you read Django's own source code, some of the rules set forth in PEP-8 aren't followed. Ironically, this is still in the interest of readability, as following every rule to the letter can sometimes cause other problems. After all, to quote the Zen of Python again, "Practicality beats purity." The examples in this book will follow the style used by Django's own source code.

Failing Loudly

"Errors should never pass silently. / Unless explicitly silenced." This may seem like a simple sentiment, but at two lines, it comprises over 10 percent of the Zen of Python, and there's something to be said for that. Dealing with exceptions is an important part of programming, and this is especially true in Python. All programming languages can generate errors, and most have a way to handle them gracefully, but each language has its own best practices for dealing with them.

One key to keep in mind is that, although the names of most Python exceptions end in Error, the base class is called Exception. To understand how they should be used and handled, it's useful to start by learning why that particular word was used. Looking at some of the dictionary definitions for the word "exception," it's easy to see variations on a theme.

- Something excepted; an instance or case not conforming to the general rule

- One that is excepted, especially a case that does not conform to a rule or generalization

- An instance that does not conform to a rule or generalization

---

[2]http://prodjango.com/pep-8/

Rather than an error, which describes a situation where a problem occurred, an exception is simply when something unexpected occurred. This may seem like a subtle distinction, but some people treat exceptions as errors, reserving them solely for unrecoverable problems like corrupted files or network failure. This is reinforced by the fact that, in some languages, raising exceptions is extremely expensive, so to prevent performance problems, exceptions are avoided whenever possible.

In Python, however, exceptions are no more expensive than simple return values, allowing them to be more accurate to their dictionary definition. If we define an exception as a violation of a rule, it stands to reason that we must first define a rule.

Defining RulesThis is the most important aspect of understanding exceptions, so it's necessary to be perfectly clear: there's no Python syntax for defining rules. It's simply not a feature of the language. Some other languages explicitly support design by contract,[3] and many can support it through framework-level code, but Python doesn't support any form of it natively.

Instead, rules are defined by programmers in what they intend their code to do. That may seem like an over-simplification, but it's really not. A piece of code does exactly what its author intends it to do, and nothing more. Anything outside the intentions of the programmer can—and should—be considered an exception. To illustrate this, here are some of the rules used by Python and Django:

- Accessing an item in a list using the bracket syntax (`my_list[3]`) returns the item at the specified position.

- A set's `discard()` method makes sure that a specified item is no longer a member of the set.

- A QuerySet's `get()` method returns exactly one object that matches the arguments provided.

Examples like these are important because even though these rules are simple, they accurately describe how the given features will behave in various situations. To further illustrate, consider the following scenarios and how the rule impacts behavior.

- If the index provided as a reference to a list item does exist, the appropriate value will be returned. If it doesn't, an exception (`IndexError`) is raised. If the value used as an index isn't an integer, a different exception (`TypeError`) is raised.

- If the item being removed from a set using `discard()` is already a member of the set, it's simply removed. If it wasn't a member of the set, `discard()` returns without raising an exception, because `discard()` only ensures that the item is not in the set.

- If the arguments passed to a QuerySet's `get()` method match one record in the database, that record is returned as an instance of the appropriate model. If no records match, an exception (`DoesNotExist`) is raised, but if more than one record matches, a different exception (`MultipleObjectsReturned`) is raised. Finally, if the arguments can't be used to query the database (due to incorrect types, unknown attribute names or a variety of other conditions), still another exception (`TypeError`) is raised.

Clearly, even simple rules can have profound effects, as long as they're defined explicitly. Although the only requirement is that they be defined in the mind of the author, rules are of little use if not conveyed to anyone else. This becomes especially important in the case of a framework such as Django, built for distribution to the masses.

---

[3]`http://prodjango.com/design-by-contract/`

Documenting Rules

There are a number of appropriate ways to document the specific rules a piece of code was written to follow. It's even quite useful to specify them in more than one way, and in varying levels of complexity. There are four main places where people look for this information, so providing it in any or all of these locations would serve the purpose quite well.

- *Documentation*—As this should be the complete collection of information about the application, it stands to reason that these rules would be included.

- *Docstrings*—Regardless of stand-alone documentation, developers will often peek at the code itself to see how it works. Docstrings allow you to provide plain-text explanations of these rules right alongside the code that implements them.

- *Tests*—In addition to providing explanations of these rules for humans to understand, it's a great idea to provide them in a way that Python can understand. This allows your rule to be verified on a regular basis. In addition, *doctests*—tests embedded inside docstrings—are also human-readable, and both purposes can be served at once.

- *Comments*—Sometimes, a function may be complicated enough that a broad overview, such as might be found in full documentation or even the docstring, doesn't give sufficient information about what a particular chunk of code is expected to do. Python's emphasis on readability makes this fairly infrequent, but it does still happen. When it does, comments can be a useful way of explaining to others what the code is intended for, and thus what should be considered an exception. In particular, comments should explain the purpose of the code, not merely outline what each line is actually doing. Think *why*, not *how*.

Regardless of how you choose to describe your rules, there's one lesson that must always take precedence: be explicit. Remember, anything not laid out in your rule should be considered an exception, so defining the rule explicitly will help you decide how the code should behave in different situations, including when to raise exceptions.

Also, be consistent. Many classes and functions will look similar in name or interface, and where at all possible, they should behave similarly. Programmers who are accustomed to a particular behavior will expect similar behavior from similar components, and it's best to meet those expectations. This is especially true when writing code that mimics types provided by Python or Django, as they're already well-documented and well-understood by many programmers.

Community

Since being released to the public in 2005, Django has achieved great success, both technically and culturally. It has amassed a tremendous following throughout the world of Python Web development, among hobbyists and professionals alike. This community is one of the greatest assets to the framework and its users, and it's most certainly worth discussing in some detail.

AN EVOLVING COMMUNITY

It's important to realize that like any social structure, the Django community will evolve and change over time. So the information in this section may not always accurately reflect current practices and expectations.

There's no reason to let that deter you, though. The one thing I don't expect to change is the community's willingness to embrace new members. You'll always be able to get in touch with a variety of people, if you're willing to put yourself out there.

Management of the Framework

One of the first things to understand about development of Django—and about Python in general—is that, while the code for the framework is available for anyone to view and manipulate (it *is* open source, after all), the overall management of the core distribution is overseen by a small group of people. These "core developers" consist of those with access to update the main code repository.

WHAT IS "CORE"?

Because Django is open source, any user may make changes to Django's code and distribute those modified copies. Many developers have done so, adding significant features and enhancements and providing their work for others to use. Advanced users can make considerable alterations to the central code without impacting those who don't need the features provided by the copy.

In addition, developers are allowed—and encouraged—to make their applications generic and distribute them to others. These sometimes become so ubiquitous that many developers include them by default in any new project they start.

In contrast, Django's core is simply the code that is distributed through the main Django web site, either as an official release or as the main trunk development code. So when a discussion includes a debate about whether something should be "in core," the dilemma is whether it should go into the official distribution or in some third-party format, such as a branch or a distributed application.

An interesting gray area is the `django.contrib` package. It's distributed inside with the main Django distribution, and thus would qualify as being part of core, but they're designed as if they could be third-party applications. The goal was that if a third-party application was written well enough, gained enough traction in the community and had a promise of continued support, it could be pulled into core eventually. In practice, though, it's more commonly gone the other direction, with `django.contrib` packages removed from core and maintained as third-party applications instead.

This structure helps ensure that those with the most experience with the framework and its history are responsible for looking over, and often tweaking, all patches before they are committed to the repository. They also regularly discuss issues concerning recent developments in the framework, major overhauls that need to be done, significant improvements that can be made, and so on.

There is still someone at the top of the management chain. This position is called the Benevolent Dictator for Life, often abbreviated BDFL, and is reserved for those who have ultimate authority over all decisions, should they need to break a tie or override a majority decision. Thankfully, they are truly benevolent dictators, a distinction not taken lightly.

In fact, the idea of a BDFL is more humorous than anything else. Though they do hold ultimate authority, this power is rarely exercised, as they tend to favor group opinion. When they do need to step in and arbitrate a decision, their ruling is based on years of experience in knowing what's best for the framework and its audience. In fact, they will often submit their own ideas to the group at large for discussion, possibly even deferring to the group if suitable counterarguments are raised.

The concept of a BDFL may seem foreign to those readers coming from corporate backgrounds, where design decisions are often made by committees, where majority rules and changes need to go through exhaustive bureaucratic processes. Instead, less direct oversight often leads to small groups of experts in different areas, who are quite capable of acting independently, producing high-quality code. This simple structure allows the process to run more quickly when it needs to, and, more importantly, helps maintain greater consistency within the framework.

In the Python world, Guido van Rossum, creator of Python itself, holds the position of BDFL. For Django, it's held by two people, each with the official title of co-BDFL: Adrian Holovaty, co-creator of the framework, and Jacob Kaplan-Moss, lead developer of the current work being done with Django. The principles and philosophies found throughout this chapter are generally reflections of the opinions and ideals of the BDFLs.

News and Resources

With a community as passionate and dynamic as Django's, it's important to keep up to date on what others are what solutions they're finding to common problems, new applications that are available and many other things. the community's size and diversity, keeping up may seem like a daunting task, but it's really quite simple.

The first thing to keep an eye on is the Django weblog[4]—the official news outlet—which contains news and updates about the framework itself, its development and its use in major endeavors. For example, the Django weblog announces new releases, upcoming development sprints and updates to the project's Web site.

Perhaps more important is the Django community news aggregator,[5] which gathers articles from developers around the world, displaying them all in one place. The variety of information available here is much more diverse, as it's generated by community members, making it an extremely valuable resource. Example content could include new and updated applications, tips and tricks for solving common problems and new Django-powered Web sites.

Reusable Applications

One of the most valuable aspects of Django is its focus on application-based development. Rather than building each site from scratch, developers should write applications for specific purposes, and then combine them to build a site. This philosophy encourages many community members to release their applications to the public, as open source, so that others can benefit from their features.Developers are free to host their applications anywhere they wish, but many choose GitHub,[6] due to its rich features and very active developer community. In fact, it's where Django itself is hosted. GitHub incorporates its own issue-tracking system, making it easy to maintain everything in one place. Many applications[7] are hosted there, so it's definitely a good idea to spend a few minutes looking around to see if someone has already written something you need. You can also find and compare third-party applications at Django Packages.[8]

After all, that's one of the primary goals of open source software: a larger community can produce better, cleaner, more functional code than a smaller group of dedicated programmers. The Django community both exhibits this behavior and encourages others to take advantage of it.

Getting Help

Despite all the knowledge contained in this and other books, it would be foolish to pretend that every potential situation can be documented ahead of time. What's more, the documentation that is available isn't always easy to find or to understand. In any of these cases, you may well find yourself needing to pose your situation to live people, with real-world experience, in hopes that someone can identify the problem and propose a solution.

The first thing to know is that *this isn't a problem*. Anyone can run into an unexpected situation, and even the best and brightest of us can get confounded by the simplest of syntax errors. If this happens to you, know that Django's community is very gentle, and you should definitely ask for help when you need it.

Read the Documentation

The first step when trying to resolve any problem is always to read the official documentation. It's quite thorough and updated regularly, as new features are added and existing behaviors are changed. When running into an error, the documentation will help ensure that you're using Django the way it's intended.

Once your code matches what the documentation shows to be appropriate, it's time to look at other common problems.

---

[4]http://prodjango.com/django-weblog/
[5]http://prodjango.com/community/
[6]http://prodjango.com/github/
[7]http://prodjango.com/github-projects/
[8]http://prodjango.com/djangopackages/

Check Your Version

As mentioned previously, the official documentation keeps up with Django's trunk development, so there's a definite possibility that the documented features don't match the features available in the code you're using. This is more likely to occur if you're using an official release, but it can still happen if you're tracking trunk, depending on how often you update your local copy.

When you're tracking trunk, the article on backwards-incompatible[9] changes should be considered an essential part of the official documentation. If you run into problems after updating, make sure that none of the features you're using have changed.

Frequently Asked Questions (FAQ)

After a few years of answering questions using the methods that follow, the Django community has heard a variety of questions that come up on a regular basis. To help answer these questions more easily, there are two articles. Although the official FAQ[10] includes many questions not related to troubleshooting problems, there are still several common issues listed there.

The Internet Relay Chat (IRC) channel has its own set of questions and answers and its own FAQ.[11]

Mailing Lists

One of the easiest ways to get help is to ask your question on the django-users mailing list.[12] Because it operates over standard email, it's accessible to everyone, without requiring any special software. Simply join the list and you'll be able to post your questions for thousands of other users to look at. There are no guarantees, but most questions get answered quickly.

One key advantage of the mailing list is that all conversations are archived for future reference. In addition to the FAQs, the django-users mailing list archive can be an invaluable resource when you're trying to track down a problem that might have occurred to someone before. Be sure to search the archives before asking your question, though, because there's a good chance someone else has run into it as well.

Internet Relay Chat (IRC)

If you need answers more quickly, the best option is the Django IRC channel,[13] where many knowledgeable members of the Django community are available for direct conversation. It's a very helpful environment, but you should be prepared to provide specific details about the problem. This may include the exact error traceback, snippets of the models, views and other code that might be involved with the problem.

This code is most often shared using an online *pastebin*—a place to temporarily put some code for others to look at. Code can be pasted onto a public Web site for a limited time, allowing it to be shared with others. GitHub provides a tool for this purpose, called gist,[14] which is a simple tool for sharing code with users on IRC and elsewhere.

Now What?

Of course, learning about philosophy and community doesn't get any code written. It helps to know how to put tools to good use, but that's nothing without a set of tools to work with. The next chapter outlines many of the less commonly used tools that Python itself has to offer, while the remaining chapters explore much of Django's own toolset.

---

[9]http://prodjango.com/backwards-incompatible-changes/
[10]http://prodjango.com/faq/
[11]http://prodjango.com/irc-faq/
[12]http://prodjango.com/django-users/
[13]http://prodjango.com/irc/
[14]http://prodjango.com/gist/

CHAPTER 2

■ ■ ■

Django Is Python

Django, like other frameworks, is built on an underlying programming language—in this case, Python—to do its work. Many people who are new to Django are also new to Python, and Python's natural-feeling syntax combined with Django's energy-saving features can make Django seem like it uses some kind of metalanguage, which isn't the case.

A proper understanding of what can be done in Django must begin with the knowledge that Django is simply Python, as are all of your applications. Anything that can be done in Python can be done in Django, which makes the possibilities nearly limitless.

This also means that Django applications have access not only to the entire Python standard library, but also to an immense collection of third-party libraries and utilities. Interfaces to some of these are provided along with Django itself, so for many cases, the existing code and documentation will be sufficient to quickly get an application up and running.

Later in this book, some additional utilities are covered, along with some tips on how to integrate them into a Django application. The possibilities aren't limited to the options outlined in this book, so feel free to look around for Python utilities that will help support your business plan, and use the techniques listed in this book to integrate them into your application.

Though learning Python is beyond the scope of this book, Django uses some of its advanced features. In this chapter, I'll discuss many of those features to help you understand how Python can contribute to the goal of making things easier for everyone.

How Python Builds Classes

Some of the most advanced Python techniques that Django relies on are related to how Python constructs its classes. This process is often taken for granted by most developers—as well it should be—but since it's at the heart of Django, it forms the basis of this exploration.

When the Python interpreter encounters a class definition, it reads its contents just as it would any other code. Python then creates a new namespace for the class and executes all the code within it, writing any variable assignments to that new namespace. Class definitions generally contain variables, methods and other classes, all of which are basically assignments to the namespace for the class. However, nearly any valid code is allowed here, including printing to console output, writing to log files or even triggering GUI interaction.

Once the contents have finished executing, Python will have a class object that is ordinarily placed in the namespace where it was defined (usually the global namespace for the module), where it is then passed around or called to create instances of that class.

```
>>> class NormalClass:
...     print('Loading NormalClass')
...     spam = 'eggs'
...     print('Done loading')
...
Loading NormalClass
```

```
Done loading
>>> NormalClass
<class '__main__.NormalClass'>
>>> NormalClass.spam
'eggs'
```

As you can see, code executes within the class definition, with any assigned variables showing up as class attributes once the class is ready.

Building a Class Programmatically

The process described in the previous section is used for any source-declared class, but the way Python goes about it offers the possibility of something far more interesting. Behind the scenes, details about the class declaration are sent off to the built-in type object, which takes care of creating an appropriate Python object for the class. This happens automatically, for every class, immediately when it finishes parsing the contents of the class declaration.

The constructor for type accepts three arguments, which represent the entire class declaration.

- name—The name provided for the class, as a string

- bases—A tuple of classes in the inheritance chain of the class; may be empty

- attrs—A dictionary of the class namespace

COMPATIBILITY: NEW-STYLE CLASSES IN PYTHON 2

The process described in this section is true for new-style Python classes, a distinction introduced in Python 2.2[1] Old-style classes have been completely removed from Python 3, but if you're working with Python 2, you'll need to make sure to force new-style classes. To do so, simply make sure that the class inherits from the built-in object type somewhere in its inheritance chain.

All the classes Django provides to be subclassed will already derive from object, so any further derivatives will automatically be new-style classes, without any extra effort on your part. Still, it's important to keep the difference in mind, so that any custom classes your application may need will exhibit the behaviors outlined in this chapter.

Like any Python object, a new type can be instantiated at any time, from any block of code. This means that your code can construct a new class based on data collected at runtime. The following code demonstrates a way to declare a class at runtime, which is functionally equivalent to the example provided in the previous section.

```
>>> DynamicClass = type('DynamicClass', (), {'spam': 'eggs'})
>>> DynamicClass
<class '__main__.DynamicClass'>
>>> DynamicClass.spam
'eggs'
```

---

[1]http://prodjango.com/new-style-classes/

A WARNING ABOUT TYPE()

Using `type()` manually makes it easy to create classes with duplicate names, and even the module location can be customized by providing a `__module__` key in the dictionary in the `attrs` argument. Although these features can be useful, as will be demonstrated later in this book, they can lead to problems with introspection.

You could reasonably have two different classes with the same name and module, but your code won't be able to tell the difference between them. This may not be a problem in some situations, but it's something to be aware of.

Metaclasses Change It Up

`type` is actually a *metaclass*—a class that creates other classes—and what we've been engaging in is called metaprogramming.[2] In essence, *metaprogramming* creates or modifies code at runtime rather than at programming time. Python allows you to customize this process by allowing a class to define a different metaclass to perform its work.

If a class definition includes a separate class for its `metaclass` option, that metaclass will be called to create the class, rather than the built-in `type` object. This allows your code to read, modify or even completely replace the declared class to further customize its functionality. The `metaclass` option could technically be given any valid Python callable, but most metaclasses are subclasses of `type`. The metaclass receives the new class as its first argument and provides access to the class object along with the details regarding its declaration.

To help illustrate how the metaclass arguments are derived from a class definition, take the following code as an example.

```
>>> class MetaClass(type):
...     def __init__(cls, name, bases, attrs):     ⟶ constructor of metaclass = constructor of type
...         print('Defining %s' % cls)
...         print('Name: %s' % name)
...         print('Bases: %s' % (bases,))
...         print('Attributes:')
...         for (name, value) in attrs.items():
...             print('    %s: %r' % (name, value))
...
>>> class RealClass(object, metaclass=MetaClass):
...     spam = 'eggs'
...
Defining <class '__main__.RealClass'>
Name: RealClass
Bases: (<class 'object'>,)
Attributes:
    spam: 'eggs'
    __module__: '__main__'
    __qualname__: 'RealClass'
>>> RealClass
<class '__main__.RealClass'>
```

Notice that the class wasn't instantiated at any time; the simple act of creating the class triggered execution of the metaclass. Notice `__module__` in the list of attributes: this attribute is a standard part of all Python classes.

---

[2]http://prodjango.com/metaprogramming/

While this example uses the __init__ method to perform special processing on the newly created class, there is another, somewhat more powerful method called __new__, with the potential for a different set of possibilities. As described in later chapters, Django uses __new__ when configuring many of its classes.

COMPATIBILITY: METACLASSES IN PYTHON 2

Python 3 introduced the ability to pass arguments into a class definition, as shown here with the metaclass option. In Python 2, metaclasses were assigned to a class variable named __metaclass__. The effect is identical in both versions; it's only a syntax change.

Using a Base Class with a Metaclass

Metaclasses can be quite useful, but the metaclass option is an implementation detail, which shouldn't need to be part of the process when defining classes. Another problem is that while each class gets processed by the metaclass, they don't inherit from any concrete class. This means that any additional functionality, such as common methods or attributes, would have to be provided during metaclass processing in order to be of any use.

With a bit of care, a concrete Python class can use a metaclass to solve both of these problems. Since subclasses inherit attributes from their parents, the metaclass option is automatically provided for all subclasses of a class that defines it. This is a simple, effective way to provide metaclass processing for arbitrary classes, without requiring that each class define the metaclass option. Following the example from the previous section, look what happens when we subclass RealClass.

```
>>> class SubClass(RealClass):  # Notice there's no metaclass here.
...     pass
...
Defining <class '__main__.SubClass'>
Name: SubClass
Bases: (<class '__main__.RealClass'>,)
Attributes:
    __module__: '__main__'
```

Notice how the subclass here doesn't have to worry about the fact that there's a metaclass in use behind the scenes. By just specifying a base class, it inherits all the benefits. Django uses this behavior to implement one of its most prominent features, described in the next section.

Declarative Syntax

Some of Django's more prominent tools feature a "declarative syntax" that is simple to read, write and understand. This syntax is designed to make minimize "boilerplate" repetitive syntax and provide elegant, readable code. For example, here's what a typical Django model and more might look like:

```
class Contact(models.Model):
    """
    Contact information provided when sending messages to the owner of the site.
    """
    name = models.CharField(max_length=255)
    email = models.EmailField()
```

This declarative syntax has become an identifying feature of Django code, so many third-party applications that supply additional frameworks are written to use a syntax similar to that of Django itself. This helps developers easily understand and utilize new code by making it all feel more cohesive. Once you understand how to create a class using declarative syntax, you'll easily be able to create classes using many Django features, both official and community-provided.

Looking at declarative syntax on its own will demonstrate how easy it is to create an entirely new framework for Django that fits with this pattern. Using declarative syntax in your own code will help you and your colleagues more easily adapt to the code, ensuring greater productivity. After all, developer efficiency is a primary goal of Django and of Python itself.

While the next few sections describe declarative syntax in general, the examples shown are for Django's object-relational mapper (ORM), detailed in Chapter 3.

Centralized Access

Typically, a package will supply a single module from which applications can access all the necessary utilities. This module may pull the individual classes and functions from elsewhere in its tree, so they can still use maintainable namespaces, but they will all be collected into one central location.

```
from django.db import models
```

Once imported, this module provides at least one class intended as the base class for subclasses based on the framework. Additional classes are provided to be used as attributes of the new subclass. Together, these objects will combine to control how the new class will work.

The Base Class

Each feature starts with at least one base class. There may be more, depending on the needs of the framework, but at least one will always be required in order to make this syntax possible. Without it, every class you ask your users to define will have to include a metaclass explicitly, which is an implementation detail most users shouldn't need to know about.

```
class Contact(models.Model):
```

In addition to inspecting the defined attributes, this base class will provide a set of methods and attributes that the subclass will automatically inherit. Like any other class, it can be as simple or complex as necessary to provide whatever features the framework requires.

Attribute Classes

The module supplying the base class will also provide a set of classes to be instantiated, often with optional arguments to customize their behavior and assigned as attributes of a new class.

```
class Contact(models.Model):
    name = models.CharField(max_length=255)
    email = models.EmailField()
```

The features these objects provide will vary greatly across frameworks, and some may behave quite differently from a standard attribute. Often they will combine with the metaclass to provide some additional, behind-the-scenes functionality beyond simply assigning an attribute. Options to these attribute classes are usually read by the metaclass when creating this extra functionality.

For example, Django's Model uses the names and options of field attributes to describe an underlying database table, which can then be created automatically in the database itself. Field names are used to access individual columns in that table, while the attribute class and options convert native Python data types to the appropriate database values automatically. More information on how Django handles model classes and fields is available in the next chapter.

Ordering Class Attributes

namespace dictionary = class attributes, which in type is dict

One potential point of confusion when using declarative syntax is that Python dictionaries are unordered, rather than respecting the order in which their values were assigned. Ordinarily this wouldn't be a problem, but when inspecting a namespace dictionary it's impossible to determine the order in which the keys were declared. If a framework needs to iterate through its special attributes, or display them to a user or programmer, it's often useful to access these attributes in the same order they were defined. This gives the programmer final control over the order of the attributes, rather than some arbitrary ordering decided by the programming language.

A simple solution to this is to have the attributes themselves keep track of the instantiation sequence; the metaclass can then order them accordingly. This process works by having all attribute classes inherit from a particular base class, which can count how many times the class is instantiated and assign a number to each instance.

```
class BaseAttribute(object):          i.e. every attribute is a sub-class & that maintains order
    creation_counter = 1
    def __init__(self):
        self.creation_counter = BaseAttribute.creation_counter
        BaseAttribute.creation_counter += 1
```

Object instances have a different namespace than classes, so all instances of this class will have a creation_counter, which can be used to sort the objects according to the order in which they were instantiated. This isn't the only solution to this problem, but it's how Django sorts fields for both models and forms.

Class Declaration

With all of these classes in a module, creating an application class is as simple as defining a subclass and some attributes. Different frameworks will have different names for the attribute classes, and will have different requirements as to which classes are required or the combinations in which they may be applied. They may even have reserved names that will cause conflicts if you define an attribute with that name, but such problems are rare, and reserving names should generally be discouraged when developing new frameworks for use with this syntax. The general rule is to allow developers to be as flexible as they'd need to be, without the framework getting in the way.

```
from django.db import models

class Contact(models.Model):
    """
    Contact information provided when sending messages to the owner of the site.
    """
    name = models.CharField(max_length=255)
    email = models.EmailField()
```

This simple code alone is enough to allow the framework to imbue the new class with a wealth of additional functionality, without requiring the programmer to deal with that process manually. Also note how all the attribute classes are provided from that same base module and are instantiated when assigned to the model.

A class declaration is never limited to only those features provided by the framework. Since any valid Python code is allowed, your classes may contain a variety of methods and other attributes, intermingled with a framework's provided features.

Common Duck Typing Protocols

You've probably heard the old adage, "If it walks like a duck and talks like a duck, it's a duck." Shakespeare played on this idea a bit more romantically when he wrote in *Romeo and Juliet*, "That which we call a rose by any other name would smell as sweet." The recurring theme here is that the name given to an object has no bearing on its true nature. The idea is that, regardless of labels, you can be reasonably sure what something is just by looking at its behavior.

In Python, and in some other languages, this concept is extended to refer to object types. Rather than relying on some base class or interface to define what an object can do, it simply implements the attributes and methods necessary to behave as expected. A common example of this in Python is a *file-like object*, which is any object that implements at least some of the same methods as a Python file object. In this way, many libraries may return their own objects that can be passed to other functions that expect a file object but while retaining special abilities, such as being read-only, compressed, encrypted, pulled from an Internet-connected source or any number of other possibilities.

Also, like interfaces in other languages, Python objects can be more than one type of duck at a time. It's not uncommon, for instance, to have an object that can behave as a dictionary in some respects, while behaving like a list in others. Django's HttpResponse object exhibits both of these behaviors, as well as mimicking an open file object.

In Django, many features utilize duck typing by not providing a particular base class. Instead, each feature defines a protocol of sorts, a set of methods and attributes that an object must provide in order to function properly. Many of these protocols are presented in the official Django documentation, and this book will cover many more. You will also see some of the special abilities that can be provided by using this technique.

The following sections describe a few common Python protocols that you'll see throughout Django, and indeed throughout any large Python library.

Callables

Python allows code to be executed from a number of sources, and anything that can be executed in the same manner as a typical function is designated as callable. All functions, classes and methods are automatically callable, as would be expected, but instances of arbitrary object classes can be designated as callable as well, by providing a single method.

__call__(self[, …])

This method will be executed when the instantiated object is called as a function. It works just like any other member function, differing only in the manner in which it's called.

```
>>> class Multiplier(object):
...     def __init__(self, factor):
...         self.factor = factor
...     def __call__(self, value):
...         return value * self.factor
...
>>> times2 = Multiplier(2)
>>> times2(5)
10
>>> times2(10)
20
>>> times3 = Multiplier(3)
>>> times3(10)
30
```

Python also provides a built-in function to assist in the identification of callable objects. The `callable()` function takes a single argument, returning `True` or `False`, indicating whether the object can be called as a function.

```
>>> class Basic(object):
...     pass
...
>>> class Callable(object):
...     def __call__(self):
...         return "Executed!"
...
>>> b = Basic()
>>> callable(b)
False
>>> c = Callable()
>>> callable(c)
True
```

Dictionaries

A dictionary is a mapping between keys and values within a single object. Most programming languages have dictionaries in some form; other languages call them "hashes," "maps" or "associative arrays." In addition to simple access to values by specifying a key, dictionaries in Python provide a number of methods for more fine-grained manipulation of the underlying mapping. To behave even more like a true dictionary, an object may provide other methods, documented in the Python Library Reference.[3]

__contains__(self, key)

Used by the `in` operator, this returns `True` if the specified key is present in the underlying mapping, and returns `False` otherwise. This should never raise an exception.

__getitem__(self, key)

This returns the value referenced by the specified key, if it exists. If the key is not present in the underlying mapping, it should raise a `KeyError`.

__setitem__(self, key, value)

This stores the specified value to be referenced later by the specified key. This should overwrite any existing value referenced by the same key, if such a mapping is already present.

```
>>> class CaseInsensitiveDict(dict):
...     def __init__(self, **kwargs):
...         for key, value in kwargs.items():
...             self[key.lower()] = value
...     def __contains__(self, key):
...         return super(CaseInsensitiveDict, self).__contains__(key.lower())
```

---

[3]http://prodjango.com/dict-methods/

18

```
...        def __getitem__(self, key):
...            return super(CaseInsensitiveDict, self).__getitem__(key.lower())
...        def __setitem__(self, key, value):
...            super(CaseInsensitiveDict, self).__setitem__(key.lower(), value)
...
>>> d = CaseInsensitiveDict(SpAm='eggs')
>>> 'spam' in d
True
>>> d['SPAM']
'eggs'
>>> d['sPaM'] = 'burger'
>>> d['SpaM']
'burger'
```

Dictionaries are also expected to be *iterable*, with the list of keys used when code loops over a dictionary's contents. Refer to the upcoming "Iterables" section for more information.

Files

As mentioned previously, files are a common way to access information, and many Python libraries provide file-like objects for use with other file-related functions. A file-like object doesn't need to supply all of the following methods, just those that are necessary to function properly. In the case of the file protocol, objects are free to implement read access, write access or both. Not all methods are listed here, only the most common. A full list of file methods is available in the Python standard library documentation, so be sure to check there for more details.[4]

read(self, [size])

This retrieves data from the object or its source of information. The optional `size` argument contains the number of bytes to be retrieved. Without this argument, the method should return as many bytes as possible (often the entire file, if available, or perhaps all the bytes available on a network interface).

write(self, str)

This writes the specified `str` to the object or its source of information.

close(self)

This closes the file so it can no longer be accessed. This can be used to free any memory resources that have been allocated, to commit the object's contents to disk or simply to satisfy the protocol. Even if this method provides no special functionality, it should be provided to avoid unnecessary errors.

---

[4]http://prodjango.com/file-methods/

A VERY LOOSE PROTOCOL

File-like objects come in many varieties, because this protocol is one of the loosest defined in all of Python. There are quite a few features, from buffering output to allowing random access to data, that are inappropriate in some situations, so objects designed for those situations will typically just not implement the corresponding methods. For example, Django's HttpResponse object, described in Chapter 7, only allows writes in sequence, so it doesn't implement read(), seek() or tell(), causing errors when used with certain file-manipulation libraries.

The common approach in situations like this is to simply leave any inappropriate methods unimplemented so that trying to access them raises an AttributeError. In other cases, a programmer may decide it's more useful to implement them but simply raise a NotImplementedError to display a more descriptive message. Just make sure to always document how much of the protocol your object obeys, so users aren't surprised if these errors occur while trying to use them as standard files, especially in third-party libraries.

Iterables

An object is considered *iterable* if passing it to the built-in iter() returns an iterator. iter() is often called implicitly, as in a for loop. All lists, tuples and dictionaries are iterable, and any new-style class can be made iterable by defining the following method.

__iter__(self)

This method is called implicitly by iter() and is responsible for returning an iterator that Python can use to retrieve items from the object. The iterator returned is often implied by defining this method as a generator function, described in the upcoming "Generators" section.

```
>>> class Fibonacci(object):
...     def __init__(self, count):
...         self.count = count
...     def __iter__(self):
...         a, b = 0, 1
...         for x in range(self.count):
...             if x < 2:
...                 yield x
...             else:
...                 c = a + b
...                 yield c
...                 a, b = b, c
...
>>> for x in Fibonacci(5):
...     print(x)
...
0
1
1
2
3
```

```
>>> for x in Fibonacci(10):
...     print(x)
...
0
1
1
2
3
5
8
13
21
34
```

Iterators

When iter() is called with an object, it's expected to return an iterator, which can then be used to retrieve items for that object in sequence. Iterators are a simple method of one-way travel through the available items, returning just one at a time until there are no more to use. For large collections, accessing items one by one is much more efficient than first gathering them all into a list.

next(self)

The only method required for an iterator, this returns a single item. How that item is retrieved will depend on what the iterator is designed for, but it must return just one item. After that item has been processed by whatever code called the iterator, next() will be called again to retrieve the next item.

Once there are no more items to be returned, next() is also responsible for telling Python to stop using the iterator and to move on after the loop. This is done by raising the StopIteration exception. Python will continue calling next() until an exception is raised, causing an infinite loop. Either StopIteration should be used to stop the loop gracefully or another exception should be used to indicate a more serious problem.

```
class FibonacciIterator(object):
    def __init__(self, count):
        self.a = 0
        self.b = 1
        self.count = count
        self.current = 0

    def __next__(self):
        self.current += 1
        if self.current > self.count:
            raise StopIteration
        if self.current < 3:
            return self.current - 1
        c = self.a + self.b
        self.a = self.b
        self.b = c
        return c
    next = __next__
```

```python
    def __iter__(self):
        # Since it's already an iterator, this can return itself.
        return self

class Fibonacci(object):
    def __init__(self, count):
        self.count = count

    def __iter__(self):
        return FibonacciIterator(self.count)
```

Note that iterators don't explicitly need to define __iter__() in order to be used properly, but including that method allows the iterator to be used directly in loops.

COMPATIBILITY: ITERATORS IN PYTHON 2

There's only one very minor change to iterators in Python 3. The __next__() method shown here used to be called next(). Note the missing underscores. This was changed to respect Python's convention of identifying magic methods like this with double underscores before and after the name of the method.

If you need to support Python 2 and 3 together, the solution is fairly simple. After you define __next__() as shown in our Fibonacci example, you can just assign the __next__() method to next on the method directly: next = __next__. This can be done anywhere inside the class definition, but it's usually best right after the end of the __next__() method, to keep things tidy.

Generators

As illustrated in the Fibonacci examples, generators are a convenient shortcut to create simple iterators without having to define a separate class. Python uses the presence of the yield statement to identify a function as a generator, which makes it behave a bit differently from other functions.

When calling a generator function, Python doesn't execute any of its code immediately. Instead, it returns an iterator whose next() method will then call the body of the function, up to the point where the first yield statement occurs. The expression given to the yield statement is used as the next() method's return value, allowing whatever code called the generator to get a value to work with.

The next time next() is called on the iterator, Python continues executing the generator function right where it left off, with all of its variables intact. This repeats as long as Python encounters yield statements, typically with the function using a loop to keep yielding values. Whenever the function finishes *without* yielding a value, the iterator automatically raises StopIteration to indicate that the loop should be ended and the rest of the code can continue.

Sequences

While iterables simply describe an object that retrieves one value at a time, these values are often all known in advance and collected on a single object. This is a *sequence.* The most common types are lists and tuples. As iterables, sequences also use the __iter__() method to return their values one by one, but since these values are also known in advance, some extra features are available.

__len__(self)

With all the values available, sequences have a specific length, which can be determined using the built-in len() function. Behind the scenes, len() checks to see if the object it's given has a __len__() method and uses that to get the length of the sequence. To accomplish this, __len__() should return an integer containing the number of items in the sequence.

Technically, __len__() doesn't require that all the values be known in advance, just how many there are. And since there can't be partial items—an item either exists or it doesn't—__len__() should always return an integer. If it doesn't, len() will coerce it to an integer anyway.

```
>>> class FibonacciLength(Fibonacci):
...     def __len__(self):
...         return self.count
...
>>> len(FibonacciLength(10))
10
>>> len(FibonacciLength(2048))
2048
```

__getitem__(self) and __setitem__(self, value)

[handwritten annotations: "index" above getitem, "index," above setitem]

All the values in a sequence are already ordered as well, so it's possible to access individual values by their index within the sequence. Since the syntax used for this type of access is identical to that of dictionary keys, Python reuses the same two methods that were previously described for dictionaries. This allows a sequence to customize how individual values are accessed or perhaps restrict setting new values to the sequence, making it read-only.

Augmenting Functions

In addition to standard declarations and calls, Python provides options that allow you to invoke functions in interesting ways. Django uses these techniques to help with efficient code reuse. You can use these same techniques in your applications as well; they are standard parts of Python.

Excess Arguments

It's not always possible to know what arguments will be provided to a function at runtime. This is often the case in Django, where class methods are defined in source even before a subclass itself is customized appropriately. Another common situation is a function that can act on any number of objects. In still other cases, the function call itself can be made into a sort of API for other applications to utilize.

For these situations, Python provides two special ways to define function arguments, which allow the function to accept excess arguments not handled by the explicitly declared arguments. These "extra" arguments are explained next.

Note that the names args and kwargs are merely Python conventions. As with any function argument, you may name them whatever you like, but consistency with standard Python idioms makes your code more accessible to other programmers.

Positional Arguments

Using a single asterisk before an argument name allows the function to accept any number of positional arguments.

```
>>> def multiply(*args):
...     total = 1
...     for arg in args:
...         total *= arg
...     return total
...
>>> multiply(2, 3)
6
>>> multiply(2, 3, 4, 5, 6)
720
```

Python collects the arguments into a tuple, which is then accessible as the variable args. If no positional arguments are provided beyond those explicitly declared, this argument will be populated with an empty tuple.

Keyword Arguments

Python uses two asterisks before the argument name to support arbitrary keyword arguments.

```
>>> def accept(**kwargs):
...     for keyword, value in kwargs.items():
...         print("%s -> %r" % (keyword, value))
...
>>> accept(foo='bar', spam='eggs')
foo -> 'bar'
spam -> 'eggs'
```

Notice that kwargs is a normal Python dictionary containing the argument names and values. If no extra keyword arguments are provided, kwargs will be an empty dictionary.

Mixing Argument Types

Arbitrary positional and keyword arguments may be used with other standard argument declarations. Mixing them requires some care, as their order is important to Python. Arguments can be classified into four categories, and while not all categories are required, they must be defined in the following order, skipping any that are unused.

- Required arguments
- Optional arguments
- Excess positional arguments
- Excess keyword arguments

This order if for definition. While calling, we cannot pass positional arguments after Keyword

```
def complex_function(a, b=None, *c, **d):
```

This order is required because *args and **kwargs only receive those values that couldn't be placed in any other arguments. Without this order, when you call a function with positional arguments, Python would be unable to determine which values are intended for the declared arguments and which should be treated as an excess positional argument.

Also note that, while functions can accept any number of required and optional arguments, they may only define one of each of the excess argument types.

Passing Argument Collections

In addition to functions being able to receive arbitrary collections of arguments, Python code may call functions with any number of arguments, using the asterisk notation previously described. Arguments passed in this way are expanded by Python into a normal list of arguments, so that the function being called doesn't need to plan for excess arguments in order to be called like this. Any Python callable may be called using this notation, and it may be combined with standard arguments using the same ordering rules.

```
>>> def add(a, b, c):
...     return a + b + c
...
>>> add(1, 2, 3)
6
>>> add(a=4, b=5, c=6)
15
>>> args = (2, 3)
>>> add(1, *args)
6
>>> kwargs = {'b': 8, 'c': 9}
>>> add(a=7, **kwargs)
24
>>> add(a=7, *args)
Traceback (most recent call last):
  ...
TypeError: add() got multiple values for keyword argument 'a'
>>> add(1, 2, a=7)
Traceback (most recent call last):
  ...
TypeError: add() got multiple values for keyword argument 'a'
```

As illustrated in the final lines of this example, take special care if explicitly passing any keyword arguments while also passing a tuple as excess positional arguments. Since Python will expand the excess arguments using the ordering rules, the positional arguments would come first. In the example, the last two calls are identical, and Python can't determine which value to use for a.

Decorators

Another common way to alter the way a function behaves is to "decorate" it with another function. This is also often called "wrapping" a function, as decorators are designed to execute additional code before or after the original function gets called.

The key principle behind decorators is that they accept callables and return new callables. The function returned by the decorator is the one that will be executed when the decorated function is called later. Care must be taken to make sure that the original function isn't lost in the process, as there wouldn't be any way to get it back without reloading the module.

Decorators can be applied in a number of ways, either to a function you're defining directly or to a function that was defined elsewhere. As of Python 2.4, decorators on newly defined functions can use a special syntax. In previous versions of Python, a slightly different syntax is necessary, but the same code can be used in both cases; the only difference is the syntax used to apply the decorator to the intended function.

```
>>> def decorate(func):
...     print('Decorating %s...' % func.__name__)
...     def wrapped(*args, **kwargs):
...         print("Called wrapped function with args:", args)
...         return func(*args, **kwargs)
...     print('done!')
...     return wrapped
...

# Syntax for Python 2.4 and higher

>>> @decorate
... def test(a, b):
...     return a + b
...
Decorating test...
done!
>>> test(13, 72)
Called wrapped function with args: (13, 72)
85

# Syntax for Python 2.3

>>> def test(a, b):
...     return a + b
...
>>> test = decorate(test)
Decorating test...
done!
>>> test(13, 72)
Called wrapped function with args: (13, 72)
85
```

The older syntax in this example is another technique for decorating functions, which can be used in situations where the @ syntax isn't available. Consider a function that's been declared elsewhere but would benefit from being decorated. Such a function can be passed to a decorator, which then returns a new function with everything all wrapped up. Using this technique, any callable, regardless of where it comes from or what it does, can be wrapped in any decorator.

Decorating with Extra Arguments

Sometimes, a decorator needs additional information to determine what it should do with the function it receives. Using the older decorator syntax, or when decorating arbitrary functions, this task is fairly easy to perform. Simply declare the decorator to accept additional arguments for the required information so they can be supplied along with the function to be wrapped.

```
>>> def test(a, b):
...     return a + b
...
>>> def decorate(func, prefix='Decorated'):
...     def wrapped(*args, **kwargs):
...         return '%s: %s' % (prefix, func(*args, **kwargs))
```

```
...     return wrapped
...
>>> simple = decorate(test)
>>> customized = decorate(test, prefix='Custom')
>>> simple(30, 5)
'Decorated: 35'
>>> customized(27, 15)
'Custom: 42'
```

However, the Python 2.4 decorator syntax complicates things. When using this new syntax, the decorator always receives just one argument: the function to be wrapped. There is a way to get extra arguments into decorators, but first we'll need to digress a bit and talk about "partials."

Partial Application of Functions

Typically, functions are called with all the necessary arguments at the time the function should be executed. Sometimes, however, arguments may be known in advance, long before the function will be called. In these cases, a function can have one or more of its arguments applied beforehand so that the function can be called with fewer arguments.

For this purpose, Python 2.5 includes the partial object as part of its functools module. It accepts a callable along with any number of additional arguments and returns a new callable, which will behave just like the original, only without having to specify those preloaded arguments at a later point.

```
>>> import functools
>>> def add(a, b):
...     return a + b
...
>>> add(4, 2)
6
>>> plus3 = functools.partial(add, 3)
>>> plus5 = functools.partial(add, 5)
>>> plus3(4)
7
>>> plus3(7)
10
>>> plus5(10)
15
```

For versions of Python older than 2.5, Django provides its own implementation of partial in the curry function, which lives in django.utils.functional. This function works on Python 2.3 and greater.

Back to the Decorator Problem

As mentioned previously, decorators using the Python 2.4 syntax present a problem if they accept additional arguments, since that syntax only provides a single argument on its own. Using the partial application technique, it's possible to preload arguments even on a decorator. Given the decorator described earlier, the following example uses curry (described in Chapter 9) to provide arguments for decorators using the newer Python 2.4 syntax.

```
>>> from django.utils.functional import curry
>>> @curry(decorate, prefix='Curried')
... def test(a, b):
```

```
...        return a + b
...
>>> test(30, 5)
'Curried: 35'
>>> test(27, 15)
'Curried: 42'
```

This is still rather inconvenient, since the function needs to be run through curry every time it's used to decorate another function. A better way would be to supply this functionality directly in the decorator itself. This requires some extra code on the part of the decorator, but including that code makes it easier to use.

The trick is to define the decorator inside another function, which will accept the arguments. This new outer function then returns the decorator, which is then used by Python's standard decorator handling. The decorator, in turn, returns a function that will be used by the rest of the program after the decoration process is complete.

As this is all fairly abstract, consider the following, which provides the same functionality as in previous examples but without relying on curry, making it easier to deal with.

```
>>> def decorate(prefix='Decorated'):
...        # The prefix passed in here will be
...        # available to all the inner functions
...        def decorator(func):
...            # This is called with func being the
...            # actual function being decorated
...            def wrapper(*args, **kwargs):
...                # This will be called each time
...                # the real function is executed
...                return '%s: %s' % (prefix, func(*args, **kwargs))
...            # Send the wrapped function
...            return wrapper
...        # Provide the decorator for Python to use
...        return decorator
...
>>> @decorate('Easy')
... def test(a, b):
...        return a + b
...
>>> test(13, 17)
'Easy: 30'
>>> test(89, 121)
'Easy: 210'
```

This technique makes the most sense in situations where arguments are expected. If the decorator is applied without any arguments, parentheses are still required in order for it to work at all properly.

```
>>> @decorate()
... def test(a, b):
...        return a + b
...
>>> test(13, 17)
'Decorated: 30'
>>> test(89, 121)
'Decorated: 210'
```

```
>>> @decorate
... def test(a, b):
...     return a + b
...
>>> test(13, 17)
Traceback (most recent call last):
  ...
TypeError: decorator() takes exactly 1 argument (2 given)
```

The second example fails because we didn't first call decorate. Thus, all subsequent calls to test send their arguments to decorator instead of test. Since this is a mismatch, Python throws an error. This situation can be a bit difficult to debug because the exact exception that will be raised will depend on the function being wrapped.

A Decorator with or without Arguments

One other option for decorators is to provide a single decorator that can function in both of the previous situations: with arguments and without. This is more complex but worth exploring.

The goal is to allow the decorator to be called with or without arguments so it's safe to assume that all arguments are optional; any decorator with required arguments can't use this technique. With that in mind, the basic idea is to add an extra optional argument at the beginning of the list, which will receive the function to be decorated. Then, the decorator structure includes the necessary logic to determine whether it's being called to add arguments or to decorate the target function.

```
>>> def decorate(func=None, prefix='Decorated'):
...     def decorated(func):
...         # This returns the final, decorated
...         # function, regardless of how it was called
...         def wrapper(*args, **kwargs):
...             return '%s: %s' % (prefix, func(*args, **kwargs))
...         return wrapper
...     if func is None:
...         # The decorator was called with arguments
...         def decorator(func):
...             return decorated(func)
...         return decorator
...     # The decorator was called without arguments
...     return decorated(func)
...
>>> @decorate
... def test(a, b):
...     return a + b
...
>>> test(13, 17)
'Decorated: 30'
>>> @decorate(prefix='Arguments')
... def test(a, b):
...     return a + b
...
>>> test(13, 17)
'Arguments: 30'
```

This requires that all arguments passed to the decorator be passed as keyword arguments, which generally makes for more readable code. One downside is how much boilerplate would have to be repeated for each decorator that uses this approach.

Thankfully, like most boilerplate in Python, it's possible to factor it out into a reusable form, so new decorators can be defined more easily, using yet another decorator. The following function can be used to decorate other functions, providing all the functionality necessary to accept arguments, or it can be used without them.

```
>>> def optional_arguments_decorator(real_decorator):
...     def decorator(func=None, **kwargs):
...         # This is the decorator that will be
...         # exposed to the rest of your program
...         def decorated(func):
...             # This returns the final, decorated
...             # function, regardless of how it was called
...             def wrapper(*a, **kw):
...                 return real_decorator(func, a, kw, **kwargs)
...             return wrapper
...         if func is None:
...             # The decorator was called with arguments
...             def decorator(func):
...                 return decorated(func)
...             return decorator
...         # The decorator was called without arguments
...         return decorated(func)
...     return decorator
...
>>> @optional_arguments_decorator
... def decorate(func, args, kwargs, prefix='Decorated'):
...     return '%s: %s' % (prefix, func(*args, **kwargs))
...
>>> @decorate
... def test(a, b):
...     return a + b
...
>>> test(13, 17)
'Decorated: 30'
>>> test = decorate(test, prefix='Decorated again')
>>> test(13, 17)
'Decorated again: Decorated: 30'
```

This makes the definition of individual decorators much simpler and more straightforward. The resulting decorator behaves exactly like the one in the previous example, but it can be used with or without arguments. The most notable change that this new technique requires is that the real decorator being defined will receive the following three values:

- func—The function that was decorated using the newly generated decorator

- args—A tuple containing positional arguments that were passed to the function

- kwargs—A dictionary containing keyword arguments that were passed to the function

An important thing to realize, however, is that the args and kwargs that the decorator receives are passed as positional arguments, without the usual asterisk notation. Then, when passing them on to the wrapped function, the asterisk notation must be used to make sure the function receives them without having to know about how the decorator works.

This is what I understand till now: Property is a function that gets called when accessing an attribute of an object. Each object has its own property.

CHAPTER 2 ■ DJANGO IS PYTHON

Descriptors take this to a extreme level - Rather than invoking a function, it invokes a class. Now since all the object share the same descriptor, the first parameter is the object instance

Descriptors

Ordinarily, referencing an attribute on an object accesses the attribute's value directly, without any complications. Getting and setting attributes directly affects the value in the object's instance namespace. Sometimes, additional work has to be done when accessing these values.

- Retrieving data from a complicated source, such as a database or configuration file

- Transforming a simple value to a complicated object or data structure

- Customizing a value for the object it's attached to

- Converting a value to a storage-ready format before saving to a database

In some programming languages, this type of behavior is made possible by creating extra instance methods for accessing those attributes that need it. While functional, this approach leads to a few problems. For starters, these behaviors are typically more associated with the type of data stored in the attribute than some aspect of the instance it's attached to. By requiring that the object supply additional methods for accessing this data, every object that contains this behavior will have to provide the necessary code in its instance methods.

One other significant issue is what happens when an attribute that used to be simple suddenly needs this more advanced behavior. When changing from a simple attribute to a method, all references to that attribute also need to be changed. To avoid this, programmers in these languages have adopted a standard practice of always creating methods for attribute access so that any changes to the underlying implementation won't affect any existing code.

It's never fun to touch that much of your code for a change to how one attribute is accessed, so Python provides a different approach to the problem. Rather than requiring the object to be responsible for special access to its attributes, the attributes themselves can provide this behavior. Descriptors are a special type of object that, when attached to a class, can intervene when the attribute is accessed, providing any necessary additional behavior.

```
>>> import datetime
>>> class CurrentDate(object):
...     def __get__(self, instance, owner):
...         return datetime.date.today()
...     def __set__(self, instance, value):
...         raise NotImplementedError("Can't change the current date.")
...
>>> class Example(object):
...     date = CurrentDate()
...
>>> e = Example()
>>> e.date
datetime.date(2008, 11, 24)
>>> e.date = datetime.date.today()
Traceback (most recent call last):
  ...
NotImplementedError: Can't change the current date.
```

How to make an attribute immutable.

Creating a descriptor is as simple as creating a standard new-style class (by inheriting from object under Python 2.x), and specifying at least one of the following methods. The descriptor class can include any other attributes or methods as necessary to perform the tasks it's responsible for, while the following methods constitute a kind of protocol that enables this special behavior.

__get__(self, instance, owner)

When retrieving the value of an attribute (value = obj.attr), this method will be called instead, allowing the descriptor to do some extra work before returning the value. In addition to the usual self representing the descriptor object, this getter method receives two arguments.

- instance—The instance object containing the attribute that was referenced. If the attribute was referenced as an attribute of a class rather than an instance, this will be None.

- owner—The class where the descriptor was assigned. This will always be a class object.

The instance argument can be used to determine whether the descriptor was accessed from an object or its class. If instance is None, the attribute was accessed from the class rather than an instance. This can be used to raise an exception if the descriptor is being accessed in a way that it shouldn't.

Also, by defining this method, you make the descriptor responsible for retrieving and returning a value to the code that requested it. Failing to do so will force Python to return its default return value of None.

Note that, by default, descriptors don't know what name they were given when declared as attributes. Django models provide a way to get around this, which is described in Chapter 3, but apart from that, descriptors only know about their data, not their names.

__set__(self, instance, value)

When setting a value to a descriptor (obj.attr = value), this method is called so that a more specialized process can take place. Like __get__, this method receives two arguments in addition to the standard self.

- instance—The instance object containing the attribute that was referenced. This will never be None.

- value—The value being assigned.

Also note that the __set__ method of descriptors will only be called when the attribute is assigned on an object and will never be called when assigning the attribute on the class where the descriptor was first assigned. This behavior is by design, and prohibits the descriptor from taking complete control over its access. External code can still replace the descriptor by assigning a value to the class where it was first assigned.

Also note that the return value from __set__ is irrelevant. The method itself is solely responsible for storing the supplied value appropriately.

Keeping Track of Instance Data

Since descriptors short-circuit attribute access, you need to take care when setting values on the attached object. You can't simply set the value on the object using setattr; attempting to do so will call the descriptor again, resulting in infinite recursion.

Python provides another way to access an object's namespace: the __dict__ attribute. Available on all Python objects, __dict__ is a dictionary representing all values in the object's namespace. Accessing this dictionary directly bypasses all of Python's standard handling with regard to attributes, including descriptors. Using this, a descriptor can set a value on an object without triggering itself. Consider the following example.

```
>>> class Descriptor(object):
...     def __init__(self, name):
...         self.name = name
...     def __get__(self, instance, owner):
...         return instance.__dict__[self.name]
...     def __set__(self, instance, value):
```

```
...            instance.__dict__[self.name] = value
...
>>> class TestObject(object):
...     attr = Descriptor('attr')
...
>>> test = TestObject()
>>> test.attr = 6
>>> test.attr
6
```

Unfortunately, this technique requires giving the attribute's name to the descriptor explicitly. You can work around this with some metaclass tricks; Django's model system (discussed in Chapter 3) shows one possible workaround.

Introspection

Many Python objects carry metadata beyond the code they execute. This information can be quite useful when working with a framework or writing your own.

Python's introspection tools can help greatly when trying to develop reusable applications, as they allow Python code to retrieve information about what a programmer wrote without requiring the programmer to write it all over again.

Some of the features described in this section rely on a powerful standard library module, inspect. The inspect module provides convenient functions to perform advanced introspection.

Only some of inspect's many uses will be detailed here, as they hold the most value to applications written using Django. For full details of the many other options available in this module, consult the Python Standard Library documentation.[5]

MORE ON OLD-STYLE CLASSES

The examples shown in this section are all for new-style classes, which, as described earlier in this chapter, will behave differently from old-style classes, especially with regards to introspection. The exact differences are beyond the scope of this book, since the usual recommendation is to simply use new-style classes.

If any of your code seems to behave differently than what's described here, make sure that all your classes inherit from object, which will make them proper new-style classes.

Common Class and Function Attributes

All classes and functions provide a few common attributes that can be used to identify them.

- __name__—The name that was used to declare the class or function
- __doc__—The docstring that was declared for the function
- __module__—The import path of the module where the class or function was declared

---

[5]http://prodjango.com/inspect-module/

In addition, all objects contain a special attribute, __class__, which is the actual class object used to create the object. This attribute can be used for a variety of purposes, such as testing to see whether the class provided a particular attribute or if it was set on the object itself.

```
>>> class ValueClass(object):
...     source = 'The class'
...
>>> value_instance = ValueClass()
>>> value_instance.source = 'The instance'
>>> value_instance.__class__
<class '__main__.ValueClass'>
>>> value_instance.source
'The instance'
>>> value_instance.__class__.source
'The class'
```

Identifying Object Types

Since Python uses dynamic typing, any variable could be an object of any available type. While the common principle of duck typing recommends that objects simply be tested for support of a particular protocol, it's often useful to identify what type of object you're dealing with. There are a few ways to handle this.

Getting Arbitrary Object Types

It's easy to determine the type of any Python object using the built-in type described earlier. Calling type with a single argument will return a type object, often a class, which was instantiated to produce the object.

```
>>> type('this is a string')
<type 'str'>
>>> type(42)
<type 'int'>
>>> class TestClass(object):
...     pass
...
>>> type(TestClass)
<type 'type'>
>>> obj = TestClass()
>>> type(obj)
<class '__main__.TestClass'>
```

type (an object) → class

type (a class) ⟶ metaclass (usually type)

This approach usually isn't the best way to determine the type of an object, particularly if you're trying to decide what branch of execution to follow based on an object's type. It only tells you the one specific class that's being used, even though subclasses should likely be considered for the same branch of execution. Instead, this approach should be used in situations where the object's type isn't necessary for a decision but rather is being output somewhere, perhaps to the user to a log file.

For example, when reporting exceptions, it's quite useful to include the exception's type along with its value. In these situations, type can be used to return the class object, and its __name__ attribute can then be included in the log, easily identifying the exception's type.

Checking for Specific Types

More often, you'll need to check for the influence of a particular type, whether a class descends from it or whether an object is an instance of it. This is a much more robust solution than using type, as it takes class inheritance into account when determining success or failure.

Python provides two built-in functions for this purpose.

- issubclass(cls, base)—Returns True if cls and base are the same, or if cls inherits from base somewhere in its ancestry

- isinstance(obj, base)—Tests if the object is an instance of base or any of its ancestors

```
>>> class CustomDict(dict):
...     pass    # Pretend there's something more useful here
...
>>> issubclass(CustomDict, dict)
True
>>> issubclass(CustomDict, CustomDict)
True
>>> my_dict = CustomDict()
>>> isinstance(my_dict, dict)
True
>>> isinstance(my_dict, CustomDict)
True
```

There's a clear relationship between issubclass and isinstance: isinstance(obj, SomeClass) is equivalent to issubclass(obj.__class__, SomeClass).

Function Signatures

As described earlier in this chapter, Python functions can be declared in a number of ways, and it can be quite useful to have access to information about their declarations directly inside your code.

Of particular importance when inspecting functions is inspect.getargspec(), a function that returns information about what arguments a function accepts. It accepts a single argument, the function object to be inspected, and returns a tuple of the following values:

- args—A list of all argument names specified for the function. If the function doesn't accept any arguments, this will be an empty list.

- varargs—The name of the variable used for excess positional arguments, as described previously. If the function doesn't accept excess positional arguments, this will be None.

- varkwargs—The name of the variable used for excess keyword arguments, as described previously. If the function doesn't accept excess keyword arguments, this will be None.

- defaults—A tuple of all default values specified for the function's arguments. If none of the arguments specify a default value, this will be None rather than an empty tuple.

Together, these values represent everything necessary to know how to call the function in any way possible. This can be useful when receiving a function and calling it with just the arguments that are appropriate for it.

```
>>> def test(a, b, c=True, d=False, *e, **f):
...     pass
...
>>> import inspect
>>> inspect.getargspec(test)
ArgSpec(args=['a', 'b', 'c', 'd'], varargs='e', keywords='f', defaults=(True, False))
```

Handling Default Values

As the previous example illustrates, default values are returned in a separate list from argument names, so it may not seem obvious how to tell which arguments specify which defaults. However, there's a relatively simple way to handle this situation, based on a minor detail from the earlier discussion of excess arguments: required arguments must always be declared before any optional arguments.

This is key because it means the arguments and their defaults are specified in the order they were declared in the function. So in the previous example, the fact that there are two default values means that the last two arguments are optional, and the defaults line up with them in order. The following code could be used to create a dictionary mapping the optional argument names to the default values declared for them.

```
>>> def get_defaults(func):
...     args, varargs, varkwargs, defaults = inspect.getargspec(func)
...     index = len(args) - len(defaults) # Index of the first optional argument
...     return dict(zip(args[index:], defaults))
...
>>> get_defaults(test)
{'c': True, 'd': False}
```

Docstrings

As mentioned previously, classes and functions all have a special __doc__ attribute, which contains the actual string specified as the code's docstring. Unfortunately, this is formatted exactly as it was in the original source file, including extra line breaks and unnecessary indentation.

To format docstrings in a more readable manner, Python's inspect module provides another useful function, getdoc(). It removes unnecessary line breaks, as well as any extra indentation that was a side effect of where the docstring was written.

The removal of indentation merits a bit of explanation. Essentially, getdoc() finds the leftmost non-whitespace character in the string, counts up all the whitespace between that character and the start of the line it's in, and removes that amount of whitespace from all the other lines in the docstring. This way, the resulting string is left-justified but retains any additional indents that exist for the sake of formatting the documentation.

```
>>> def func(arg):
...     """
...     Performs a function on an argument and returns the result.
...
...     arg
...         The argument to be processed
...     """
...     pass
...
>>> print(func.__doc__)

    Performs a function on an argument and returns the result.
```

```
    arg
        The argument to be processed

>>> print(inspect.getdoc(func))
Performs a function on an argument and returns the result.

arg
    The argument to be processed
```

In situations where docstrings should be displayed to users, such as automated documentation or help systems, getdoc() provides a useful alternative to the raw docstring.

Applied Techniques

There are innumerable combinations of Python features that can be used to accomplish a vast multitude of tasks, so the few shown here should by no means be considered an exhaustive list of what can be done by combining the many features of Python. However, these are useful tactics in terms of Django, and serve as a solid basis for the other techniques listed throughout this book.

Tracking Subclasses

Consider an application that must, at any given time, have access to a list of all subclasses of a particular class. Metaclasses are a terrific way to go about this, but they have one problem. Remember, each class with a metaclass option will be processed, including this new base class, which doesn't need to be registered (only its subclasses should be registered). This requires some extra handling, but it's fairly straightforward:

```
>>> class SubclassTracker(type):            ⌐→ cls is parameter
...     def __init__(cls, name, bases, attrs):   as its self
...         try:
...             if TrackedClass not in bases:
...                 return
...         except NameError:
...             return
...         TrackedClass._registry.append(cls)
...
>>> class TrackedClass(metaclass=SubclassTracker)
...     _registry = []
...
>>> class ClassOne(TrackedClass):
...     pass
...
>>> TrackedClass._registry
[<class '__main__.ClassOne'>]
>>> class ClassTwo(TrackedClass):
...     pass
...
>>> TrackedClass._registry
[<class '__main__.ClassOne'>, <class '__main__.ClassTwo'>]
```

Handwritten notes:
Doing similar thing in --new-- would also work, but --new-- is called when objects are created.

Metaclass is called when it reads code.

The metaclass performs two functions. First, the `try` block makes sure that the parent class, `TrackedClass`, has already been defined. If it hasn't been, a `NameError` is raised, indicating that the metaclass is currently processing `TrackedClass` itself. Here, more processing could be done for `TrackedClass`, but the example simply ignores it, allowing it to bypass the registration.

In addition, the `if` clause makes sure that another class hasn't specified `SubclassTracker` explicitly as its `metaclass` option. The application only wants to register subclasses of `TrackedClass`, not other classes that might not fit the proper requirements for the application.

Any application author who wants to use a declarative syntax similar to Django's could use this technique to provide a common base class, from which specific classes can be created. Django uses this process for both its models and its forms so that its declarative syntax can be fairly consistent throughout the framework.

If Python makes it through those tests without bailing out early, the class is added to the registry, where all subclasses of `TrackedClass` can be retrieved at any time. Any subclasses of `TrackedClass` will show up in this registry, regardless of where the subclass is defined. Executing the class definition will be sufficient to register it; that way, the application can import any modules that might have the necessary classes and the metaclass does the rest.

Though its registry provides many more features than a simple list, Django uses an extension of this technique to register models, since they must each extend a common base class.

In the previous example, registry was defined in main class, here plugin is defined in metaclass.

A Simple Plugin Architecture

In reusable applications, it's usually desirable to have a well-defined core set of features, combined with the ability to extend those features through the use of plugins. While this may seem like a tall order that might require extensive plugin architecture libraries, it can be done quite simply and entirely in your own code. After all, a successful, loosely-coupled plugin architecture comes down to providing just three things:

- A clear, readable way to declare a plugin and make it available to code that needs to use it

- A simple way to access all the plugins that have been declared

- A way to define a neutral point between plugins and the code that uses them, where the plugins should be registered and accessed

Armed with this simple list of requirements and a healthy understanding of what Python has to offer, a few simple lines of code can combine to fulfill these requirements.

```
class PluginMount(type):
    def __init__(cls, name, bases, attrs):
        if not hasattr(cls, 'plugins'):
            # This branch only executes when processing the mount point itself.
            # So, since this is a new plugin type, not an implementation, this
            # class shouldn't be registered as a plugin. Instead, it sets up a
            # list where plugins can be registered later.
            cls.plugins = []
        else:
            # This must be a plugin implementation, which should be registered.
            # Simply appending it to the list is all that's needed to keep
            # track of it later.
            cls.plugins.append(cls)
```

That's all it takes to get the whole thing working, keeping track of registered plugins and storing them in a list on the `plugins` attribute. All that's left is to work out how to achieve each of the points listed earlier. For the following examples, we'll create an application for validating the strength of a user's password.

The first step will be the neutral access point, which I'll call a *mount point*, from which each side of the equation can access the other. As mentioned before, this relies on metaclasses, so that's a good place to start.

```python
class PasswordValidator(metaclass=PluginMount):
    """
    Plugins extending this class will be used to validate passwords.
    Valid plugins must provide the following method.

    validate(self, password)
        Receives a password to test, and either finishes silently or raises a
        ValueError if the password was invalid. The exception may be displayed
        to the user, so make sure it adequately describes what's wrong.
    """
```

You could add more to this if you want, but what's here is the only part that's essential to get the process working properly. When looking to add more to it, just know that individual plugins will subclass it and will thus inherit anything else you define on this class. It's a handy way of providing additional attributes or helper methods that would be useful for all the plugins to have available. Individual plugins can override them anyway, so nothing would be set in stone.

Also note that the plugin mount point should contain documentation relating to how plugins will be expected to behave. While this isn't expressly required, it's a good practice to get into, as doing so will make it easier for others to implement plugins. The system only works if all the registered plugins conform to a specified protocol; make sure it's specified.

Next, set up your code to access any plugins that were registered, using them in whatever way makes sense for the application. Since the mount point already maintains its own list of known plugins, all it takes is to cycle through the plugins and use whatever attributes or methods are appropriate for the task at hand.

```python
def is_valid_password(password):
    """
    Returns True if the password was fine, False if there was a problem.
    """
    for plugin in PasswordValidator.plugins:
        try:
            plugin().validate(password)
        except ValueError:
            return False
    return True

def get_password_errors(password):
    """
    Returns a list of messages indicating any problems that were found
    with the password. If it was fine, this returns an empty list.
    """
    errors = []
    for plugin in PasswordValidator.plugins:
        try:
            plugin().validate(password)
        except ValueError as e:
            errors.append(str(e))
    return errors
```

These examples are a bit more complicated than most, since they require error handling, but it's still a very simple process. Simply iterating over the list will provide each of the plugins for use. All that's left is to build some plugins to provide this validation behavior.

```python
class MinimumLength(PasswordValidator):
    def validate(self, password):
        "Raises ValueError if the password is too short."
        if len(password) < 6:
            raise ValueError('Passwords must be at least 6 characters.')

class SpecialCharacters(PasswordValidator):
    def validate(self, password):
        "Raises ValueError if the password doesn't contain any special characters."
        if password.isalnum():
            raise ValueError('Passwords must contain at least one special character.')
```

Yes, it really is that easy! Here's how these plugins would look in practice.

```python
>>> for password in ('pass', 'password', 'p@ssword!'):
...     print(('Checking %r...' % password), end=' ')
...     if is_valid_password(password):
...         print('valid!')
...     else:
...         print()  # Force a new line
...         for error in get_password_errors(password):
...             print('  %s' % error)
...
Checking 'pass'...
  Passwords must be at least 6 characters.
  Passwords must contain at least one special character.
Checking 'password'...
  Passwords must contain at least one special character.
Checking 'p@ssword!'... valid!
```

Now What?

With a solid understanding of what Python has to offer, you're ready to dive into some of the ways Django uses these tools for many of its features and how you can apply the same techniques in your own code. Forming the foundation of most Django applications, models make use of many of these advanced Python features.

CHAPTER 3

■ ■ ■

Models

Data is at the center of most modern Web applications, and Django aims to provide support for a variety of data structures and persistence options. Models are the primary aspect of the traditional MVC model that Django uses as expected. Models are an essential part of any application that needs to persist data across multiple requests, sessions or even server instances.

Django models are defined as standard Python classes, with a wealth of additional features added in automatically. Behind the scenes, an object-relational mapper (ORM) allows these classes and their instances access to databases. Without this ORM, developers would be required to deal with the database directly, using Structured Query Language (SQL), the standard way to access content in databases.

The primary goal of SQL is to describe and access the relationships that are stored in a relational database. SQL does not generally provide high-level relationships for applications, so most applications include handwritten SQL for data activities. This is definitely possible, but it tends to lead toward lots of repetition, which in and of itself violates the DRY principle outlined in Chapter 1.

These bits of SQL littered throughout an application's code quickly become unmanageable, especially since the programmers who have to manage the code aren't typically experts in relational databases. That also means that these databases are quite prone to bugs, which are often troublesome to track down and fix.

That still doesn't factor in the biggest issue of all: security. SQL injection[1] attacks are a common way for malicious attackers to access or even modify data they shouldn't have access to. This occurs when hand-written SQL doesn't take appropriate precautions with regard to the values that are passed into the database. The more SQL statements that are written by hand, the more likely they are to be susceptible to this type of attack.

All of these problems are extremely common in Web development, regardless of language, and ORMs are a common way for frameworks to mitigate them. There are other ways to avoid some of these problems, such as SQL injection, but Django's ORM was written with these concerns in mind and handles much of it behind the scenes. By accessing data using standard Python objects, the amount of SQL is minimized, reducing the opportunity for problems to crop up.

How Django Processes Model Classes

Described in Chapter 2, one of Django's most recognizable features is its declarative syntax for model definitions. With this, model definitions can be simple and concise, while still providing a vast array of functionality. The basic process of using metaclasses for declarative syntax is described in detail in Chapter 2, but there are more specific steps taken when handling models, which deserve some extra attention.

The metaclass responsible for processing model definitions is `ModelBase`, living at `django.db.models.base`. This provides a few key features, listed here in the order in which the actions are performed.

---

[1]`http://prodjango.com/sql-injection/`

1. A new class is generated to be used for the actual model, preserving the module location where the original model was defined.

2. If a custom app_label wasn't provided for the model, it's determined based on the module where it was declared.

3. Meta options are pulled out of the model and placed in a special Options object, which is described in more detail later in this chapter.

4. Two special exception classes, DoesNotExist and MultipleObjectsReturned, are created and customized for the new model.

5. A default manager is assigned to the model if one wasn't already provided.

6. If the model was already defined—which can happen because of differences in how the module was imported at different stages—the existing model is retrieved from the application cache and returned, making sure that the same class object is always used.

7. Attributes and methods defined on the original model are added to the newly-created model class.

8. Settings from inherited parent models are set on the new model.

9. The new model is registered with the application cache for future reference.

10. The newly-created model is returned to be used in place of the class that was defined in the source file.

Abstract models and inherited models are special cases, where not all of these actions occur. Specific differences for these cases are covered later in this chapter.

Setting Attributes on Models

Python provides useful tools for getting and setting attributes on objects without knowing the name in advance, but while getattr() and setattr() represent the standard way of accessing attributes on objects, one of Django's hooks for model fields requires some additional handling. Django provides a class method, add_to_class(), on all of its models, which should be used as a substitute for setattr().

The syntax and semantics of add_to_class() are slightly different than the traditional functions. It's actually a class method, rather than a built-in or even module-level function, which means the class is provided implicitly, rather than being an explicit first argument. This method checks the provided value for the presence of a contribute_to_class() method, and calls it if it exists. Otherwise, the standard setattr() function is used to add the value to the model. These behaviors are mutually exclusive; only one will happen in a given add_to_class() call. It's important to realize that this isn't just for Django's own internal code. If an application has need to add arbitrary objects as attributes to models, they must call add_to_class(). This way, developers working with the application can pass any object in, and be assured that it will be handled the same as if it had been applied directly on the model's class definition.

This whole process changes what the classes look like when using the introspection techniques described in Chapter 2. In order to determine the declared fields, the database table being used or the display name for the model, some additional knowledge is required.

Getting Information About Models

Once a model has been processed by Python, along with Django's ModelBase metaclass, its original structure can still be determined by using an attribute that exists on every Django model and its instances called _meta.

There are a number of attributes available on _meta, which combine to describe the model, how it was defined, and what values were provided to customize its behavior. These can also be classified into two separate groups: attributes that are determined by looking at the actual structure of the original class and those that are specified directly as part of a Meta class defined inside the model.

REGARDING THE STABILITY OF _META

Names beginning with underscores typically refer to private attributes that shouldn't be used directly. They're often used internally by functions and methods that are more public in nature, and are generally accompanied by warnings about likely changes and undocumented behavior. In most cases, these warnings are valid; programmers usually write tools for their own use, and find little need in documenting their behavior or securing their longevity.

However, _meta is a bit of an exception to the rule. While it is indeed part of a private API, which isn't necessary for the vast majority of situations, it shares something with many tools described in this book; it can prove extremely useful if understood and used properly. In fact, _meta goes one better, by being quite stable and highly unlikely to change without considerable effort to keep it backwards-compatible. It's the foundation of much of Django's own internal code, and is already being accessed directly by many third-party applications as well.

So, while names beginning with underscores do generally spell danger, potential incompatibilities and lack of support, you can rely on _meta quite safely. Just make sure to keep up with Django's list of backwards-incompatible changes. Anything new that would break _meta will be listed there.

Class Information

While most of the basic introspection techniques covered in Chapter 2 apply to Django models, there are a number of details that are also made available on the _meta attribute. Most of this is information Django itself needs in order to properly deal with models, but as with many other features, it can be quite useful for other applications as well.

One important distinction to make with models is whether they're "installed" or not. This means checking whether the application that contains them is listed in the site's INSTALLED_APPS setting. Many Django features, such as syncdb and the built-in admin interface, require an application to be listed in INSTALLED_APPS in order to be located and used.

If an application is designed to accept any Django model directly, rather than iterating through INSTALLED_APPS, it will often need some way to determine whether the model is properly installed. This is necessary in case the application needs to handle models differently, depending on whether database operations should be performed on the table, for instance. For this purpose, Django provides the installed attribute, which will be True only if the model belongs to an application listed in INSTALLED_APPS, and False otherwise.

There are two other attributes of model-level information that are commonly useful to application developers. As described in Chapter 2, all Python classes provide an easy way to get the name of the class and the module where it was defined, using the __name__ and __module__ attributes, respectively. However, there are some situations where these can be misleading.

Consider a situation where a model may be subclassed without inheriting all the Django-specific model inheritance processing. This requires a bit of tweaking with metaclasses, but can prove useful for solving certain types of problems. When doing this, the __name__ and __module__ attributes will refer to the child class, rather than the actual model that sits underneath.

Often, this is the desired behavior, as it's just how standard Python works, but when attempting to interact with the Django model, or other areas of Django that may need to work with it, it may be necessary to know the details of the model itself, rather than the child class. One way to go about this would be to use class introspection to get the various parent classes that are in use, checking each to see if it's a Django model.

This is a fairly unsightly process that takes time to code, time to execute, makes maintenance and readability more difficult and adds boilerplate if it needs to be done often. Thankfully, Django provides two additional attributes on _meta to greatly simplify this. The module_name attribute contains the __module__ attribute from the underlying model, while object_name pertains to the __name__ attribute of the model.

Field Definitions

A major challenge involved in using and manipulating Django models is the process of locating and using fields that are defined for them. Django uses the creation_counter technique described in Chapter 2 to keep track of the order of fields, so they can be placed inside a list for future reference. This list is stored in the fields attribute of the model's _meta attribute.

As a list, this can be iterated to retrieve all the field objects in order, which is extremely useful when looking to deal with models generically. As described later in this chapter, field objects have attributes containing all the options that were specified for them, so each item in the list can provide a wealth of information.

With this, we can create a custom form or template output, or any other feature that needs to work with fields on an arbitrary model. Consider the following example, which prints out the display names and current values for each field in a given object, without having to know in advance what model is being used.

```
from django.utils.text import capfirst

def get_values(instance):
    for field in instance._meta.fields:
        name = capfirst(field.verbose_name)
        value = getattr(instance, field.name)
        print('%s: %s' % (name, value))
```

Going about it this way allows the function to ignore the details of the model behind the object. As long as it's an instance of a proper Django model, the _meta attribute will be available and all the fields will be accessible in this way. Since Django automatically adds an AutoField to any model that doesn't declare a primary key, the created AutoField will also be included in the fields list.

While being able to iterate through a list is great for those situations where all the fields will be taken into account, sometimes only a single field is needed, and the name of that field is known in advance. Since fields is a list instead of a dictionary, the only way to get a field by its name would be to loop over the fields, checking each to see if its name matches.

To cater to this need, Django provides a utility method, _meta.get_field(). By providing the field name to the _meta.get_field(), it's easy to retrieve just the specified field. If no field with that name exists, it will raise a FieldDoesNotExist exception, which lives at django.db.models.fields.

To get a better understanding of how these methods work together to identify the fields that were declared on a model, consider the following model declaration.

```
class Product(models.Model):
    sku = models.CharField(max_length=8, verbose_name='SKU')
    name = models.CharField(max_length=255)
    price = models.DecimalField(max_digits=5, decimal_places=2)

    def __unicode__(self):
        return self.name
```

Then, the model could be inspected to get more information about this declaration, without having to know what it looked like in advance.

```
>>> from django.utils.text import capfirst
>>> for field in Product._meta.fields:
...     print('%s: %s' % (capfirst(field.verbose_name), field.__class__))
...
ID: <class 'django.db.models.fields.AutoField'>
SKU: <class 'django.db.models.fields.CharField'>
Name: <class 'django.db.models.fields.CharField'>
Price: <class 'django.db.models.fields.DecimalField'>
>>> Product._meta.get_field('name').__class__
<class 'django.db.models.fields.CharField'>
```

Primary Key Fields

Any field can be specified as a primary key, by setting `primary_key=True` in the field's definition. This means that if code is to handle a model or a model instance without prior knowledge of its definition, it's often necessary to identify which field was defined as a primary key.

Much like getting a field by name, it would be possible to just iterate over all the fields, looking for one with its `primary_key` attribute set to True. After all, Django only allows one field to be specified as a primary key. Unfortunately, this again introduces a fair amount of boilerplate that slows things down and makes it more difficult to maintain.

To simplify this task, Django provides another `_meta` attribute, pk, which contains the field object that will be used as the primary key for the model. This is also faster than iterating over all the fields, since pk is populated once, when the model is first processed. After all, Django needs to determine whether it needs to provide an implicit primary key. The `_meta.pk` attribute is also used to enable the pk shortcut property on model instances, which returns the primary key value for an instance, regardless of which field is the primary key.

Typically, models don't need to declare an explicit primary key, and can instead let Django create one automatically. This can be a useful way to avoid repeating such a common declaration, while still allowing it to be overridden if necessary. One potential problem with this, however, is the task of determining whether a model was given an automatic field, and what that field looks like.

It's possible to make certain assumptions about a model, based on how Django provides this automatic field, and what it would typically look like. However, it's easy to create a custom field that looks a lot like the implicit field, and it'd be very difficult to tell the difference if your code only looks at its structure and options.

Instead, Django provides two attributes on the `_meta` attribute that help with this situation. The first, `_meta.has_auto_field`, is True if the model let Django provide an id field implicitly. If it's False, the model has an explicit primary key, so Django didn't have to intervene.

The second attribute related to the automatic primary key field is `_meta.auto_field`, which will be the actual field object Django provided for use as the primary key. If `_meta.has_auto_field` is True, this will be an AutoField, and will always be configured the same way for all models that use it. It's important to look at this attribute instead of making assumptions about the field's structure, in case Django makes any changes in the future. It's an easy way to help make sure your application keeps working properly in the future. If a model provides its own primary key field, and thus `_meta.has_auto_field` is False, `_meta.auto_field` will be set to None.

Configuration Options

In addition to providing access to the fields declared on the model, `_meta` also acts as a container for all the various options that can be set on a model using the Meta inner class. These options allow a model to control a variety of things, such as what the model is named, what database table it should use, how records should be ordered, and a number of others.

These options all have defaults, so that even those attributes that aren't specified on the model are still available through the `_meta` attribute. The following is a list of the many options that are available in this way, along with their default values and a brief description what the option is intended for.

- abstract—A Boolean that indicates whether the model was defined as abstract, a process that is described in more detail in Django's model inheritance documentation.[2] The default value is False.

- app_label—A string containing the name Django uses to recognize the application where the model was defined. It's easiest to understand what this means by looking at the default value, which is the name of the module containing the models.py the model is specified in. For a model located at corporate.accounts.models.Account, the app_label would be "accounts".

- db_table—The name of the database table that Django will use to store and retrieve data for the model. If not defined explicitly, it's determined as a function of the model's name and location. That is, the db_table for a model called Account with an app_label of accounts would be "accounts_account".

- db_tablespace—In the case of Oracle, and perhaps other database backends in the future, tables can be placed in different parts of the disk, or different disks entirely. By default, this is simply an empty string, which tells the database to store the table in its default location. This option is ignored for backends that don't support it.

- get_latest_by—The name of a date-based field, such as a DateField or a DateTimeField, which should be used to determine the most recent instance of a model. If not provided, this will be an empty string.

- order_with_respect_to—An instance of a field relating to another model, which is used when ordering instances of this model. This defaults to None, which implies that the model's ordering is determined solely by fields within the model itself, rather than any related models.

- ordering—A tuple containing the names of fields to be used when ordering instances of the model. By default, this is an empty tuple, which relies on the database to determine the ordering of model instances.

- permissions—A sequence of tuples of additional permissions to be added to the model. Each tuple in the sequence contains two values, the first being the name of the permission to be used in code and in the database, and the second being the text to be displayed in the admin interface when selecting permissions for a user or group.

- unique_together—A sequence of tuples indicating any groups of fields that must, when combined, be used in only one record in the database. Each tuple in the sequence contains the names of the fields that must be unique together for a particular index. Multiple tuples don't have any relation to each other; they each represent a separate index at the database level.

- verbose_name—The display name for a single instance of the model. By default, this is determined by the name of the class itself, by splitting up each capitalized portion into a separate uncapitalized word; Article would become "article", while AddressBook would become "address book".

- verbose_name_plural—The display name for multiple instances of the model. By default, this will be simply the verbose_name with an "s" at the end. Article would be "articles" and AddressBook would be "address books".

- verbose_name_raw—The raw, untranslated version of verbose_name. Occasionally, it's necessary to use the same display name for everyone, without Django applying a translation. This is particularly useful when storing it away in the cache or database for later access, especially if it'll be translated at a later point in time.

---

[2]http://prodjango.com/model-inheritance/

Accessing the Model Cache

Once models have been processed by the ModelBase metaclass, they're placed in a global registry called AppCache, located at django.db.models.loading. This is instantiated automatically, immediately when the module is imported, and is accessed using the name cache. This special cache provides access to the various models that are known to Django, as well as installs new ones if necessary.

Because ModelBase handles registration of new models whenever the class is processed by Python, the models it contains aren't guaranteed to be part of applications present in the INSTALLED_APPS setting. This fact makes it even more important to remember that the _meta attribute on the model contains an installed attribute indicating whether the model belongs to an installed application.

Whenever code accesses one of the features in this section, AppCache will automatically load applications that are listed in INSTALLED_APPS, making sure that whenever some of the features are accessed, the cache includes all applications and models that should be made available. Without this, the results of these methods would be wildly unpredictable, based solely on which applications were loaded in which order.

As might seem obvious, the application cache can only be fully populated once all the applications have been loaded. Therefore, if an application's models.py makes any calls to AppCache as part of this loading process, it's possible that the cache might not be fully populated yet.

To protect against this problem, AppCache provides a method to determine whether the cache itself has been populated and is ready to be accessed. Calling cache.app_cache_ready() will return True or False depending on whether all of the installed applications have been processed correctly. Using this, applications that could benefit from having their own cache of known models can check if this cache is available for that purpose. If so, it can use this cache directly, while if not, it can manually determine what it needs to know.

Retrieving All Applications

When looking to introspect a site's contents, it's also very useful to look at the structure of applications themselves. After all, looking at models is only useful if there are models to look at, and sometimes it's necessary to just collect all the models currently in use. It's also useful to have them arranged by the application that declares them. Django already needs to have this information handy, so AppCache is designed to specifically manage this information.

HOW DOES DJANGO SEE APPLICATIONS?

One important thing to keep in mind is that Django needs an object to use as a reference for the application. A Django application is essentially a standard Python package, which is just a collection of modules contained in a single folder. While Python provides an object to use as a reference for individual modules, it doesn't offer anything to refer to a package.

Because of this, the closest notion Django can have to an application object is the __init__.py module that Python uses to recognize it as a package. In that case, Django would be using a module object as an application reference.

Unfortunately, few projects store anything useful in __init__.py, so Django isn't likely to find anything of interest in it. In order to get at anything really useful, it would have to perform some extra work to traverse the package structure to get a module that contained some pertinent information.

Instead, since Django has to use a module object anyway, it makes more sense to use a module that contains useful information right off the bat. For the majority of applications, the most useful module in a package is models.py, where all the Django models are defined. Therefore, Django uses this module to recognize an application. Some of the following methods return an application, and in each case, it returns the models module within the application's package.

The first step in a site-wide introspection is to determine what applications are installed. Calling `cache.get_apps()` will return such a list, containing the application module for each application in the INSTALLED_APPS setting that contains a models module. That's not to say that it only returns applications that have models. It actually checks for the presence of a models module, so even an empty `models.py` will cause an application to be included in this list.

Take, for example, the following INSTALLED_APPS setting, showing several of Django's own contributed applications, as well as some in-house applications and the `signedcookies` application described in Chapter 7.

```
INSTALLED_APPS = (
    'django.contrib.admin',
    'django.contrib.auth',
    'django.contrib.contenttypes',
    'django.contrib.sessions',
    'django.contrib.sites',
    'news',
    'customers',
    'callcenter',
    'signedcookies',
)
```

Most of these applications will, by necessity, contain various models. Chapter 7's `signedcookies`, however, only interacts with the site's HTTP traffic, so it has no use for the database. Therefore, when looking through the results of `cache.get_apps()`, the `signedcookies` application won't show up.

```
>>> from django.conf import settings
>>> from django.db.models.loading import cache
>>> len(settings.INSTALLED_APPS)
9
>>> len(cache.get_apps())
8
>>> for app in cache.get_apps():
...     print(app.__name__)
...
django.contrib.admin.models
django.contrib.auth.models
django.contrib.contenttypes.models
django.contrib.sessions.models
django.contrib.sites.models
news.models
customers.models
callcenter.models
```

Retrieving a Single Application

With a list of applications, it's straightforward to get models from each, so they can be handled appropriately. The next section describes that process in more detail. However, looking at *all* models isn't always the best approach; sometimes an application might be given the label of a specific application, so it can deal with just the models in that application.

While it would certainly be possible to just loop through the results from `cache.get_apps()`, checking the module names against the application module's __name__ attribute, that technique quickly runs into a few problems. First, the application's label isn't the same as its __name__ attribute, so trying to compare the two results in a good bit of extra code, most of which is already being done by Django. Also, that code must be tested and maintained, which increases the risk of introducing bugs into the application.

Instead, Django provides a utility for handling this situation. By passing the known label to cache.get_app(), an application can retrieve the application module for just the application matching that particular label. The label referred to here is determined as a specific part of the application's import path.

Typically referenced as app_label, an application's label is usually formed from the last part of the application module's import path before the models portion. To illustrate a few examples, consider the following application labels, corresponding to the entries in the INSTALLED_APPS setting.

```
admin
auth
contenttypes
sessions
sites
news
customers
callcenter
signedcookies
```

There's one important note to mention here. As part of the Meta options described in the official documentation, and briefly touched on earlier in this chapter, any model may override its own app_label setting to behave as though it was declared inside a different application. This option *does not* affect the behavior of cache.get_app() in any way. The get_app() method simply maps the app_label to an application module, without regard to what options the modules inside it may have declared.

As demonstrated earlier with cache.get_apps(), applications without models are viewed slightly differently within Django itself than others. By default, cache.get_app() will raise an ImproperlyConfigured exception if the application doesn't contain a models.py file. Sometimes it may still be useful to process applications without models, so cache.get_app() accepts an optional second argument to control how such applications are handled.

This second argument, called emptyOK, takes a Boolean indicating whether the application is allowed to not contain any models. This defaults to False, which will raise the ImproperlyConfigured exception, but if True is given instead, cache.get_app() will simply return None, allowing the calling code to continue managing the application.

```
>>> from django.db.models.loading import cache
>>> print(cache.get_app('admin'))
<module 'django.contrib.admin.models' from ...>
>>> print(cache.get_app('signedcookies'))
Traceback (most recent call last):
  ...
django.core.exceptions.ImproperlyConfigured: App with label signedcookies could not be found
>>> print(cache.get_app('signedcookies', emptyOK=True))
None
```

Dealing with Individual Models

Once an application is known, the next step is to deal with individual models within that application. Once again, AppCache comes through with a few methods to handling this situation. Retrieving models from the cache typically takes one of two forms, depending on how much is known about the model in advance.

In the first case, consider pure introspection. Remember from the previous section that AppCache provides access to all known applications with a single call to the get_apps() method, which returns application modules. Since these modules are actually the models modules within each application, it may seem easy to just use dir(app_module) or iterate over app_module.__dict__ to get the models that were defined.

Unfortunately, like many uses of simple iteration, that would require the loop to check each individual object in the module to see if it is in fact a model or if it's something else entirely. After all, Python modules can contain anything, and many models make use of tuples and module-level constants to help do their work, so there's no guarantee that each item in the module's namespace is in fact a Django model.

Instead, `cache.get_models()` retrieves a list of proper Django models that are specific to the given application module. It's no coincidence that both `cache.get_apps()` and `cache.get_app()` return application modules; `cache.get_models()` is suitable for use with both of these methods. That means that a list of models can be retrieved even without an application, but knowing the application in advance reduces the number of models retrieved.

The following code demonstrates how these techniques can be used in combination to retrieve a list of models for each of the known applications in use on the site.

```
>>> from django.db.models.loading import import cache
>>> for app in cache.get_apps():
...     app_label = app.__name__.split('.')[-2]
...     for model in cache.get_models(app):
...         print('%s.%s' % (app_label, model.__name__))
...
admin.LogEntry
auth.Message
auth.Group
auth.User
auth.Permission
contenttypes.ContentType
sessions.Session
sites.Site
news.News
customers.Customer
callcenter.Agent
callcenter.Call
callcenter.Case
```

As an additional option, `get_models()` can also be called with no argument, which will cause it to return all the models that are known to AppCache. This is a useful shortcut to avoid some of the overhead associated with the extra loop in this example, as a quick way to grab all the models.

There's a catch, however.

When using `get_models()` directly, with no argument, *all* registered models are returned. This may sound like a great idea, and sometimes it is, but remember that AppCache registers all models as they're encountered, regardless of where they were found. The full list may include models that aren't part of an installed application. Contrast that with the `get_apps()`/`get_models()` combination, which only retrieves models if their applications are found in the INSTALLED_APPS setting.

In practice, `get_models()` may return different results if called without an argument than if it were called with each of the applications returned from `get_apps()`. Typically, this could mean that an application may get access to extra models that it might not want to know about. Sometimes this is indeed the desired behavior, but it's always important to understand the difference.

One way a model could be in AppCache, but not be installed, is if the application is imported from a separate, installed application, which would cause its model classes to be processed by Django and registered, regardless of whether or not it was in INSTALLED_APPS. Also, if any model specifies an app_label on its Meta class and that application label doesn't match up with any installed application, the same situation would occur. If an application does wish to access all the models, regardless of whether they're installed or not, remember that it can use the _meta.installed attribute to identify which models were installed properly.

Sometimes, the name of both the application and the model are provided, perhaps as part of a URL or other configuration. In these cases, it doesn't make much sense to iterate over all the models for the given application. For this case, AppCache provides another method, get_model(), which retrieves a model class based on an application label and model name. The application name is case-sensitive, but the model name isn't.

```
>>> from django.db.models.loading import cache
>>> cache.get_model('auth', 'user')
<class 'django.contrib.auth.models.User'>
```

Using Model Fields

One of the most important aspects of models is the set of fields that are available to hold data. Without fields, a model would just be an empty container with no way to do anything useful. Fields provide a way to organize a model's values and validate against specific data types, providing a bridge between the database and native Python data types.

Normally, when accessing a field as an attribute of a model instance, the value will be a standard Python object representing the value found in the database. Previous sections in this chapter have described a variety of ways to get access to the actual field objects themselves, rather than this converted value. There are a variety of useful things that can be done with field objects.

Common Field Attributes

Different field types will have different attributes according to their needs, but there are several attributes that are common across most built-in Django fields. These can be used to generically access various details of fields, and by association, the values and behaviors they're meant to interface with. Note that there are more attributes used internally than those listed here, but these are the most useful and stable, and will provide the greatest value to applications looking to work with fields.

The descriptions listed here are how Django itself uses these attributes, and how developers will expect them to behave. Other applications will likely find use for them as well, to control certain types of behaviors, so the following descriptions will help illustrate their intended usage.

Some applications may find uses that are slightly different from what Django itself expects to use them for, but the general semantics of the values should remain intact. Remember that developers will build their expectations for these values based on how Django itself behaves, and third-party applications should avoid violating these expectations.

- attname—The name of the attribute on model instances where the database-related value is stored. This is typically the same as the name attribute, for simple cases where the value from the database is stored directly on the model. In other cases, it's more appropriate to expose a more complex object, such as another model instance, to other code when the actual field name is accessed. For those cases, attname and name will be different, with the attribute referenced by name being the complex object, while the attribute referenced by attname contains the raw data required to create it.

- blank—A Boolean value indicating whether the field must have a value supplied when using a form generated automatically based on the model. This is purely validation-related behavior; the null attribute controls whether a model can actually be saved in the database without a value for the given field.

- choices—A sequence of 2-tuples indicating the valid choices for the field. The first item in each tuple is the actual value that would be stored in the database if selected, while the second item is the text that will be displayed to the user for that value.

- column—The name of the database column that will be used to hold the field's value. This will either match db_column, if the field declared its database column explicitly, or will have been generated automatically, based on the field's name. Normally, this can be ignored, since Django manages the database interaction directly, but some applications may have need to communicate directly with the database or interface with some other database adapter that will need this information.

- db_column—The name explicitly supplied as the database column name for the field's values. This is different from column in that db_column refers to what the model itself declares, rather than what will actually be used. This will only have a value if the model field specified its db_column argument explicitly; it will be None otherwise.

- db_index—A Boolean indicating whether the field was declared to have an index created for it in the database. This only indicates whether the field was configured to instruct Django to create the index. Other indexes may have been added directly in the database itself, which won't necessarily be reflected in the value of this attribute.

- db_tablespace—The tablespace directive indicating where the field's data will be stored. Currently only supported for the Oracle backend, the format of its contents will depend on which database backend is in place. It will always have a string value, defaulting to the value of the DEFAULT_INDEX_TABLESPACE setting if not set explicitly.

- default—The default value for the field, to be used if no value has yet been supplied to the field itself. In addition to being inserted into the database in such a case, this value will be used as the field's initial value for any forms generated based on the model. The type of value stored in this attribute will be whatever native Python data type the field is intended to interact with, such as a string or an integer.

- description—A simple text description of the field or its purpose. A docstring is generally useful as well, but this description can be used when displaying information about the field inside an application, such as admindocs.

- editable—A Boolean indicating whether the field should be presented to users for editing when generating forms based on the model. This doesn't make the field itself read-only from within Python so this is far from a guarantee that the field won't be edited. It's simply a directive to control the default behavior of forms, though other applications can—and should—use it to control other behaviors as well, if they provide editing capabilities.

- empty_strings_allowed—A Boolean indicating whether the field allows an empty string as a possible value. This isn't an option specified as the configuration of a specific field instance, but is rather defined in the field's class itself. Many fields, such as CharField and EmailField, treat empty strings separately from None, so this attribute allows backends to decide how to handle empty strings for databases, such as Oracle, that might otherwise lose that distinction.

- help_text—The informative text provided in the field definition, to be displayed to users when the field is presented for editing. This will be passed in for forms that are generated based on the model, such as the provided admin interface.

- max_length—The maximum length the field's value can contain. Most string-based fields, such as CharField and EmailField, use this to limit the length of string content, both in form fields and the underlying database column. Other field types, such as IntegerField and DateField, simply ignore it, as it has no meaning in those cases.

- name—The name of the field, as defined when assigning the field to the model. This is set as part of the `contribute_to_class()` process, to maintain DRY by avoiding having to type the name twice. This will be the name of the attribute where the field's native Python value will be assigned and retrieved. Contrast this with `attname`, which stores the raw data necessary to populate name. Often, the two values will be the same, but the distinction is important to understand, for cases where they're different.

- null—A Boolean indicating whether the field can be committed to the database without a value assigned. This primarily controls how the underlying database column is created, but some applications may find other uses, as long the semantics remain the same.

- primary_key—A Boolean indicating whether the field should be used as the primary key for the database table. In addition to instructing the database to generate the primary key index, Django uses this indicator to determine which field's value to use when looking up specific instances, such as related objects through foreign key relationships. See the section on "Primary Keys" earlier in this chapter for details on the _meta.pk shortcut for determining which field has this value set to True.

- rel—In the case of fields that relate one model to another, this will be a special object describing the various aspects of that relationship. For all non-relationship field types, this will be set to None.

- serialize—A Boolean indicating whether the field should be included when model instances are serialized using the serialization framework.[3]

- unique—A Boolean indicating the field must be unique among all instances of the model. This is primarily used to create the proper constraints in the database to enforce this condition, but it can also be used by applications. For instance, a content editing application that provides detailed feedback about whether the user-entered values are valid for the model can also take this into account when making that determination.

- unique_for_date—The name of a date-related field, such as a `DateField` or `DateTimeField`, for which this value should be unique. This is essentially like `unique`, except that the constraint is limited to records that occur on the same date, according to the field referenced by this attribute. This can't be enforced at the database level, so Django manages the constraint manually, as should any other applications that need to provide detailed information about whether a given object can be committed to the database.

- unique_for_month—Like unique_for_date, except that the uniqueness is only required for objects that occur within the same month, according to the date-related field referenced by the name contained by this attribute.

- unique_for_year—Like unique_for_date, except that the uniqueness is only required for objects that occur within the same year, according to the date-related field referenced by the name contained by this attribute.

- verbose_name—The full name of the field, in plain English, to be displayed to users. Django's documentation recommends that this begin with a lower-case letter, so that applications can capitalize it as necessary. If an application needs this value capitalized, be sure to use the `capfirst()` utility method, described in Chapter 9.

---

[3]http:/prodjango.com/serialization/

Common Field Methods

Like the attributes described in the previous section, these methods are common to most field types, and provide a wealth of functionality that might otherwise be difficult to come by. Not all field types will implement all of these methods, and their exact behavior may change depending on the field type involved, but the general semantics described here will remain the same.

There are more methods that get used even more internally, which aren't listed here, because they're primarily responsible for simply populating the attributes described in the previous section. Therefore, it's generally best to simply reference the generated attributes, rather than attempting to recreate them manually after the fact.

- `clean(value, instance)`—Validates the given `value` is appropriate for the model, and the `instance` it's assigned to. Internally, this defers to both `to_python()` and `validate()`, as well as processing a list of validators that were defined when the field was instantiated. It will return a corrected value if everything was valid, and will raise `django.core.exceptions.ValidationError` otherwise.

- `contribute_to_class(cls, name)`—Configures the field for the class it's attached to. One of the most important methods on fields, this is called when `ModelBase` is processing the attributes that were assigned to the model's class definition. The `cls` argument is the model class it was assigned to, and `name` is the name it was given when it was assigned there. This allows fields the opportunity to perform any additional setup or configuration, based on this information. It usually doesn't need to be called directly, but can be a useful way of applying a field to a previously-processed model.

- `db_type(connection)`—Returns the database-specific column definition necessary for this field to store its data. Typically, this is only used internally, but as with some of the other attributes listed, if an application needs to access the database directly using some other tool, this can be a useful way to determine what the underlying column looks like.

- `formfield()`—Returns a form field based on the field's data type and verbose name, suitable for inclusion on any standard form. It optionally takes one explicit argument, `form_class`, which is a form field class to be instantiated, which defaults to whatever form field is most appropriate, as defined by the model field itself. It also accepts any number of additional keyword arguments, which are simply passed through the form field's constructor before returning the instantiated form field. This is normally called automatically by Django when constructing a form based on a model, but may be used manually as well for other situations. More information can be found in Chapter 5.

- `get_attname()`—Returns the name that should be used for the `attname` attribute. This is only called once, while the field is being configured for the class.

- `get_attname_column()`—Returns a two-item tuple containing the values to be used for the `attname` attribute as well as the `column` attribute.

- `get_cache_name()`—Returns a name suitable for use as a cache for the field, if caching is necessary. This is typically only required for fields that generate complex Python data types, which would suffer significant performance penalties if such a complex object had to be generated on every access, or in cases where it won't be used. See the applied techniques at the end of this chapter for details on how to use this method in such cases.

- `get_choices()`—Returns a sequence of 2-tuples that should be used for displaying choices to users looking to enter data into this field. Unlike the `choices` attribute, this may also include an empty option that would indicate no choice has been made. This behavior is controlled by two optional arguments: `include_blank`, a Boolean indicating whether it should be included, and `blank_choice`, a list of tuples containing the values and display text that should be used for the empty options. By default, these arguments are configured so that a single choice of (`""`, `"---------"`) is included.

- `get_db_prep_lookup(value, lookup_type, connection, prepared=False)`—Returns a representation of the supplied value that's suitable for comparing against existing values in the database.

- `get_db_prep_save(value, connection)`—Returns a representation of the supplied value that's suitable to be stored in the database.

- `get_db_prep_value(value, connection, prepared=False)`—Returns a representation of the supplied value that's ready for general use with the database. This is called internally by both `get_db_prep_lookup()` and `get_db_prep_save()`.

- `get_default()`—Returns the default value that would be used for the field. This takes care of all the necessary logic, checking if a default value was provided, executing it if a callable was provided as the default, and differentiating between empty strings and None, for database backends needing that behavior.

- `get_internal_type()`—Returns a string representing a high-level idea of what type of data the field contains. This is primarily used, along with a mapping provided by each database backend, to determine the actual database column to be used.

- `get_prep_lookup(lookup_type, value)`—Like `get_db_prep_lookup()`, except that this method is used for simpler conversions that don't require knowing which type of database is used.

- `get_prep_value(value)`—Like `get_db_prep_value()`, except that this method is used for simpler conversions that don't require knowing which type of database is used.

- `has_default()`—Returns True if the field has a default value associated with it, or False if the default behavior will be left to the database backend.

- `pre_save(model_instance, add)`—Returns a value for the field just prior to being saved in the database. By default, this simply returns the value that is already set on the supplied `model_instance`, but it could return a value derived from some other field or perhaps completely unrelated to the instance, such as the current time. The add argument is a Boolean indicating whether the provided instance is being added for the first time.

- `save_form_data(instance, data)`—Stores the supplied data to the appropriate attribute on the supplied instance. This is a shortcut for forms to be able to adequately populate a model instance based on form data.

- `set_attributes_from_name(name)`—Uses the supplied name argument to set the field's name, attname, column and verbose_name attributes as necessary. This method defers to get_attname_column() for the attname and column values, while verbose_name is only set here if it wasn't explicitly defined when instantiating the field.

- `to_python(value)`—Coerces the supplied value to a native Python data type that can be used when accessing the field's value on a model instance. See its description later in this chapter for further details.

- `validate(value, instance)`—Returns without error if the field's value is appropriate for the field's configuration and other data on a model instance, or raises `django.core.exceptions.ValidationError` otherwise. This is called internally by `clean()`.

- `value_from_object(obj)`—Returns the field's value as it appears on the supplied object.

Subclassing Fields

One of the more useful things that can be done with Django models, particularly with regard to reusable applications, is to tie into a model's ability to process individual types of fields in a generic fashion. This allows fields themselves to have considerable control over how they interact with the database, what native Python data type is used to access their contents and how they're applied to the model classes that use them.

The majority of this section assumes that the custom field will need to retain much of the same functionality of existing fields, such as interacting with the database and generated forms. There are many other applications, such as the historical records application described in Chapter 11, which use the hooks described in this section to provide much more functionality than just a simple field.

The term "field" here is used loosely to describe any object that uses some of these techniques to present itself to a Django developer as something resembling a standard Django model field. In reality, such an object could encapsulate complex relationships, such as a tagging application, or even control the creation of entire new Django models on the fly, based on the model to which they're assigned. The possibilities are nearly limitless.

The key to remember is that Django uses duck typing principles with regard to fields. It simply accesses whatever attributes and methods it expects in each situation, without regard to what those actually do behind the scenes. In fact, there's not even any requirement that objects be a subclass of `django.db.models.fields.Field` to make use of these hooks. Inheriting from `Field` simply provides an easy way to reuse much of the existing functionality, if that behavior is required.

Deciding Whether to Invent or Extend

One of the first things to consider when writing a new field is whether to try to invent an entire new type of field, starting perhaps from scratch without the aid of `Field` at all, or to extend some existing field type and inherit much of its behavior. There are advantages and disadvantages to each approach, and which is most appropriate depends very much on the demands of the new field being created.

By inheriting from `Field` or one of its subclasses, most of the behaviors in the following sections will be inherited, potentially reducing the amount of new code the custom field must include. If its behavior is similar to an existing field type, this can be a very useful way not only to cut down on new code, which helps reduce bugs, but also to automatically receive any new or updated functionality provided by Django itself in future releases. After all, by relying on Django itself for much of this behavior, updates to that code will automatically be reflected in the behavior of the custom field.

On the other hand, if the new field varies considerably from any existing field type, the standard behaviors will need to be rewritten for its own use anyway, negating any value of inheriting from a parent class. If most—or all—of these behaviors have to be written from scratch, inheriting from an existing field will simply create an extra step in the process Python uses to manage the class, even though that extra step offers little or no benefit. In these cases, it's best, therefore, to simply start from scratch, implementing just those behaviors that make sense for the custom field, and Django will still process it properly, due to its use of duck typing.

Of course, there is some middle ground between the two approaches. For instance, a custom field may interact with a completely unique data type, bearing little resemblance to any existing field types, but it may still store its data in the database like a standard field, and could benefit from reusing many of Django's more basic field methods, such as assigning names and storing itself in `_meta.fields`. In these cases, it's quite reasonable to inherit from `Field` itself, rather than a specific subclass, and inherit just this most basic functionality.

Performing Actions During Model Registration

The first step any field goes through is being processed by the `ModelBase` metaclass, whenever Python encounters a model class that utilizes the field in question. For standard Python objects, this means simply getting assigned to the model class as normal, with no additional processing. Fields take a different path, however, and each field gets the chance to customize how it's applied to a model class.

contribute_to_class(self, cls, name)

This is perhaps the most important method a field can contain, as it provides an essential feature: the ability for a field to know what class it was assigned to, and what name it was given. This may seem like a simple requirement, but Python itself doesn't normally have a way to facilitate this.

You may recall that descriptors, described in Chapter 2, have a way to identify what class—and even what instance of that class—was used to access the object, but this is only available at the time the attribute is accessed; there's still no way to know this information at the time the assignment took place. More importantly, even descriptors don't provide any way to identify what name was used to access them, which can be a considerable problem when trying to cache information or interact with other features that require the use of a name, such as that of a database column.

Instead, by using a metaclass, Django can intercede at the point where Python is processing the class, and use the presence of a `contribute_to_class()` method to identify objects that need to be handled differently. If this method exists, it's called instead of the standard `setattr()`, allowing the field to register itself in whatever way is most appropriate for its purpose. When doing so, Django also provides the class itself as an argument, as well as the name it was given, which was discovered while looking through the attributes assigned to the class. Therefore, in addition to the usual `self`, this method receives two arguments.

- `cls`—The actual class object of the model the field was assigned to. This can be used to customize the field based on the name or other attributes of the model itself.

- `name`—The name, as a string, of the attribute as it was assigned to the model's class. Fields will typically store this away as an attribute of the field itself, for future reference.

Once these two arguments have been processed in whatever way is appropriate for the field, the method shouldn't return anything, as its return value is ignored by Django.

CONTRIBUTE_TO_CLASS() VS SETATTR()

There is one very important thing to keep in mind when dealing with `contribute_to_class()`. It's been mentioned a few times already in various places, but it's so important that it merits driving home very explicitly. If Django identifies an object as having a `contribute_to_class()` method, *only that method will be called.*

Normally, `setattr()` is used to set attributes on an object such as a class, but since model fields don't get set in the standard namespace, that step is skipped intentionally. Therefore, if a custom field does in fact need to be set as an attribute on the model class itself, doing so is the sole responsibility of the field itself, during the execution of its `contribute_to_class()` method.

Sometimes, fields will instead need to set some other object, such as a descriptor, as the attribute on the class, to provide additional customizations for other types of access. This, too, is the responsibility of the field class, and the only time to do so in a way that will maintain the appearance of a standard field is during the execution of its `contribute_to_class()` method.

In the case of standard Django fields, and perhaps for many types of custom fields and other objects that behave as fields, this avoidance of `setattr()` is quite intentional. If that behavior is desired, `contribute_to_class()` should simply avoid setting anything on the model class, and Django's own behavior will make sure that nothing is assigned to the class itself.

contribute_to_related_class(self, cls, related)

For fields that relate themselves to other models, this is called once the related model is available, so that attributes can be added to that model as well. For example, this is how Django provides a reverse attribute on a related class when a ForeignKey is applied.

The two arguments it receives are cls, the model class the relationship was actually applied to, and related, the model the relationship points to, where other attributes may yet need to be applied. Like contribute_to_class(), this shouldn't return anything, as it would simply be ignored anyway.

Altering Data Behavior

Given that most field types exist to interact with specific data types, one of the first things to consider is how to tell Django to handle that data type. This includes how to store it in the database, how to ensure validity of its value and how to represent that value in Python. These are some of the most fundamental aspects of field behavior, and properly altering them can open up a world of possibilities.

get_internal_type(self)

This method returns a string, which helps determine how the database should store values for the field. The string itself isn't an actual database column type, but instead it's applied to a mapping provided by the database backend to determine what type of column to use. This way, fields can be written without being tied to a specific database backend.

Because the return value for this function gets applied to a known dictionary of types to retrieve the database column name, that value must be a valid entry in that dictionary. Therefore, there's a finite set of possible return values, which are listed here.

- AutoField
- BigIntegerField
- BooleanField
- CharField
- CommaSeparatedIntegerField
- DateField
- DateTimeField
- DecimalField
- FileField
- FilePathField
- FloatField
- ImageField
- IntegerField
- IPAddressField
- NullBooleanField
- OneToOneField

- PositiveIntegerField

- PositiveSmallIntegerField

- SlugField

- SmallIntegerField

- TextField

- TimeField

validate(self, value, instance)

When a model is being checked for the accuracy of its values, this method is used to determine whether the field's contents are correct. The arguments it receives are the value of the field itself, and also the model with all of its fields. This allows it the option of validating not only the field's own value, but also that it makes sense in the context of the greater model.

It should be obvious why this would be of use when validating an individual field's value, but it's less clear what value lies in using the rest of the model's values. After all, when writing a field, there's typically no way to know what other fields will be used alongside it.

Sometimes, however, a field may be written specifically for a particular model, and can therefore know in advance what the entire model will look like. In these cases, the field can, for example, check to see what type of account a person has, because the maximum value for the field depends on that other field.

to_python(self, value)

The value of a field can be stored in a number of different ways, depending on where it's being stored. In a database, it can be one of a few basic types, such as strings, integers and dates, while when serializing a model, all values will be coerced to strings. That means that often, when instantiating a model, its value has to be forced back into its proper Python representation. This behavior is handled by the to_python() method, though it's not quite as straightforward as it may seem on the surface.

The first thing to consider is that the value passed to to_python() could be one of a number of representations of the data. For instance, it could be whatever format is returned from the database adapter, such as a string, integer or native Python date, but it could also be a string retrieved from a serializer, or if the field manages a more complex custom data type that needs to be initialized, the value could actually be a fully-initialized instance of that type.

To illustrate this, consider the situation of BooleanField. Values that get passed into it could come in a variety of forms, so it's to_python() method needs to anticipate this and make sure that it always returns a Boolean value or throws an exception indicating that the value wasn't suitable for the field.

```
def to_python(self, value):
    if value in (True, False): return value
    if value in ('t', 'True', '1'): return True
    if value in ('f', 'False', '0'): return False
    raise exceptions.ValidationError(_("This value must be either True or False."))
```

As you can see, it has to check for a few different types of values that could all be coerced into Boolean values reliably. In addition to the native True and False, it checks for the string representations of the same, as well as a couple single-character representations that might turn up in various situations. If it finds something suitable, it simply returns the appropriate native Boolean value, raising the ValidationError described in the previous section if a suitable value couldn't be found.

Unfortunately, to_python() is an extra method call that's not always necessary, so it's not *always* called when it seems like it would be. In particular, it's provided mainly for validating data prior to committing to the database and when retrieving content from serialized data, so when retrieving from the database, it's assumed that the data has already been validated, and the database backends generally suffice for returning the proper type.

Because of this, Django doesn't call to_python() when retrieving data from the database. For the built-in types, and many potential add-on fields, this is sufficient, but for other data types or complex objects, some more work will be done to convert the database value to something appropriate to work with. To support these types of fields, Django provides a special way to force to_python() to be called when populating the field's value.

Supporting Complex Types with SubfieldBase

Sometimes databases just don't have the necessary data types to support certain types of applications. For example, most databases don't have a way to store a length of time and present it to Python as a datetime.timedelta[4] object. PostgreSQL has a column type called interval[5] for this purpose, which does map directly to a Python timedelta as it should, but other databases don't, which makes this impractical in terms of reusability. It would work suitably for PostgreSQL, but in order to make an application portable, it needs to be usable with more than one database.

Thankfully, timedelta stores its values in days, seconds and microseconds, and can write the entire value based on just a number of seconds passed in as a float. Therefore, it's possible for a new DurationField to use a DecimalField to store a value in the database, convert to a float in Python, then pass it into timedelta for use on the model instance.

```
import datetime
import re

from django.core.exceptions import ValidationError

def to_python(value):
    if isinstance(value, datetime.timedelta):
        return value
    match = re.match(r'(?:(\d+) days?, )?(\d+):(\d+):(\d+)(?:\.(\d+))?', str(value))
    if match:
        parts = match.groups()
        # The parts in this list are as follows:
        # [days, hours, minutes, seconds, microseconds]
        # But microseconds need to be padded with zeros to work properly.
        parts[4] = groups[4].ljust(6, '0')
        # And they all need to be converted to integers, defaulting to 0
        parts = [part and int(part) or 0 for part in groups]


        return datetime.timedelta(parts[0], parts[3], parts[4],
                                  hours=parts[1], minutes=parts[2])
    try:
        return datetime.timedelta(seconds=float(value))
    except (TypeError, ValueError):
        raise ValidationError('This value must be a real number.')
```

---

[4]http://prodjango.com/timedelta/
[5]http://prodjango.com/postgresql-interval/

```
except OverflowError:
    raise ValidationError('The maximum allowed value is %s' % \
                          datetime.timedelta.max)
```

This is the type of process that simply can't be handled without using to_python(), and it must take place every time the model is instantiated, even when coming from the database. However, calling an extra method call on every access from the database can get quite expensive, so it's essential to be able to handle this without penalizing those fields that don't use it.

As will be shown at the end of this chapter, a descriptor can be used to customize what happens when a field's value is accessed, which can be an excellent way to control this type of behavior. Of course, descriptors can be tricky if they're just a means to an end, and the to_python() behavior described here is a fairly common need for these complex data types, so Django provides a shortcut to ease the creation of this descriptor.

Located at django.db.models.fields.subclassing, the SubfieldBase metaclass is Django's way of easing the creation of model fields whose to_python() method will always be called. By simply applying this to a model class, it takes care of the rest, setting up a descriptor that calls to_python() the first time the field is loaded. Therefore, the DurationField example would use this in the field definition as follows:

```
from django.db import models
from django.db.models.fields.subclassing import SubfieldBase

class DurationField(models.DecimalField, metaclass=SubfieldBase):
    pass

    # Field logic then continues here
```

Controlling Database Behavior

Another important aspect of fields is how they interact with the database. This can include how the data itself is stored, how it's prepared before being sent to the database and how it's prepared for comparison with values already in the database. This process is already taken by Django itself, with every existing field type providing a few methods to define this behavior.

For custom fields, it's often necessary to override this behavior, interacting with the database in ways other than how Django itself would expect to do so. The following methods define nearly every aspect of how a field works with the database, so fields have a great deal of control over how the database interaction is handled.

db_type(self, connection)

Rarely overridden by individual fields, this method returns a database-specific string that controls how the column is created for use with the given field. Django internally uses the result of the get_internal_type() method in conjunction with a mapping provided by each individual backend to provide a return value from this method. That functionality is enough for the vast majority of field applications.

The most important thing to remember when considering the use of this method is that its return value is specific to a particular database backend. In order to use this field in projects with different backends, the connection argument is provided to help you decide what to use. In a simple case, you can use connection.settings_dict['ENGINE'] to determine what type of database the field is being used on, and behave accordingly. For example, if DurationField could in fact use interval in PostgreSQL, while still supporting other databases:

```
class DurationField(models.Field):
    def db_type(self, connection):
        engine = connection.settings_dict['ENGINE']
```

```
    if engine == 'django.db.backends.postgresql_psycopg2':
        return 'interval'
    else:
        return connection.creation.data_types['DecimalField']
```

One other feature of this method is that if you return None instead of a string, Django will skip the creation of this particular field. This can be necessary if the field must be created in a more complicated fashion than a single string can represent. Django will still attempt to reference the column when executing queries, though, so you'll need to make sure you do in fact create the column before attempting to use this field.

Most of time, you'll want to leave this method to Django, but it does provide a way to override the default behavior when you really need to. Just be careful doing this in a distributed application, because you'll end up having to support multiple types of databases, not just the one you're most familiar with.

get_prep_value(self, value)

There are a few methods that deal with preparing a value for different kids of use within the database, but they typically share the same code for preparing a value for use in the database at all. The get_prep_value() method is used by both of the following methods to perform this basic conversion.

In most cases, converting a Python object to some more basic type will suffice to allow a custom field to pass values to the database. By overriding get_prep_value(), the other database preparation methods can typically use their default implementations without issue. For example, DurationField requires this type of conversion, since timedelta objects can't be passed directly to most databases, which led to using a DecimalField to control the column's behavior. A custom get_prep_value() method can convert timedelta objects to Decimal values, which can then be passed to the database normally.

```
from django.db import models
from django.db.models.fields.subclassing import SubfieldBase
from django.utils import _decimal

class DurationField(models.DecimalField, metaclass=SubfieldBase):
    def get_prep_value(self, value):
        return _decimal.Decimal('%s.%s' % (value.days * 86400 + value.seconds,
                                           value.microseconds))

    # Field logic then continues here
```

get_db_prep_value(self, value, connection, prepared=False)

In cases when you need to prepare the value differently for different database connections, this method will allow you the flexibility to do so. The connection argument again represents the database connection being used, and can be used to make the necessary decisions about how to proceed. The prepared argument indicates whether the value has already been passed through get_prep_value(). If False, you should call that method before proceeding further. Here's what DurationField could look like if it continued to split up its behavior between PostgreSQL and other databases:

```
from django.db import models
from django.db.models.fields.subclassing import SubfieldBase
from django.utils import _decimal
```

```
class DurationField(models.DecimalField, metaclass=SubfieldBase):
    def get_prep_value(self, value):
        # Nothing to do here, because get_db_prep_value() will do the dirty work
        return value

    def get_db_prep_value(self, value, connection, prepared=False):
        if not prepared:
            value = self.get_prep_value(value)
        engine = connection.settings_dict['ENGINE']
        if engine == 'django.db.backends.postgresql_psycopg2':
            # PostgreSQL can handle timedeltas directly
            return value
        else:
            return _decimal.Decimal('%s.%s' % (value.days * 86400 + value.seconds,
                                               value.microseconds))

    # Field logic then continues here
```

get_db_prep_save(self, value, connection)

This works much the same as get_db_prep_value(), but offers a way to offer separate behavior when actually saving values into the database, as opposed to other operations. In fact, if you don't provide an implementation for this method, the default behavior will simply defer to get_db_prep_value(), which will usually suffice.

get_prep_lookup(self, lookup_type, value)

Another area where fields have to interact with the database is when making comparisons between Python objects and values already stored in the database. This takes place every time a QuerySet's filter() method is used, for instance, in order to generate the necessary database query. Since comparisons might require different handling than saving, Django uses the get_prep_lookup() method to manage this task.

When called, this method receives two explicit arguments, detailing how the lookup is expected to take place. The first, lookup_type, is the type of comparison that was requested in the filter() method. The second, value, is the Python object that was provided for comparison against database values.

While value is fairly straightforward, lookup_type is a little different, because it's a string containing the requested comparison type. There are several of these available as part of Django's database API,[6] each having its own expectations. This is the full list, including the purpose of each:

- exact and iexact—The supplied value must match exactly with what's present in the database, with iexact being case-insensitive. Django assumes a filter without a lookup type to mean exact, which will be passed in to get_prep_lookup().

- contains and icontains—The supplied value must be present in at least part of the value present in the database, with icontains being case-insensitive.

- gt and gte—The database value must compare as greater than the value supplied to the lookup, while gte also allows for the values to be equal.

- lt and lte—The database value must compare as less than the value supplied to the lookup, while lte also allows for the values to be equal.

- `in`—The database value must exactly match at least one of the values present in a list supplied as the lookup value.

- `startswith` and `istartswith`—The database value must begin with the string supplied as the lookup value, with `istartswith` being case-insensitive.

- `endswith` and `iendswith`—The database value must end with the string supplied as the lookup value, with `iendswith` being case-insensitive.

- `range`—The database value must with the range specified by a 2-tuple of beginning and ending limits supplied as the lookup value.

- `year`, `month` and `day`—The database value must contain the specified lookup value as its year, month or day portion, depending on which lookup type was used. This is valid for dates only.

- `isnull`—The database value must be equivalent to `NULL` in order to be matched.

- `search`—The database value must pass a full-text index search. This is valid only for MySQL, and only if the database has been modified to enable the necessary indexing.

- `regex` and `iregex`—The database value must match the format specified by the regular expression supplied as the lookup value, with `iregex` being case-insensitive.

Fields that inherit from some existing field can usually avoid overriding this method, as the parent class usually does the right thing. Other times, unfortunately, the child class needs specific handling for certain lookup types, where this can be quite useful. Still other times, it's necessary to restrict certain types of lookups entirely.

One useful side effect of having Python code executed as part of the lookup process is that it allows exceptions to be thrown for lookups that aren't valid for that field. This works just like anywhere else, where if you raise an exception, it will bail out of the query early, displaying a message indicating what happened.

WHERE'D MY ERROR GO?

Unfortunately, even though it's possible—and often quite useful—to raise exceptions within `get_prep_lookup()`, sometimes you may find that they get suppressed. If this happens, the query will appear to execute, but you'll likely receive just an empty list as its result, rather than seeing your error.

Due to the some of the hoops QuerySets have to jump through internally, certain types of errors—including `TypeError`, which seems like an obvious choice to use—get caught and suppressed, causing Django to move on with the process in spite of not getting a valid value for that field.

In order to make sure that the error gets raised to its fullest and works as expected, be sure to use `ValueError` instead of `TypeError`, as it doesn't get caught in the same trap.

get_db_prep_lookup(self, lookup_type, value, connection, prepared=False)

This performs essentially the same task as `get_prep_lookup()`, except that its output will be fed directly into the database query. It receives the same arguments, with the addition of `connection` and `prepared`, which work just like the arguments passed into `get_db_prep_value()`. The default implementation defers to `get_prep_lookup()`, which will be sufficient for most needs.

Dealing with Files

Many applications have need to manage content that goes beyond what's traditionally stored in database. Beyond the usual numbers and strings, there's a world of other data formats, from audio and video to print-ready Portable Document Format (PDF) files and plenty more. Content like this isn't well suited for being stored directly in the database—though in some cases it's at least possible—but it's still useful to tie it to other content that is in the database.

To handle this, Django provides a special `FileField`, with extra methods designed to facilitate access to files. It also uses many of the hooks described in this chapter to store a reference to the file in the database, as well as provide a special object that can access files in a portable manner. Django also provides an `ImageField`, which inherits much of its functionality from `FileField`, while adding some of its own, specifically tailored for dealing with the special needs of images.

Subclasses of `FileField` shouldn't generally need to override many of its methods, since they're mostly related to those features of a file that are common to all file types. This includes things like the filename and relative path, which don't have anything to do with the specifics of a particular type of file. Some, however, such as `save_file()`, can be overridden to provide special handling of attributes related to a specific type of file.

get_directory_name(self)

This method simply returns a relative path that will be stored in the database along with the filename. By default, this looks at the `upload_to` attribute of the field to determine what the directory should be, and even subclasses should respect this behavior. Exactly how that attribute is used, however, is where subclasses can customize this method to great effect.

Normally, Django creates a directory name using two pieces of information: the `upload_to` string itself and the current date. The date the file was uploaded is applied to the directory name, replacing certain characters with portions of the date. This allows individual fields to more accurately control where their files are stored, which helps keep directories smaller, and can possibly even make better use of disk capacity.

In a subclass, however, it may be more useful to generate the directory name based on some other type of information, such as the current site's domain name in multisite setups, or the Internet Protocol (IP) address of the machine where the upload was received, in larger production environments where there are multiple Web servers sharing common storage.

Essentially, anything's fair game here, as long as it only requires information that can be determined by only having access to the `FileField` instance. The current site or IP address can be obtained without regard to the current model at all, as can the current time. Other information, however, such as the user who submitted the file, the IP address of his or her remote computer, or the object the file will be attached to, is not accessible from this function, and thus can't be used.

Of course, there is another option to specify some of this additional information, but doing so bypasses this method entirely. By specifying a callable for `upload_to`, as described in Django's file documentation,[7] the directory can be generated based on the object it will be attached to, which may include the `User` who owns the object.

Note that when using a callable as `upload_to`, that callable is expected to return the *entire* path, including the directory and filename, so `get_directory_name()` won't be called at all in such cases, unless that callable explicitly calls it. Also, the incoming request still isn't available, even to that callable, so making directory naming decisions based on that information will require a custom view.

get_filename(self, filename)

This works in much the same way as `get_directory_name()`, except that it's responsible for specifying the filename portion of the path instead of the directory. It receives the original filename that was specified with the incoming file, and returns a new filename that will be used in the database, as well as the underlying storage system.

---

[7]http://prodjango.com/file-api/

If a `FileField` subclass has need to customize the filename that will be used for a particular file, such as stripping out certain characters or altering the file's extension, this would be the place to do it. That's also why it receives the original filename as well, so that it has a way to create a filename that's at least partially related to the one provided by the user.

By default, its output is combined with that of `get_directory_name()` to form the full path to be stored in the database and passed to the storage system. Like its counterpart, however, this is only true if the `upload_to` argument to the field was not a callable. If a callable was specified, it's responsible for specifying the entire path, including the filename. Therefore, in such cases, this method will only be called if the `upload_to` callable specifically requests it.

generate_filename(self, instance, filename)

This is the default method used to generate the entire path. It uses the same function signature as a callable `upload_to` argument, because it plays the exact same role. In fact, internally to `FileField`, all references for generating the filename to be used for the file reference this method; if a callable was supplied to `upload_to`, it's simply assigned to this same name, replacing the default behavior.

The default behavior is to use `os.path.join()` to combine the output of both the `get_directory_name()` and `get_filename()` methods, ignoring the model instance provided as an argument. If a `FileField` subclass needs the ability to specify the file's entire path all at once, this method would be the place to do it.

Of course, remember that if a callable was supplied as the `upload_to` argument, this method will get replaced. This is true regardless of what behavior is supplied by a `FileField` subclass; the needs of a specific instance always win over the behavior of its class. So, while overriding this behavior can provide a more useful default, it doesn't remove an individual developer's ability to replace it entirely.

save_form_data(self, instance, data)

This is a utility method for forms to use as a shortcut for saving a file associated with a model instance. It accepts an instance of the model the field was attached to, as well as the uploaded file data provided by the form. By default, it just extracts the necessary information from the uploaded file object, and passes it through to the standard file saving methods.

The `instance` argument is an instance of the model where the `FileField` was defined, and the `data` argument is an `UploadedFile` object, as described in Chapter 8. The uploaded file contains a `name` attributes, which contains the filename and a `read()` method, which is used to access the file's contents, so that it can be saved properly.

As this is the primary way files are handled by most areas of Django itself, overriding this field provides an excellent opportunity to tie into extended functionality based on specific field types. For example, Django's own `ImageField` uses this as an opportunity to store the width and height of an image in separate fields, so they can be indexed and searched in the database directly. Other file types could take this same approach, storing certain attributes of the file in other fields for easier access later on.

Since this method gets access to the entire file's contents, it's possible to pass those contents into most libraries that deal with files. Anything that can read an open file object can process uploaded content by simply wrapping it in a `StringIO`[8] object. That way, the contents can be accessed without having to write them to the storage system first, only to have to read them back again.

delete_file(self, instance, sender)

While this may look like simply a way to delete a file, it actually serves a very particular purpose, which is alluded to by the presence of a `sender` argument. The `contribute_to_class()` method of `FileField` sets up this method as a listener for the `post_delete` signal. It's not intended to be called individually, but instead it gets called every time a model instance with a `FileField` is deleted. As described for `post_delete`, the `instance` argument is the object that was just deleted, and the `sender` argument is the model class for that instance.

---

[8]`http://prodjango.com/stringio/`

When triggered, it checks to see if the file referenced by this field on the specified instance should be deleted. After all, if no other instances are referencing the same file, and it's not the default values for new instances, it's quite likely that no references to the file remain. In those cases, the file is permanently removed from the storage system.

The uses for overriding this are clear, because the logic for when to delete the file are included directly within this method. If a FileField subclass needs to have different rules for this, simply overriding this method is enough to make it happen.

The obvious example is if files should always remain, for historical reasons, even after the model instances associated with them have been deleted. Providing that behavior is a simple matter of just defining an empty implementation of this method.

```python
from django.db import models

class PermanentFileField(models.FileField):
    def delete_file(self, instance, sender, **kwargs):
        pass
```

Of course, there are other possible use cases for this as well, but the specifics of what those would look like will depend very much on the needs of an individual application.

attr_class

As a simple attribute, rather than a method, attr_class might not seem like it would provide much power or flexibility. Thankfully, looks are often deceiving, as it's actually the gateway to some very useful features. The attr_class attribute is set to a class that will be used to represent the field's value when referenced in Python. That means that the value of this simple attribute is actually the primary way of specifying what features are available on the public API for data entered into a particular FileField instance.

The following section describes the behavior of the class specified by default for this attribute, and how its methods can be overridden to provide additional functionality.

Customizing the File Class

When a model defines a FileField, the value made available as the attribute on actual model instances is a special object designed specifically for managing files. Located at django.db.models.fields.files, the File class provides a number of platform-independent and storage-independent methods for accessing a file's content and properties of that content, as well as for saving new files and deleting existing ones.

Because it's the public-facing API for accessing files, it's often quite useful to provide additional functionality for file types that have common qualities that will need to be referenced often. This provides a nice, clean, object-oriented way to encapsulate that common code in one place, rather than requiring the rest of the application to write it over and over again.

For example, Django's own ImageField provides its own subclass, ImageFile, which contains additional methods for accessing the width and height of an image, as well as caching it to speed up subsequent accesses. It's an excellent example of how easy it is to provide this extra functionality.

In addition to providing new methods, though, there are a number of existing methods that could benefit from being overridden. These are a bit less likely to be of use directly, but as ImageFile shows, they can be used to perform some important tasks, such as updating or invalidating cached values.

For the most part, the methods described next map directly to file storage methods described in Chapter 8. The main difference is that these are specific to a particular file type, and can be customized for aspects that are unique to that file type, while storage systems are just designed to work with files, without regard to what type of content gets handled.

path(self)

This returns the path of the file, if it's stored on the local filesystem. For files stored on other backends, which can't be accessed with Python's built-in open() function, this will raise an AttributeError, because the corresponding method isn't available on the related storage system object.

This is provided mostly as a compatibility layer with older versions of Django, for those projects that were written before the introduction of this new file handling system. In the real world, projects written for newer versions of Django should avoid the use of this method, and instead use the open() method listed in this section to access files in a more portable fashion. Overriding it will also be of little use, so it's listed here for completeness with the rest of the API.

url(self)

This method returns the URL where the file can be retrieved on the Web. It might be served up from the Django project itself, a media server operated by the site's owners, or even a storage service operated by a third party. The exact details of where this URL comes from are specified by the storage system, so this method is a portable way to access the URL for the file.

Overriding this provides little benefit for the most situations, but there are a few reasons to do so, depending on the situation. One example might be a FileField subclass that manages HTML files with a specific structure, so that the URL might contain a name reference, to direct browsers to a specific point in the file.

size(self)

This retrieves the size of the underlying file, caching it for future reference. While this can be a very useful feature, there's little value in overriding it in a subclass. The nature of file size is such that it doesn't vary depending on file type, and there's not really anything that can be done to customize how the size is obtained, so it's just included here for completeness.

open(self, mode='rb')

This retrieves the file's content and returns an open file or file-like object, which allows access to the file. This is the preferred method of accessing a file's contents in a portable fashion, since it passes through to the storage system for the majority of its functionality.

The mode attribute takes all the same options as Python's own open() function,[9] and can be used to open the file for read or write access. One use of overriding this method could be to change the default access mode, but only for changing whether it should be opened in binary mode by default or not. The default should always at least be to open the file for reading, rather than writing.

Another potential reason to subclass this would be to provide custom behaviors to the returned file-like object. By default, this method will return whatever object is returned by the storage system, but particular file types might have use for customizing methods on that object, such as write() or close() to alter how and when the file is written. Because this method is responsible for returning an open file-like object, it can wrap the true file-like object in another, passing through to the real object after doing whatever extra work needs doing.

save(self, name, content, save=True)

As the name implies, this saves a new file to the storage system, replacing the file currently in place on the model instance. The arguments should be mostly self-explanatory, with name being the name the new file should be saved as, and content being the actual contents of the file to written using that name.

---

[9]http://prodjango.com/open/

- Of course, invalid characters in the filename or existing files with the same name could result in the filename being changed by the storage system. Such changes will be reflected in the filename that's stored on the model instance.

- The save argument, however, merits further explanation. Because this saves a file that's related to a model instance, the new filename will be stored on that instance for future reference. However, it's not always beneficial to commit that change to the database immediately.

- By default, it does save the instance right away, but if save is set to False, this will be bypassed, allowing additional changes to take place before committing to the database. Take care when doing this, however. The file will already have been committed to the storage system, so failing to eventually save the instance with the new filename will result in a file with no references to it.

- Overriding this can provide a way to customize or record the filename that will be used, to change the default database commitment behavior, or perhaps most commonly, to retrieve information about the file's contents and update any cached information accordingly. The default File object does this for the filesize, and ImageFile also updates its dimensions cache.

delete(self, save=True)

Also fairly self-explanatory, this deletes the file directly from the storage system, regardless of which storage system is being used. It also removes the filename from the model instance, so that it no longer references the file.

The save argument works just like the one from the save() method, determining whether the model instance is saved or not. Also like save(), if False is provided, it's important to make sure the instance is in fact saved eventually. Otherwise, it will contain a reference to a file that has already been deleted. Perhaps worse yet, if another instance saves a file with the same name, the reference from the first instance will no longer be orphaned, but will in fact point to the wrong file entirely.

Overriding this provides most of the same benefits as overriding save(), by being able to remove any cached information so it doesn't cause confusion if accessed later.

Signals

Chapter 2 described the signal dispatching system bundled with Django, and how signals work in general. As explained, signals can be created and made available from any Python module, and can be used for any purpose. For dealing with models, several signals provided out of the box, and can be used in a number of situations.

The following signals are all available at django.db.models.signals, and each sends the model class as the standard sender argument to the listener. In addition, many signals include a model instance as an additional argument. These and other additional arguments are detailed in the descriptions of each individual signal listed here.

class_prepared

This signal fires when Django's ModelBase metaclass has finished processing a model class, indicating that the class is completely configured and ready to be used. Since the metaclass operates as soon as Python encounters the class declaration, class_prepared is fired before Python even continues processing the module that contains that declaration.

One important note to consider, however, is that this fires just prior to the model being registered with AppCache. Therefore, if a listener for class_prepared looks through AppCache to inspect the models that have been processed up to that point, the model that fired the signal won't yet be present. There may be some uses for inspecting the application cache at this point in the process, but without a full application cache, its value is quite limited.

Unlike most of the other signals listed in this section, `class_prepared` only sends the standard `sender` argument. Since there isn't any instance available at the point in time when the signal is fired and the `_meta` attribute on the new model class contains all the information about how it was declared, the model itself is enough to obtain all the information that's available at that point in time.

```
>>> from django.db import models
>>> def listener(sender, **kwargs):
...     print('%s.%s' % (sender._meta.app_label, sender._meta.object_name))
...
>>> models.signals.class_prepared.connect(listener)
>>> class Article(models.Model):
...     title = models.CharField(max_length=255)
...     class Meta:
...         app_label = 'news'
...
news.Article
```

Like all signals, listeners for `class_prepared` can be registered with or without a specific model to listen for, though it may not seem like this would be possible. After all, if the listener must be registered prior to the signal being fired, and the signal is fired before Python even continues with the rest of the module, how can it possibly be registered with a class to listen for? Even if it could, what possible purpose could it serve?

The answer to both of these questions is `contribute_to_class()`. Remember that attributes on a model are given the opportunity to customize how they're applied to the model. When an object with a `contribute_to_class()` method is encountered, that's called instead of the usual `setattr()`, where it's passed the model class and the attribute name, allowing the object to perform whatever functionality it wants to.

The key here is that `contribute_to_class()` receives the model class as an argument. It makes for an excellent opportunity to register a listener for `class_prepared` specifically for the class being processed. In fact, depending on the need at hand, this is not only possible, but could be downright essential.

Consider a situation where a field-like object needs to know everything about the model it's attached to in order to properly configure itself. Since there's no guarantee that all the other fields have been processed by the time `contribute_to_class()` is called on the object in question, it's necessary to defer the rest of the configuration until the class has finished processing.

pre_init and post_init

When a model is instantiated, `pre_init` fires before any other work is performed. It gets dispatched even before any of the arguments passed into the model are assigned to their appropriate attributes. This is a good opportunity to inspect the arguments that will be assigned to the instance prior to that actually happening, especially since this allows a listener to fire before encountering any errors that might come as a result of the arguments specified.

Because this takes place prior to any of the field values being populated on the object itself, it doesn't send the new object along when the signal is fired. Instead, it passes along two additional arguments besides `sender` that correspond to the positional and keyword arguments that were passed in to the model.

- `args`—A tuple containing the positional arguments that were passed to the model constructor
- `kwargs`—A dictionary containing the keyword arguments that were passed to model constructor

Note that even though these are the same names as those usually given to the excess argument technique described in Chapter 2, these are passed to the listener as explicit keyword arguments, rather than using * and **. Listeners must define these arguments explicitly in order for them to work properly.

```
>>> from django.db.models.signals import pre_init
>>> from news.models import Article
>>> def print_args(sender, args, kwargs, **signal_kwargs):
...     print('%s(*%s, **%s)' % (sender._meta.object_name, args, kwargs))
...
>>> pre_init.connect(print_args, sender=Article)
>>> article = Article(title=u'Testing')
Article(*(), **{'title': u'Testing'})
```

Similarly, `post_init` gets fired as part of the model instantiation process, but at the end instead of the beginning, once all the arguments have been mapped to the appropriate attributes based on the fields that were defined on the model. Therefore, as the name implies, the object is completely initialized at this point.

It would make sense, then, that when `post_init` fires, it gets passed the fully configured model instance as well as the standard `sender`, which is the model class. The new object is passed in as the `instance` argument to the listener, which can then do with it whatever is necessary, according to the application.

```
>>> from django.db.models.signals import post_init
>>> from news.models import Article
>>> def print_args(sender, args, kwargs, **signal_kwargs):
...     print('Instantiated %r' % instance)
...
>>> post_init.connect(sender=Article)
>>> article = Article(title=u'Testing')
Instantiated <Article: Testing>
```

pre_save and post_save

When a model instance is being committed to the database, Django provides two ways to hook into that process, both at the beginning and at the end. The primary difference, therefore, between the two is that `pre_save` is called before the object was committed to the database, while `post_save` is called afterward. This simple distinction can be very important, depending on the needs of the application.

When triggered by `pre_save`, a listener receives the model class as `sender`, and also the instance of the model as `instance`. This allows the listener to get access to—and even modify—the instance that's about to be saved, before it hits the database. This can be a useful way to provide or override default arguments for models provided by third-party applications.

On the other hand, `post_save` is called after the save has been performed, and the instance has been committed to the database. This is a useful step in two ways, because it not only ensures that the data is in fact present in the database, which is necessary when dealing with related models, but it also occurs after Django has made the decision about whether to insert a new record into the database or update an existing record.

In addition to the sender and instance arguments that work the same way as in `pre_save`, listeners for `post_save` can receive another argument. The `created` argument is a Boolean indicating whether or not the instance had to be created from scratch. A value of `True` means it was newly inserted into the database, while `False` means an existing record was updated. When using the `post_save` signal to track database changes, this is an important distinction, and can be used to determine the behavior of other applications. To see this in action, see the history example in Chapter 11 of this book.

Because a model manager's `create()` method does in fact commit a new instance to the database, it fires both of these signals. It's also safe to assume that any time `create()` is used, the `created` argument will be `True`, but just remember that there may well be other times when that argument is also `True`.

```
>>> from django.db.models import signals
>>> from news.models import Article
>>> def before(instance, **kwargs):
...     print('About to save %s' % instance)
...
>>> signals.pre_save.connect(before, sender=Article)
>>> def after(instance, created, **kwargs):
...     print('%s was just %s' % (instance, created and 'created' or 'updated'))
...
>>> signals.post_save.connect(after, sender=Article)
>>> Article.objects.create(title='New article!')
About to save New article!
New Article! was just created<Article: New article!>
```

A NOTE ABOUT COMBINING PRE_SAVE() AND POST_SAVE()

There's another very important difference between pre_save and post_save, because they're not always called as a pair. Because pre_save is triggered at the beginning of the process, you can reliably assume that it will always be called every time a save() is initiated. However, post_save only happens at the end, so if anything goes wrong during the save itself, post_save won't get triggered.

This is an important distinction, because it may seem convenient to register a pair of listeners for the model saving signals, expecting that both will always be called every time. While that may be true for the majority of cases, and certainly when nothing goes wrong, things do go wrong sometimes. Examples include an entry with a duplicate primary key or other unique column, data being of the wrong type or a timeout connecting to the database.

In situations where this type of behavior is required, the only reasonably sane way to go about it is to override the save() method on the model. This allows custom code to be run before and after the actual database interaction, but it also provides a way to identify problems that occurred in the process. In addition, it allows the code a better opportunity to pair the two pieces of functionality more fully, since if something does go wrong, it's easier to identify, and thus any pending actions can be canceled as a result.

pre_delete and post_delete

Similar to the previous section in spirit, pre_delete and post_delete are the pair of signals relating to the deletion of model instances. They function almost identically to their saving counterparts, except that they both provide just the sender and instance arguments.

When using post_delete, keep in mind that the instance passed in to the listener will have already been removed from the database, so many of its methods will raise exceptions if used. This is especially true if it had previously related to instances of other models. Those relationships will have been lost by the time post_delete is triggered, so any handling of those situations should be done in pre_delete or by overriding the delete() method on the model. If you do override the model's delete() method, you'll need to make sure to access the model and its relationships prior to calling the delete() method on the parent class. Once you delete it through the parent class, you'll be in the same situation as when using the post_delete signal.

Also, because the instance will have been deleted, its primary key value will no longer match up with anything in the database. However, in order to more accurately keep track of which object was deleted, the primary key value is left intact on the instance, and can be read using the pk shortcut described earlier in this chapter.

post_syncdb

Unrelated to a specific model, post_syncdb is instead triggered as part of the syncdb management command's normal process. It provides a way for applications to identify when an application's models have been installed into the database, in order to perform other tasks based on their definitions.

While there are likely other uses for this as well, the primary use for post_syncdb is to either configure the application itself the first time its models are installed in the database, or to identify other applications that are being installed, taking action appropriately. Within Django itself, there are examples of both types of functionality.

- The django.contrib.auth application uses it to install permissions for new models into the database, as soon as the models are installed, as well as to create a new superuser if the auth application itself was just installed.

- The django.contrib.contenttypes application uses it to maintain its own record of what models are in use, so it can provide relationships to any installed model.

- The django.contrib.sites application uses it to install a default site for all new projects that use the application.

The key to making post_syncdb considerably effective is that it uses a different type of value for the sender argument that accompanies all signals. Instead of using a specific model, this signal sends the application's models module, which is the object Django uses to identify an application. This allows a listener to be configured either for all applications or just the one that registered it.

All applications listed in the INSTALLED_APPS setting emit a post_syncdb signal every time the command is executed, even if nothing has changed. Therefore, in addition to sender, listeners of post_syncdb receive three additional arguments to indicate with more detail the circumstances under which syncdb was called, and help control their behavior in response.

- app—The application object (its models module) representing the application that was just synchronized with the database. This is exactly the same as the sender argument, but is named app here to make listener functions a bit more readable.

- created_models—A Python set containing all the models for the application that were actually installed into the database during the execution of syncdb. This is how a listener can identify just those models that are new, which is usually the most important thing a post_syncdb handler needs to know. This will always be provided, but in the case of an application where nothing is new, it will simply be an empty set.

- verbosity—An integer identifying the verbosity level requested by the user who executed syncdb. Valid values are 0, 1 and 2, with 0 being minimal output (nothing in most cases), 1 being normal output and 2 being all output (including messages indicating actions being performed, even they don't require user input). Listeners for post_syncdb should always be prepared to output what activities they're performing, and should use this argument to identify when different messages should be displayed.

```
from django.db.models import signals

def app_report(app, created_models, verbosity, **kwargs):
    app_label = app.__name__.split('.')[-2]

    if verbosity == 0:
        # Don't do anything, because the
        # user doesn't want to see this.
        return
```

```
# Get a list of models created for just the current application
app_models = [m for m in created_models if m._meta.app_label == app_label]

if app_models:
    # Print a simple status message
    print('Created %s model%s for %s.' % (len(app_models),
                                          len(app_models) > 1 and 's' or '',
                                          app_label))
    if verbosity == 2:
        # Print more detail about the
        # models that were installed
        for model in app_models:
            print('  %s.%s -> %s' % (app_label,
                                     model._meta.object_name,
                                     model._meta.db_table))

elif verbosity == 2:
    print('%s had no models created.' % app_label)

signals.post_syncdb.connect(app_report)
```

Code for `post_syncdb` listeners is generally placed in an application's management package, which is automatically loaded whenever `manage.py` is used for a project containing that application. This ensures that it doesn't get unnecessarily loaded for situations where it's not needed, while also making sure that it does get loaded whenever it might be necessary. Also, since it's Python, code in your management package can do other things as well, such as inspect the `INSTALLED_APPS` setting and decide whether the listener should even be registered at all.

Applied Techniques

Given the wide array of tools available for individual models to customize their behavior, their interaction with the database, and that of the field associated with it, the options are nearly limitless. The techniques that follow represent just a small portion of what's possible.

Loading Attributes on Demand

When working with certain types of data, it's sometimes quite expensive to construct a complex Python object to represent a given value. Worse yet, some parts of the application might not even use that object, even though the rest of the model might be necessary. Some examples of this in the real world are complex geographic representations or large trees of nested objects.

In these cases, we must be able to get access to the full object when necessary, but it's very important for performance to not have that object constructed if it won't be used. Ideally, the data would be loaded from the database when the model is instantiated, but the raw value would just sit on the instance without being loaded into the full object. When the attribute is accessed, it would be constructed at that point, then cached so that subsequent accesses don't have to keep reconstructing the object.

Looking back again to Chapter 2, descriptors are the perfect tool for this task, since they allow code to be run at the exact moment an attribute is accessed. Some care must be taken to make sure that the fully constructed object is cached properly for future use, but by using a separate name and `attname`, this is also fairly straightforward.

To illustrate how this would work in practice, consider a field designed to store and retrieve a pickled copy of any arbitrary Python object. There's no way to know in advance how complicated the Python representation will be, so this is a situation where it's ideal to delay the construction of that object until it's actually necessary.

Storing Raw Data

The first step is to tell Django how to manage the raw data in the database, using a standard field. Since pickled objects are just strings, some form of text field would clearly be prudent, and since there's no way to know in advance how large the pickled representation will be, the nearly limitless TextField seems like an obvious choice.

Of course, given that there will be some extra work going on for this new field, TextField alone won't suffice. Instead, we'll create a subclass that inherits the database functionality of TextField, while allowing extra customizations where necessary. Since fields are just Python classes like any other, this works just like you'd expect, but with one addition. In order to interact with the database using a different value than is used to interact with other Python code, the attname attribute needs to be different than the name attribute. This is controlled by a custom get_attname() method.

```
from django.db import models

class PickleField(models.TextField):

    def get_attname(self):
        return '%s_pickled' % self.name
```

This much alone will suffice for getting the field set up properly for the database. At this point, it's even possible to assign a PickleField instance to a model and sync it with the database, and the column created will be perfectly usable for the duration of this example. Of course, it only manages the raw data so far; it won't be able to handle real Python objects at all, much less deal with pickling and unpickling as necessary.

Pickling and Unpickling Data

To make the translation between a full Python object and a string representation that can be stored in the database, Python's pickling modules[10] will be the tool of choice. There are actually two separate modules provided by Python for this purpose: cPickle, written in C for improved performance, and pickle, written in pure Python for flexibility and portability. There are some minor differences between the two,[11] but they can be used interchangeably.

Having two modules available makes importing a bit trickier than usual. For obvious reasons, it's very valuable to have the greater performance when it's available, but a key aspect of Python and Django is the ability to be used across multiple platforms and environments. Therefore, when looking to import a pickling module, it's best to try the more efficient module first, falling back to the more portable module when necessary.

```
try:
    import cPickle as pickle
except ImportError:
    import pickle
```

With a pickle module available, we can give PickleField the ability to actually pickle and unpickle data. By providing a couple basic methods, it's possible to interface with the underlying module in a more object-oriented manner. In addition, it's safe to assume that when preparing to commit to the database, the field's value will be the full Python object, which obviously must be pickled.

---

[10]http://prodjango.com/pickle/
[11]http://prodjango.com/cpickle/

On the other hand, when using a QuerySet's `filter()` method to make comparisons against values in the database, pickled data will be quite useless. It would technically be possible to pickle the query's value to compare against that found in the database, but it would be comparing the pickled values, not the original Python objects, which could lead to incorrect results.

More importantly, even though a pickled value is guaranteed to be unpickled properly when necessary, it's quite possible that the same value, pickled on different occasions or possibly on different machines, will have different strings representing the original object. This is a documented side effect of the way pickling works, and must be taken into account.

With all of this in mind, it's unreasonable to allow any kind of comparison against pickled data, so an exception should be thrown if such a comparison is attempted. As described previously in this chapter, that behavior is controlled by get_db_pre_lookup(), which can be overridden to throw such an exception. The full field thus far follows:

```
class PickleField(models.TextField):
    def pickle(self, obj):
        return pickle.dumps(obj)

    def unpickle(self, data):
        return pickle.loads(str(data))

    def get_attname(self):
        return '%s_pickled' % self.name

    def get_db_prep_lookup(self, lookup_type, value):
        raise ValueError("Can't make comparisons against pickled data.")
```

Note that `pickle` and `cPickle` only support pickled data strings as plain byte strings, not as full Unicode strings. Since everything in Django gets coerced to Unicode wherever possible, including retrieving from the database, `unpickle()` needs to take the extra step of forcing it back to a byte string in order to be unpickled properly.

WHY THE EXTRA METHODS?

It may seem odd to define separate `pickle()` and `unpickle()` methods, when the pickling module is already available in the module's namespace. After all, it's not only extra lines of code for you, the developer, to write, but it's also an extra function call that Python has to go through to get the job done, which slows things down slightly, and seemingly unnecessarily.

The biggest advantage of doing it this way is that if any other application has need to subclass `PickleField` and wishes to override exactly how the data gets pickled and unpickled, having explicit methods for it makes that process considerably easier. They can just be overridden like normal, and as long as the rest of `PickleField` just references the methods, the subclass will work quite well.

This gets us one step closer, now that `PickleField` can store values in the database properly. However, it still doesn't solve the main issue of loading data into a Python object, and doing so only when it's really necessary.

Unpickling on Demand

If we weren't concerned with performance, it'd be easy to perform the unpickling step in the to_python() method and just use SubfieldBase to make sure it happens every time an object is instantiated, regardless of where it came from. Unfortunately, that would incur a good deal of unnecessary overhead for those cases where this field wouldn't be accessed, so it's still well worth loading it up on demand, only when it's requested.

As mentioned earlier, Python descriptors are particularly well suited for this scenario. They get called when an attribute is accessed, and can execute custom code at that time, replacing standard Python behavior with something designed for the task at hand.

The first step is determining how to instantiate the descriptor, which also means identifying what data it will need in order to get the job done. In order to retrieve the raw data from the model instance properly, it'll need access to the field object, from which it can gather the name of the field itself.

```python
class PickleDescriptor(property):
    def __init__(self, field):
        self.field = field
```

That will store references to all the features of the field that will be useful later on. With those in place, it's possible to write the __get__() and __set__() methods that will actually do the hard work in the long run. Actually, __set__() is the easier of the two to implement; it just has to assign the raw data to the instance's namespace directly.

```python
def __set__(self, instance, value):
    instance.__dict__[self.field.name] = value
    setattr(instance, self.field.attname, self.field.pickle(value))
```

With that in place, the trickiest bit of this whole process is the descriptor's __get__() method, which must be able to perform the following tasks in order to work properly.

- Identify whether or not the full Python object needs to be created.

- Generate a full Python object, by way of unpickling the raw data, only when necessary.

- Cache the generated Python object for future use.

- Return the cached copy of the object if it's available, or the new one otherwise.

That last one's actually a bit of a red herring, since it's easy to make sure that a Python object is available at the end of the method, and just return that, without regard to where it came from. The rest, though, may look like quite a laundry list, but it's really not that difficult to perform all those tasks in a small, readable method.

```python
def __get__(self, instance, owner):
    if instance is None:
        return self

    if self.field.name not in instance.__dict__:
        # The object hasn't been created yet, so unpickle the data
        raw_data = getattr(instance, self.field.attname)
        instance.__dict__[self.field.name] = self.field.unpickle(raw_data)

    return instance.__dict__[self.field.name]
```

It should be fairly clear how this method performs each of the requirements. The first block checks for accesses from the model class, raising an appropriate exception. The second block does three more tasks, by first checking for the presences of a cached copy, and continuing otherwise. Then, it does two more in one line, unpickling the raw data and storing it in the cache if the cache wasn't already populated. At the end, it simply returns whatever's in the cache, regardless of whether it was in the cache when the method began.

Putting It All Together

The only thing left to make the whole thing work is to get the descriptor on the model at the right time, so it's in place to get called when the attribute is accessed. This is precisely the intent of contribute_to_class(), where Django already provides a way for third-party code, such as this, to tie into the model creation process. Just make sure to always call the conribute_to_class() method on the parent class as well, to make sure that all the standard Django functionality is applied as well as the application's more specialized requirements.

```python
def contribute_to_class(self, cls, name):
    super(PickleField, self).contribute_to_class(cls, name)
    setattr(cls, name, PickleDescriptor(self))
```

With all of that now in place, we have a total of three import statements, two new classes and one new field that performs a very useful task. This is just one example of how this technique can be put to use, and there are as many more as there are applications using complicated Python data structures. The important thing to take away from this example is how to use descriptors to populate those complex objects only when necessary, which can be a big win in situations where they might not always be used.

```python
try:
    import cPickle as pickle
except ImportError:
    import pickle

from django.db import models

class PickleDescriptor(property):
    def __init__(self, field):
        self.field = field

    def __get__(self, instance, owner):
        if instance is None:
            return self

        if self.field.name not in instance.__dict__:
            # The object hasn't been created yet, so unpickle the data
            raw_data = getattr(instance, self.field.attname)
            instance.__dict__[self.field.name] = self.field.unpickle(raw_data)

        return instance.__dict__[self.field.name]

    def __set__(self, instance, value):
        instance.__dict__[self.field.name] = value
        setattr(instance, self.field.attname, self.field.pickle(value))
```

```python
class PickleField(models.TextField):
    def pickle(self, obj):
        return pickle.dumps(obj)

    def unpickle(self, data):
        return pickle.loads(str(data))

    def get_attname(self):
        return '%s_pickled' % self.name

    def get_db_prep_lookup(self, lookup_type, value):
        raise ValueError("Can't make comparisons against pickled data.")

    def contribute_to_class(self, cls, name):
        super(PickleField, self).contribute_to_class(cls, name)
        setattr(cls, name, PickleDescriptor(self))
```

Creating Models Dynamically at Runtime

Chapter 2 demonstrated how Python classes are really just objects like any other, and can be created at runtime by using the built-in type() constructor and passing in some details about how it should be defined. Since Django models are really just Python declared in a specific way, it's reasonable to expect that they could also be created at runtime using this same feature. Some care must be taken, but this can be an extremely useful technique in a variety of situations.

The trick is to remember how Python processes classes, and how Django processes its models. Chapter 2 already illustrated the basic tools necessary to make this work, so it's now just a matter of applying that to the specific details of Django models. There are a few things that set models apart from other Python classes:

- All models subclass django.db.models.Model.
- Fields are specified as class attributes in the model's declaration.
- Additional options are specified in a Meta class inside the model's declaration.

With these requirements outlined, it's fairly easy to map a model declaration onto the arguments for type(). In particular, remember that there are three arguments required to construct a class: name, bases and attrs. The model's name is clearly mapped to name, while the single subclass of models.Model can be wrapped in a tuple and passed into bases. The remainder of the class declaration would go into attrs, including a Meta class for any additional model-level configuration options.

A First Pass

To make a first pass at what this function might look like, let's start with just the most basic aspect of class creation and work our way out from there. To begin with, consider a function that generates a class with the correct name and base class, to illustrate the basic technique for creating a class dynamically and returning it for use elsewhere.

```python
from django.db import models

def create_model(name):
    return type(name, (models.Model,), {})
```

Unfortunately, that's actually a little too simplistic. Trying this out in Python will result in a KeyError, because Django expects the attribute dictionary to include a __module__ key, with its value being the import path of the module where the model was defined. This is normally populated by Python automatically for all classes defined in source files, but since we're generating a model at runtime, it's not available.

This is just one of the minor details that dynamic models have to face, and there's really no way of avoiding it entirely. Instead, create_model() needs to be updated to provide a __module__ attribute directly. This is also another example of why it's a good idea to put this code in one place; imagine having to deal with this every time a dynamic model is required. Here's what it looks like to include a module path for the class:

```python
def create_model(name, module_path):
    return type(name, (models.Model,), {'__module__': module_path})
```

Now it can accept a module path and keep Django happy. Well, it can keep Django happy as long as the module path has already been imported, which means it has to actually exist. Under normal circumstances, the model's __module__ attribute is set to the path of the module where it was defined. Since the model will only be processed while executing that module, it's always guaranteed that the module will exist and have been imported successfully. After all, if it hadn't, the model would've been encountered in the first place.

For now, since the only requirement of the module path is that it be valid and already imported, Django's own django.db.models will make a reasonable candidate. It should be overridden where appropriate, of course, but it's a decent default until things get rolling.

```python
def create_model(name, attrs={}, module_path='django.db.models'):
    attrs = dict(attrs, __module__=module_path)
    return type(name, (models.Model,), attrs)
```

Clearly, these dynamic models shake things up quite a bit, bypassing much of how Python normally works with a process like this. The __module__ issue is just the first issue encountered, and one of the easiest to work around. Thankfully, even though there are a few others to be handled, it can be well worth it if used properly.

The next step in this basic example is to include a dictionary of attributes to be set as if they were declared directly on a class definition. This will allow fields to be included on the model, as well as custom managers and common methods like __unicode__(). Since we're already passing a dictionary to be used as attributes, assigning additional items to that dictionary is a simple process.

```python
def create_model(name, attrs={}, module_path='django.db.models'):
    attrs = dict(attrs, __module__=module_path)
    return type(name, (models.Model,), attrs)
```

Ordinarily, it's not advisable to supply a mutable object, such as a dictionary, as a default argument, since modifications to it would affect all future executions of the function. In this example, however, it's used only to populate a new dictionary, and is immediately replaced by that new dictionary. Because of this, it's safe to use as the default argument, in an effort to keep the method reasonably succinct.

So far, we've set up a 3-line function to create basic models with any number of attributes, which can then be used in other areas of Django. Technically, this function alone could be used to generate any model imaginable, but it already provides a shortcut for setting up __module__, so it would make sense to provide another shortcut for setting up the model configuration by way of a Meta inner class. That way, code to create a model won't have to set up that class directly.

Adding Model Configuration Options

Django models accept configuration through an inner class called Meta, which contains attributes for all the options that are specified. That should sound familiar, since that's basically what models themselves do as well. Unfortunately, because of how Django processes the Meta class, we have to take a different approach.

The attributes defined within Meta are passed along into a special Options object, which lives at django. db.models.options. As part of this process, Options makes sure that no attributes were supplied that it doesn't know how to handle. Unfortunately, because the fact that Meta is a class is just a way to separate its namespace from that of the main model. Options only knows how to handle old-style Python classes—that is, classes that *don't* inherit from the built-in object type.

This is an important distinction, because calling type() directly creates a new-style class, even if it doesn't inherit from object, or any subclasses for that matter. This ends up creating two additional attributes on the class that Options doesn't know how to deal with, so it raises a TypeError to indicate the problem. That leaves two options for creating a Meta class: removing the additional attributes or creating an old-style class using some other means.

While it would be possible to just remove the attributes that offend Options, an even better idea would be to provide it exactly what it expects: an old-style class. Clearly, using type() is out of the question, which leaves us with just declaring a class using standard syntax. Since this is possible even within functions, and its namespace dictionary can be updated with new attributes, it's a decent way to go about solving this problem.

```
from django.db import models

def create_model(name, attrs={}, meta_attrs={}, module_path='django.db.models'):
    attrs['__module__'] = module_path
    class Meta: pass
    Meta.__dict__.update(meta_attrs, __module__=module_path)
    attrs['Meta'] = Meta
    return type(name, (models.Model,), attrs)
```

This will now accept two attribute dictionaries, one for the model itself, and another for the Meta inner class. This allows full customization of Django models that can be created at any time. While this may seem like a rather abstract concept at the moment, see Chapter 11 for a full example of how this can be used in practice to automatically record all changes to a model.

Now What?

With a solid foundation of Django's models under your belt, the next step is to write some code that will allow users to interact with those models. The next chapter will show how views can provide your users with access to these models.

CHAPTER 4

■ ■ ■

URLs and Views

Much of this book is split into fairly self-contained chapters, but this one covers two seemingly unrelated concepts together, because each relies very much on the other. URLs are the primary entry points to your site, while views are the code that respond to incoming events. What goes on in a view is very open-ended. Aside from accepting a request and returning a response, there's no particular protocol that views should adhere to, and no rules about what they are or aren't allowed to do.

The possibilities for views are too vast to consider describing in detail, and there aren't any utilities designed explicitly for views to use while executing. Instead, it's possible to hook into the process Django uses to map Web addresses to the views they should execute. This makes the link between URLs and views extremely important, and a thorough understanding of it can enable further advanced techniques.

Also, in terms of how Django manages incoming requests, URL configurations exist solely to dispatch a request to a view that can handle it. Discussing URLs and URL configurations independently of views would be of little value.

URLs

Since all incoming requests to a Web server originate with the Web browser accessing a URL, a discussion of URLs is an important place to start. The process taken by the browser to transform a URL into a message to be sent to the Web server is beyond the scope of this chapter, but Chapter 7 provides more information.

One common point of confusion is whether a Web address should be called a Uniform Resource Identifier (URI) or a Uniform Resource Locator (URL). Many people use these two terms interchangeably, regardless of whether they know the difference. In a nutshell, a URI is a complete addressing mechanism that includes two pieces of information.

- The name of the scheme or protocol to be used to connect to the resource. This is always followed by a single colon.

- The path where the resource can be found. The exact format of this path may be different for different schemes, so not all URI paths look alike.

URLs, on the other hand, are addresses from a small set of connection schemes whose path portions all conform to a single format. Included in this set are such common protocols as HTTP, HTTPS and FTP—essentially the common protocols found on the Web today. The path format shared by these protocols is as follows.

- The protocol to be used to access the resource, such as `http://` for standard HTTP. This is a slight extension to the scheme portion of the URI because it is assumed that all URL protocols will include two forward slashes following the colon.

- The host domain where the resource can be found, such as `prodjango.com` or `www.prodjango.com`.

- Optionally, the port number the server responds to. Each protocol has a default port that will be used if one isn't supplied. For standard HTTP, this is 80, while for encrypted HTTP using the Secure Sockets Layer (SSL), it will be 443.

- The path of the resource on the server, such as /chapter4/.

So while all URLs are certainly URIs, not all URIs are URLs. That subtle distinction can be confusing when working on the Web because either term can be used to describe the addresses found everywhere. Since Django is built for the Web—and thus the addresses covered under URL schemes—the rest of this book will refer to these addresses as URLs, as the full range of URIs might not be suitable for Django's dispatching mechanism.

DESIGNING CLEAN URLS

In an ideal world, the URLs you choose when setting up a site the first time will never change,[1] remaining intact until the documents—or the entire server—are no longer maintainable. Changing URLs simply because of a redesign or reorganization of the site is generally bad form and should be avoided.

The key to making URLs maintainable for the long haul and making it easier for your users to keep track of them, is to design them well in the first place. Django makes this easy, allowing you to design your URLs in whatever hierarchy you like, assigning variables right in the URL and splitting the URL structure into manageable chunks.

Above all, URLs are part of your application's user interface, since users have to see them, read them and often type them in manually. Keep this in mind when designing your URLs.

Standard URL Configuration

Django doesn't provide any features for automatically discovering or generating a URL structure for any site. Instead, each site and application is expected to explicitly declare whatever addressing scheme is most appropriate using URL configurations. This isn't a limitation—it's a feature that allows you to define your site's addresses the way you'd like. After all, sites on the Web are like real estate; your Web framework shouldn't determine your floor plan.

Defining a URL configuration may seem quite simple, but there's a bit going on that merits some special attention, especially since Django's own tools aren't the only way to define this configuration. The implementation lives at django.conf.urls.defaults and provides two functions that work together to manage URL configurations.

The patterns() Function

A URL configuration consists of a list of patterns that each map a particular type of URL to a view. These patterns each have a few components but all of them are specified together as arguments to the patterns() function.

```
from django.conf.urls.defaults import *

urlpatterns = patterns('',
    (r'^$', 'post_list'),
    (r'^(?P<id>\d+)/$', 'post_detail'),
    (r'^(?P<id>\d+)/comment/$', 'post_comment', {'template': 'comment_form.html'}),
)
```

---

[1]http://prodjango.com/cool-uris-dont-change/

The arguments for this function can be placed in two groups:

- A single import path prefix for any views that are specified as strings
- Any number of URL patterns

Historically, all views were specified as strings, so the prefix was a great way to reduce the amount of duplication required to map URLs to views from a single application. More recently, URL patterns are allowed to specify views as callables, in which case the prefix would be ignored. It is still often useful to specify views as strings using a prefix, as it reduces the overall code by not requiring a set of imports for the views.

The URL patterns are traditionally passed in as tuples, though "The url() Function" section later in this chapter describes a more recent addition. Details of each portion of this tuple are as follows:

- A regular expression used to match against the URL
- The view function to be called for a request matching this pattern
- Optionally, a dictionary of arguments to be passed to the function

This tuple contains all the information necessary to map an incoming request to a view function. The URL's path will be checked against the regular expression, and if a match is found, the request is passed along to the specified view. Any arguments captured by the regular expression are combined with the explicit arguments in the extra dictionary, then passed along to the view along with the request object.

■ **Note**   Like most regular expressions, URL patterns are typically described using raw strings, indicated by the r prefix. Raw strings don't go through standard escaping, which is useful here because regular expressions offer their own forms of escaping. If we didn't use raw strings, we'd have to escape each backslash in order to pass it through to the regular expression. The example here would be written `'^(?P<id>\\d+)/$'` without a raw string.

MULTIPLE ARGUMENTS WITH THE SAME NAME

A single URL configuration can provide values in two separate ways: in the URL's regular expression and in the dictionary attached to the pattern. Accepting arguments from two different sources makes it possible to provide two different values for the same key, which needs to be resolved somehow. If you try doing this with keyword arguments to a standard function, Python will raise a TypeError as described in Chapter 2.

Django allows these multiple arguments to be specified without raising an exception, but they can't be all passed to the view together. As the second portion of this chapter shows, views are called just like any normal Python function, so these multiple arguments would cause the same TypeError described in Chapter 2. To resolve this issue without an error, Django has to reliably choose one instead of the other. Any argument provided with a dictionary in the URL configuration will take priority over anything found in the URL.

It's bad form to provide multiple arguments with the same name in this manner, since it relies heavily on Django's handling of the situation to work properly. While that behavior isn't likely to change on a whim, relying on it could cause problems in the future. More importantly, specifying the same argument name in multiple places greatly reduces the readability of your URL configurations. Even in closed-source applications, someone else will likely need to read your code long after you're done with it.

The url() Function

In an effort to provide better flexibility in the long run, URL pattern tuples have been deprecated in favor of the url() utility function. url() takes the same arguments that are passed into the tuple, but can also take an extra keyword argument to specify the name of the URL pattern being described.

This way, a site can use the same view multiple times, yet still be able to be referenced using reverse URL lookups. More information on that can be found later in this section.

The include() Function

Rather than supplying all your URL patterns in a single file, the include() function allows them to be split up among multiple files. It takes a single argument: an import path where another URL configuration module can be found. This not only allows the URL configuration to be split across multiple files, but it also allows the regular expression to be used as a prefix for the included URL patterns.

One important thing to remember when using include() is to not specify the end of the string in the regular expression. The expression should never end in a dollar sign ($). The dollar sign ($) causes the expression to only match the full URL. This wouldn't leave any additional URL fragments to pass along to the included configuration. This means that the extra URL patterns would only be matched if they check specifically for an empty string.

Resolving URLs to Views

Views are rarely called directly by your own code but are instead invoked by Django's URL dispatch mechanism. This allows views to be decoupled from the particular URLs that trigger them, and the details of how those two aspects are linked can be safely ignored for most projects. But since views don't always have to just be simple functions, knowing how Django goes from URL to view is important in order to determine what views are truly capable of.

Mapping URLs to views is a simple, well-documented process, but it's worth covering the basics here for reference. A typical URL pattern consists of a few distinct items:

- A regular expression to match against the incoming URL being requested

- A reference to the view to be called

- A dictionary of arguments to be passed along every time the view is accessed

- A name to be used to reference the view during reverse lookups

Since URL patterns are expressed in regular expressions, which can capture certain portions of a string for later use, Django uses this as a natural way to pull arguments out of a URL so they can be passed to a view. There are two ways these groups can be specified, which determine how their captured values are passed into the view.

If groups are specified without names, they're pulled into a tuple, which is passed along as excess positional arguments. This approach makes the regular expression a bit smaller, but it has some drawbacks. Not only does it make the regular expression a bit less readable, it also means that the order of arguments in your view must always match the order of the groups in the URL, because Django sends them in as positional arguments. This couples the URL to the view more than is usually preferable; in some situations, such as the object-based views described later in this chapter, it can still be quite useful.

If groups are given names, Django will create a dictionary mapping those names to the values that were extracted from the URL. This alternative helps encourage looser coupling between URLs and views by passing captured values to the view as keyword arguments. Note that Django doesn't allow named and unnamed groups to be used together in the same pattern.

Resolving Views to URLs

As alluded to in the previous section, there's another URL resolution process that Django provides, which can be of even more use if applied properly. Applications often need to provide links or redirects to other parts of the application or elsewhere on the site, but it's not usually a good idea to hard-code those links directly. After all, even proprietary applications can change their URL structure, and distributed applications may not have any idea what the URL structure looks like in the first place.

In these situations, it's important to keep the URLs out of the code. Django offers three distinct ways to specify a location without needing to know its URL in advance. Essentially, these all work the same way, as they all use the same internal machinery, but each interface is suited for a particular purpose.

The permalink Decorator

One of the most obvious places for code to reference a URL is in the get_absolute_url() method of most models. Providing this method is a common convention, so templates can easily provide a direct link to an object's detail page without having to know or care what URL or view is used to display that page. It doesn't take any arguments and returns a string containing the URL to be used.

To accommodate this situation, Django provides a decorator, living at django.db.models.permalink, which allows a function to return a set of values describing a view to be called, transforming it into a URL that calls the view. These values are provided as the return value from a function such as the get_absolute_url() method and follow a specific structure—a tuple containing up to three values.

- The first value is the name of the view to be called. If the view was named, that name should be used here. If not, the import path of the view should be used instead. This is always required.

- The second value is a tuple of positional arguments that should be applied to the view. If there are no arguments to be applied to the view at all, this value doesn't need to be provided, but if keywords are needed, this should be an empty tuple.

- The third value in this tuple is a dictionary mapping keyword arguments to their values, all of which will be passed to the specified view. If no keyword arguments are necessary, this value can be left out of the tuple.

Given the following URL configuration:

```
from django.conf.urls.defaults import *
from django.views.generic.detail import DetailView
from library.import models

class LibraryDetail(DetailView):
    queryset = models.Article.objects.all()

urlpatterns = patterns('django.views.generic',
    url(r'^articles/(?P<object_id>\d+)/$', LibraryDetail.as_view(),
        name='library_article_detail'),
)
```

a corresponding model (located in a `library` application) might look like this:

```
from django.db import models

class Article(models.Model):
    title = models.CharField(max_length=255)
    slug = models.SlugField()
    pub_date = models.DateTimeField()

    def get_absolute_url(self):
        return ('library_article_detail',
            (), {'object_id': self.id})
    get_absolute_url = models.permalink(get_absolute_url)
```

The url Template Tag

Another common need is to have templates provide links to views that aren't based on models but still shouldn't have a hard-coded URL. For instance, a link to a contact form doesn't necessarily have any ties to the database or any models, but will still need to be linked to in a way that can accommodate future changes or distribution.

The syntax for this template looks quite similar to the `permalink` decorator because it passes values to the same utility function. There are some slight differences, because as a template tag, it doesn't use true Python code.

```
{% url library_article_detail object_id=article.id %}
```

The reverse() Utility Function

Django also provides a Python function that provides the translation from a description of a view and its arguments to a URL that will trigger the specified view. Living at `django.core.urlresolvers`, the `reverse()` function does exactly that. It takes all the same arguments described for the previous two techniques, but also one other, allowing it to specify which URL configuration module should be used to resolve the URL. This function is used internally by both the `permalink` decorator and the `url` template tag. The `reverse()` function takes up to four arguments.

- `viewname`—The name of the view to be called or the import path if no name was specified. This is always required.

- `urlconf`—The import path of a URL configuration module to use for lookups. This is optional and if it's absent or None, the value is taken from the ROOT_URLCONF setting.

- `args`—A tuple of any positional arguments that will be passed to the view.

- `kwargs`—A dictionary of any keyword arguments that will be passed to the view.

Using the same example as in the previous section, here's how `reverse()` would be used to obtain a URL for a specific object.

```
>>> from django.core.urlresolvers import reverse
>>> reverse('library_article_detail', kwargs={'object_id': 1})
'/articles/1/'
```

Keep in mind that `args` and `kwargs` are separate, distinct arguments. The `reverse()` utility function does not use any form of the argument expansion described in Chapter 2.

POSITIONAL VS. KEYWORD ARGUMENTS

To illustrate best practice, the examples in this section all use named groups in the URL's regular expression, which allows—in fact, requires—the reverse resolution to specify arguments using keywords. This greatly improves the readability and maintainability of your code, which is a primary goal of writing Python. It is possible, though, to specify URLs without naming the capture groups, which requires reverse resolution to use positional arguments only.

For example, if the URL pattern was defined as `r'^articles/(d+)/$'`, here's how the previous examples would have to be written in order to work properly:

- The `permalink` decorator—`return ('library_article_detail', (self.id,), {})`

- The `url` template tag—`{%url library_article_detail article.id %}`

- The `reverse()` function—`reverse('library_article_detail', args=(1,))`

Since a URL configuration only allows positional arguments *or* keyword arguments, but not both, there's no need to specify both types together in the same reverse resolution call.

Function-Based Views

One point of confusion for programmers coming from other environments is the fact that Django uses the term "view" a bit differently than others. Traditionally, the view in a Model-View-Controller (MVC) architecture refers to the display of information to a user—essentially, the output portion of a user interface.

The Web doesn't work like that. Viewing data is typically a direct result of a user action, and updates to that view only take place as responses to subsequent actions. This means that the output process is irrevocably linked to the user input process, which can cause some confusion about how even the traditional MVC pattern should define a view.

So there is no simple answer to the question of how Django's views compare to those of other environments because there isn't anything solid to compare against. People from different backgrounds are likely to have different expectations about what a view should be. The bad news is that Django probably doesn't line up with any of them. The good news is that once you start working with Django, the notion of a view is clearly defined, so there's little confusion when communicating with other Django developers.

Templates Break It Up a Bit

Django's views do perform the basic function of the output interface, because they're responsible for the response that is sent to the browser. In a strict sense, this response is the entire output, and it contains all the information about what the user will see. This is often too much work to do in Python while still making it readable, so most views rely on templates to generate the bulk of the content.

The most common practice is to have each view call a single template, which may make use of a number of tools to minimize the amount of template code that must be written for use by a particular view. Chapter 6 includes further details on the template language and the tools that can be used, but the important thing to know for this section is that templates are a great way to simplify the coding process as a whole. They help cut down on the amount of code that must be written, while simultaneously making that code more readable and maintainable for the future.

While Chapter 1 listed templates as a separate layer, remember that they're really just a tool that Django makes available to other parts of an application, including views. Ultimately, whether or not templates are used to generate content, the view alone is responsible for generating the final response. Django's template system has no concept of requests or responses; it just generates text. It's up to views to handle the rest.

Anatomy of a View

A view is a function that takes an HTTP request and returns an HTTP response. That is a bit simplistic, given the potential power of views, but that's really all there is to it. A view always receives, as its first argument, the HttpRequest created by Django, and it should always return an HttpResponse, unless something went wrong. Full details on those objects, their purpose and their properties are covered in Chapter 7.

The first aspect of that definition is the notion that a view must be a standard function. This definition is a bit flexible because in reality, any Python callable can be used as a view; it just happens that basic functions are easy to work with and provide everything that's necessary for most situations. Methods—both on classes and instances—and callable objects, using the protocol described in Chapter 2, are all perfectly valid for use as views. This opens up a variety of other possibilities, some of which will be described later in this chapter.

The next point is the one immutable when it comes to views. Whenever a view is called, regardless of what other arguments are passed along, the first argument is always an HttpRequest object. This also means that all views must accept at least this one object, even those views that don't have use for any explicit arguments. Some simple views, such as those that display the server's current time, may not even use the request object, but must always accept it anyway to fulfill the basic protocol of a view.

On the subject of arguments, another point is that a view must be able to accept whatever arguments are passed to it, including those captured from the URL and those passed into the site's URL configuration. This may seem obvious, but a common point of confusion is the presumption that Django uses some kind of magic to allow a URL configuration to specify which template should be used, without requiring any supporting code in the view.

Django's generic views all allow you to specify the template name, and many users assume that Django somehow passes this straight through to the template system to override whatever name the view uses by default. The truth is that the generic views have special handling for this argument, and the view itself is responsible for telling the template system which template to use. Django relies on standard Python, so there's no magic behind the scenes that tries to interpret what your arguments are supposed to mean. If you plan to supply an argument to a function, make sure that the view knows how to deal with it.

The last notion from that original description of views is that a view must return an HttpResponse object, and even that isn't entirely accurate. Returning a response is definitely the primary goal of all views, but in certain situations it's more appropriate to raise an exception, which will be handled in other ways.

What goes on between request and response is largely unrestricted, and views can be used for as many purposes as there are needs to be met. Views can be built to serve a specific purpose or they can be made generic enough to be used in distributed applications.

Writing Views to Be Generic

A common theme in Django development is to make code as reusable and configurable as possible so that applications and snippets are useful in more than one situation, without having to rewrite code for every need. That's the whole point of DRY: Don't Repeat Yourself.

Views present a bit of a challenge with regards to DRY, since they're only called by incoming requests. It may seem like it wouldn't be possible to write a view that could be called for anything other than the request it was originally intended for. Django itself, however, is full of examples of generic views, which can be used for a variety of applications and situations with only a small amount of configuration necessary for each new use.

There are a few guidelines that can greatly aid the reuse of views, making them generic enough to be used throughout a variety of applications. Views can even be made so generic that they can be distributed to others and included in projects the original author had no concept of.

Use Lots of Arguments

Typically, a view could perform quite a few different tasks, all combining to solve a particular problem. Each of these tasks often has to make assumptions about how it should work, but these assumptions can typically be pulled out into a configurable option using arguments. Consider the following view, designed to retrieve a blog post and pass it along to a template.

```python
from django.shortcuts import render_to_response
from django.template import RequestContext

from blog.models import Post

def show_post(request, id):
    post = Post.objects.get(id=id)
    context = RequestContext(request, {'post': post})
    return render_to_response('blog/detail.html', context)
```

This view will work perfectly well for its intended purpose, but it's quite tightly connected to a specific blog application. It's still loosely coupled in the sense that it doesn't need to deal with the details of how to retrieve the blog post or render the template, but still relies on details specific to the blog application, such as the model and template.

Instead, it's possible to move these assumptions into arguments that can be swapped out for other situations. While initially this will involve some extra work, it can save a lot of time later, if this view is used in a great number of situations. More importantly, the more complex the view, the more code that can be reused using this technique. Once these options have been moved out into arguments, specific values can be passed in with a URL configuration, so a view doesn't have to be written for each purpose.

For this particular view, a few things can be factored out in this way. The model doesn't need to be known in advance and the view should also be able to work with a QuerySet so that a particular URL could operate on a limited set of data. Also, the field name shouldn't be hard-coded, and the template name should be provided outside the view.

```python
from django.shortcuts import render_to_response
from django.template import RequestContext

def show_object(request, id, model, template_name):
    object = model._default_manager.get(pk=id)
    context = RequestContext(request, {'object': object)})
    return render_to_response(template_name, context)
```

Then, when it comes time to use this view, it's easy to customize by providing these details using a URL configuration. Simply supply the argument values as an extra dictionary in the URL configuration, and they'll be passed along each time the view is called from that URL pattern.

```python
from django.conf.urls.defaults import *

from blog.models import Post

urlpatterns = patterns('',
    (r'^post/(?P<id>\d+)/$', 'blog.views.show_object', {
        'model': Post,
        'template_name': 'blog/detail.html',
    }),
)
```

This approach can even be used with models that use other types of IDs, such as a music database using catalog numbers in the format of DJNG-001; anything that can be guaranteed unique among all objects can be used as an object's primary key. Since our new generic view simply passes the ID straight through to the database API, it's easy to support these other types of IDs by simply adjusting the URL pattern appropriately.

```
r'^album/(?P<id>[a-z]+-[0-9])/$'
```

This particular view shouldn't have to be written in the first place, because Django provides one out of the box for this purpose, DetailView, and it's even more versatile than the example shown here. It uses nearly a dozen different arguments, all of which are expected to be customized in URL configurations.

Once you have a view that accepts a number of arguments for customization, it can become quite easy to require far too many arguments be specified in each URL configuration. If every use of a view requires all the configuration options to be specified, it could quickly become just as much work to use the generic view as it would be to write the view from scratch each time. Clearly, there needs to be a better way to manage all these arguments.

Provide Sensible Defaults

Since functions can define default values for any arguments that can use them, the most reasonable way to manage this complexity is to provide decent defaults wherever possible. Exactly what defaults can be provided and what they look like will be different for each view, but it's usually possible to come up with some sensible values for them.

Sometimes you have a number of views that each serve a different purpose but may have some code in common. This is often boilerplate, which every view needs to use, but isn't geared toward the true functionality of any individual view.

For example, views for private pages must always verify that users are logged in and that they have the appropriate permissions. An application may have a dozen different types of views, but if they're all private, they must all use that same code every time. Thankfully, we're working in Python, which provides a useful alternative.

View Decorators

Most boilerplate in views is either at the very beginning or the very end. Usually it handles such tasks as initializing various objects, testing standard prerequisites, handling errors gracefully or customizing the response before it goes out to the browser. The real meat of the view is what sits in the middle, and that's the part that's fun to write. Described in Chapter 2, decorators are a great way to wrap several functions in some common code that can be written once and tested easily, which reduces both bugs and programmer fatigue. Since views are typically just standard Python functions, decorators can be used here as well.

Chapter 2 illustrated how decorators can be used to write a wrapper around the original function, which can then access all the arguments that were intended for that function, as well as the return value from the function itself. In terms of views, this means that decorators always have access to the incoming request object and the outgoing response object. In some cases, a decorator can be special-cased for a particular application, which would allow it to anticipate a greater number of arguments that are specific to that application.

There are a number of things decorators can offer views, and a few of them are common enough to warrant inclusion in Django itself. Living at django.views.decorators are a few packages containing decorators you can use on any view in any application. The following packages are listed with just the trailing portion of their full import path provided, given that they all live at the same location.

- cache.cache_page—Stores the output of the view into the server's cache so that when similar requests come in later, the page doesn't have to be re-created each time.

- cache.never_cache—Prevents caching for a particular view. This is useful if you have site-wide caching set up but certain views can't afford to go stale.

- `gzip.gzip_page`—Compresses the output of the view and adds the appropriate HTTP headers so the Web browser knows how to handle it.

- `http.conditional_page`—Only sends the whole page to the browser if it has changed since the last time the browser got a copy of it.

- `http.require_http_methods`—Accepts a list of HTTP methods (described in detail in Chapter 7) that the view is limited to. If the view is called with any other method, it sends a response telling the browser it's not allowed, without even calling the view. Two included shortcut variations are `http.require_GET` and `http.require_POST`, which don't take any arguments and are hard coded for GET and POST requests, respectively.

- `vary.vary_on_header`—Helps control browser-based caching of pages by indicating that the page's content changes, depending on the values of the headers passed into the decorator. A simple variant specific to the `Cookie` header is available at `vary.vary_on_cookie`.

Additional decorators are provided as part of the bundled applications living at `django.contrib`. These decorators all live below that path, so as in the previous list, only the relevant path is supplied:

- `admin.views.decorators.staff_member_required`—A simple decorator that checks the current user to see if it has staff access. This is used automatically for all the views in Django's built-in admin, but could also be used for any other staff-only views on your site. If the user doesn't have staff permissions, the decorator redirects the browser to the admin's login page.

- `auth.decorators.user_passes_test`—Accepts a single argument, which is a function to test the current user against some arbitrary condition. The provided function should accept just the `User` object and return `True` if the test passes or `False` if it fails. If the test passes, the user will be granted access to the page, but if it fails, the browser will redirect to the site's login page, as determined by the `LOGIN_URL` setting.

- `auth.decorators.login_required`—A specialized version of `user_passes_test`, this decorator simply checks that the user is logged in before allowing access to the view.

- `auth.decorators.permission_required`—Another specialization of `user_passes_test`, this checks that the user has a given permission before the view is loaded. The decorator takes a single argument: the permission to be checked.

These are just the decorators that are bundled with Django itself. There are many other purposes for decorators, and third-party applications can provide their own as well. In order for these decorators to be of any use, however, they must be applied to views.

Applying View Decorators

Chapter 2 described how decorators can be applied to standard Python functions. Applying decorators to views works the same way, but there's a notable difference: views aren't always under your control.

The techniques described in Chapter 2 assume that the functions you decorate are your own. While that's often the case, the number of distributed applications means that many Django-powered Web sites will use code from other sources, with views of their own. Applying decorators as described previously would require changes to the third-party code.

The goal is to apply decorators to third-party views without actually modifying third-party code. The key to doing this lies in the older-style decorator syntax from Python 2.3 and earlier. Remember that the new syntax allows decorators to be applied above the function definition, but the older syntax relies on passing the function to the decorator directly. Since Python functions can be imported from anywhere and can be passed in as arguments at any time, this is an excellent way to create decorated views from third-party code.

Also remember that the URL configuration is defined in a Python module, which gets executed when it is read. This makes the wide array of Python available to this configuration, including the ability to pass functions into decorators to create new functions.

```python
from django.conf.urls.defaults import *
from django.contrib.auth.decorators import login_required
from thirdpartyapp.views import special_view

urlpatterns = patterns('',
    (r'^private/special/$', login_required(special_view)),
)
```

Writing a View Decorator

Chapter 2 covered how decorators themselves work and how they can be written to work in a variety of situations, though decorators for views have a few specific details that should be noted. These have less to do with the technical side of writing decorators and more with the nuances of how to achieve certain useful effects when working with views specifically.

The most common task decorators are used for with views is to create a wrapper function around the original view. This allows the decorator to perform extra work beyond what the view itself would ordinarily do, including

- Performing additional work based on the incoming request or altering its attributes

- Altering the arguments to be passed to the view

- Modifying or replacing the outgoing response

- Handling errors that occur inside the view

- Branching to some other code, without even executing the view

The first thing to consider when writing a decorator is that it receives all the arguments intended for the view itself. Previous sections covered this, but only in the usual context of using *args and **kwargs to receive the arguments and pass them straight through to the wrapped function. With views, you know in advance that the first argument will always be the incoming request object, so a wrapper function can anticipate this and receive the request separately from the other arguments.

By interacting with the request object prior to executing the view, decorators can do two important things: make decisions based on the incoming request and make changes to the request to alter how the view operates. These tasks aren't mutually exclusive and many decorators do both, such as the following example from Django.

```python
from django.utils.functional import wraps

def set_test_cookie(view):
    """
    Automatically sets the test cookie on all anonymous users,
    so that they can be logged in more easily, without having
    to hit a separate login page.
    """
    def wrapper(request, *args, **kwargs):
        if request.user.is_anonymous():
            request.session.set_test_cookie()
        return view(request, *args, **kwargs)
    return wraps(view)(wrapper)
```

PRESERVING A VIEW'S NAME AND DOCUMENTATION

The built-in admin interface generates documentation for your application's views using the name and docstring of the view function itself. By using decorators to wrap the function, we're essentially replacing the original view function with the wrapper. This causes the admin interface to see the wrapper instead of the view.

Ordinarily, this would cause the name and docstring of the view to be lost in the shuffle, so the admin's documentation feature doesn't work properly with these views. To get the right documentation, those attributes of the function must remain intact throughout the wrapping process.

Django provides an additional decorator, living at `django.utils.functional.wraps`, which is designed to copy these attributes onto the wrapped function so it looks more like the original view. This process is described in more detail in Chapter 9, but all the examples in this section use it to illustrate best practices for decorating views.

Another common use of decorators is to extract some common code from the beginning or end of a set of views. This can be especially useful when looking at incoming arguments, as decorators can perform any lookups and initializations prior to calling the view. Then, decorators can simply pass fully prepared objects to the view, rather than raw strings captured from a URL.

```
from django.utils.functional import wraps
from django.shortcuts import get_object_or_404

from news.models import Article

def get_article_from_id(view):
    """
    Retrieves a specific article, passing it to the view directly
    """
    def wrapper(request, id, *args, **kwargs):
        article = get_object_or_404(Article, id=int(id))
        return view(request, article=article, *args, **kwargs)
    return wraps(view)(wrapper)
```

The great thing about a decorator like this is that, even though the logic it contains is fairly minimal, it does cut down on the amount of code that has to be duplicated for views that all get an Article object according to an ID provided in the URL. This not only makes the views themselves a bit more readable, but any time you can cut down on code that has to be written, you can help reduce bugs.

Also, by having access to the response, decorators can make some interesting decisions about how that response should behave. Middleware classes, described in Chapter 7, have much more use for accessing the response, but there are still useful things decorators can do.

Of note is the ability to set the content-type of the response, which can control how the browser deals with the content once it receives it. Chapter 7 describes this in more detail and also how it can be set when creating the response. However, it's also possible to set it after the response has already been created and returned from a view.

This technique can be a good way to override the content-type for specific types of views. After all, if no content-type is specified, Django pulls a value from the DEFAULT_CONTENT_TYPE setting, which defaults to 'text/html'.

For certain types of views, especially those intended for Web services, it may be better to serve them using another content-type, such as 'application/xml', while still being able to use generic views.

```
from django.utils.functional import wraps

def content_type(c_type):
    """
    Overrides the Content-Type provided by the view.
    Accepts a single argument, the new Content-Type
    value to be written to the outgoing response.
    """
    def decorator(view):
        def wrapper(request, *args, **kwargs):
            response = view(request, *args, **kwargs)
            response['Content-Type'] = c_type
            return response
        return wraps(view)(wrapper)
    return decorator
```

This decorator could then accept a content-type when applying it to a view.

```
@content_type('application/json')
def view(request):
    ...
```

A lesser-used feature of view decorators is the ability to catch any exceptions that are raised by the view or any code it executes. Views typically just return a response directly, but there are still many situations where a view may opt to raise an exception instead. One common example, found in many of Django's own generic views, is raising the Http404 exception to indicate that an object couldn't be found.

Chapter 9 covers the exceptions Django provides in its standard distribution, many of which can be raised by views for one reason or another. In addition, many of the standard Python exceptions could be raised for various situations, and it can be useful to catch any of these. A decorator can perform a variety of additional tasks when an exception is raised, from simply logging the exception to the database to returning a different type of response in the case of certain exceptions.

Consider a custom logging application with a log entry model like this:

```
from datetime import datetime

from django.db import models

class Entry(models.Model):
    path = models.CharField(max_length=255)
    type = models.CharField(max_length=255, db_index=True)
    date = models.DateTimeField(default=datetime.utcnow, db_index=True)
    description = models.TextField()
```

The application providing this model could also provide a decorator for projects to apply to their own views that logs exceptions to this model automatically.

```python
from django.utils.functional import wraps

from mylogapp.models import Entry

def logged(view):
    """
    Logs any errors that occurred during the view
    in a special model design for app-specific errors
    """
    def wrapper(request, *args, **kwargs):
        try:
            return view(request, *args, **kwargs)
        except Exception as e:
            # Log the entry using the application's Entry model
            Entry.objects.create(path=request.path,
                                 type='View exception',
                                 description=str(e))

            # Re-raise it so standard error handling still applies
            raise
    return wraps(view)(wrapper)
```

The recurring theme with all these examples is that view decorators can encapsulate some common code that would otherwise have to be duplicated in every instance of the view. In essence, view decorators are a way to extend the view's code before or after the original code. It's important to generalize these examples in order to realize just how much is possible with view decorators. Any boilerplate you find yourself duplicating at the beginning or end of your views is fair game to be placed in a decorator to save some time, energy and trouble.

Class-Based Views

Views don't have to be limited to functions. In the end, all that matters to Django is that it gets a callable; how that callable is created is still up to you. You can also define your views as classes, which provides a few key advantages over traditional functions.

- Higher degree of configurability
- Easier customization for specialized applications
- Reuse of objects that may be used for other purposes

Even though the end result must be a callable, there are even more ways to create classes than there are for functions. Django's own generic views follow a particular structure though, and in the spirit of maintaining similarity where possible, it's a good idea to try to match up with that. Just remember that you can write your classes differently if this format doesn't suit your needs as easily as something else.

django.views.generic.base.View

The easiest way to get the basics into your class is to subclass Django's own View class. It won't do everything you'll need out of the box, of course, but it provides the basics:

- Validates arguments passed into the view configuration

- Prevents using arguments named after HTTP methods

- Collects arguments passed in the URL configuration

- Keeps request information in a convenient place for methods to access

- Verifies that a requested HTTP method is supported by the view

- Automatically handles OPTIONS requests

- Dispatches to view methods based on the requested HTTP method

Some of this functionality is specific to it being a class, such as making convenient request information conveniently available to various view methods. Others, such as enforcing specific HTTP methods and handling OPTIONS requests directly, are really just good HTTP practices that are made easier by the fact that a class can provide such functionality without you having to remember to defer to it in your own code.

Classes offer a chance for multiple methods to interact, so Django uses a few standard methods to do the common items, while providing you a way to add in other methods that now only need to worry about the specifics of your application. And since it's just a class, you can also add other methods as you see fit. Django won't do anything with them, so you'll have to call them yourself, but it does give you a chance to abstract out common code more easily than if you were working with raw functions.

All of Django's generic views inherit from a common ancestor to provide all these hooks, and it's easy for yours to do the same. Let's take a look at some of the methods Django provides on a default generic view.

__init__(self, **kwargs)

As a class designed to create objects, __init__() is obviously where instances of the class start out. Its keyword arguments are options defined in the URL, but you don't actually call this directly at any time. Instead, your URL configuration will use the as_view(), which does a few things, including initializing the class.

The default implementation of __init__() simply sets all supplied keyword arguments as instance variables on the view object.

BE CAREFUL OVERRIDING __INIT__()

As you'll see in the following sections, the view class doesn't get instantiated until a request arrives and is sent to the generated view function. This means that __init__() fires for every incoming request, rather than just once at the time Django processes your URL configuration.

Therefore, if you need to perform any changes to the configuration options or react to them in any way that doesn't require access to any information from an actual request, you'll want to override as_view() and add your logic there instead. In fact, __init__() doesn't even see the request object itself; it only receives the arguments that were captured from the URL.

So while __init__() is typically a good place to provide additional configuration features, in this case it tends not to work out so well. It's best to override as_view() if you need to work with the configuration and dispatch() if you need to work with anything related to an incoming request.

---

as_view(cls, **initkwargs)

This class method is the primary entry point into your view. When you configure a URL to use this view, you'll call this method, which will return a view function for Django to use. You'll also pass the configuration options into the method call, rather than placing them in a dictionary alongside the view itself. For example:

```
from django.views.generic.base import View

urlpatterns = patterns('',
    (r'^example/', View.as_view(template_name='example.html')),
)
```

When called, as_view() is responsible for a few things:

- It verifies that none of the provided options match the names of HTTP methods. If any are found, it raises a TypeError immediately, rather than waiting for a request to come in.

- It also verifies that all of the provided options match existing named attributes on the class. This enforces a pattern where default options are established as class attributes, then overridden by individual URL configurations, as necessary. For instance, the preceding example would raise a TypeError because template_name isn't named as an attribute on the built-in View class.

- Then it creates a simple view function that will be returned to the URL configuration, for use when an actual request comes in. This view then gets updated with a few attributes from the class and any applied decorators, to make it more useful when introspecting it later.

- Lastly, it returns the newly-created view function, so Django has something to work with when requests start coming in.

The view function created by as_view() is even simpler still. It accepts a request, as well as *args and **kwargs, so it can receive anything captured from the URL, according to the regular expression in the URL configuration. This is identical to how any other view would work; there is nothing special about how Django's URL dispatching handles a class-based view.

Once it has this information, it's only responsible for a little bit of record-keeping and a call to something more useful:

- First, it creates an instance of the view class, passing in the configuration options supplied to as_view(). This is where __init__() finally comes into play, because the instance of a view is only good for a single request. Each subsequent request will get a new instance of the view class.

- Next, it checks to see if the view has get() and head() methods. If it has get() but not head(), it sets the view up so that HEAD requests will get sent to the get() method. In general, HEAD should act just like GET but without returning content, so this is a reasonable default behavior.

- Then, it sets the request and URL-captured information onto the object, as instance attributes named request, args and kwargs. You may not need to access this information as attributes on the object, but they're there if you do need them.

- Lastly, it defers execution to the dispatch() method, passing in the request and all captured arguments, exactly as they were passed into the view itself.

dispatch(self, request, *args, **kwargs)

This is the point where requests are properly handled. Like any view, it's responsible for accepting a request and returning a response. Its default implementation handles some of the complexities of different HTTP methods, while allowing you to just write your code in additional view methods.

- It first checks to see if the requested HTTP method is valid and has a matching view method on the class to handle the request. If not, it returns a response with a status code of 405 Method Not Allowed, rather than even trying to serve it in any additional capacity.

- If the class does have a matching view method, dispatch() simply defers to that, passing all the arguments into it.

The first test for HTTP methods checks a lower-cased copy of the method string against a list of known methods, stored as a class attribute called http_method_names:

- get
- post
- put
- delete
- head
- options
- trace

Notice that newer options, such as PATCH, aren't present in this list. If you do have need for a different method and are hosting in an environment that will pass it through to Django, you can override this list to add any additional methods you need. If an HTTP method comes in that's not in this list, Django won't allow it, even if you have a view method of the same name.Django's behavior here is generally preferred, but you can override dispatch() to provide other functionality if you'd like. For example, if you have an API that can return data in various formats, you might use the dispatch() method to format the output as needed, leaving the individual methods to just retrieve and return the raw data.

Individual View Methods

After dispatch() determines that the view can handle the request, it sends that request off to one of several possible functions, named according to HTTP methods. For example, a GET request will get routed off to get(), POST requests go to post(), and so on. Each of these would behave just like a standard view function, accepting a request and additional arguments and returning a response.

To demonstrate how this helps your code in practice, consider the following example of form processing in traditional function-based views:

```python
def view(request, template_name='form.html'):
    if request.method == 'POST':
        form = ExampleForm(request.POST)
        if form.is_valid():
            # Process the form here
            return redirect('success')
        else:
            return render(request, template_name, {'form': form})
```

```
    else:
        form = ExampleForm()  # no data gets passed in
        return render(request, template_name, {'form': form})
```

This view services both GET and POST requests, so it has to deal with requests that form data that needs to be processed, while also managing requests without any data, to present the form in the first place. Here's how that view would look with a class-based view instead.

```
class FormView(View):
    template_name = 'form.html'

    def get(self, request):
        form = ExampleForm()
        return render(request, self.template_name, {'form': form})

    def post(self, request):
        form = ExampleForm(request.POST)
        if form.is_valid():
            # Process the form here
            return redirect('success')
        else:
            return render(request, self.template_name, {'form': form})
```

This is a much cleaner separation of concerns, and as an added bonus, the class-based version will automatically handle HEAD and OPTIONS requests properly, while rejecting requests for PUT, DELETE and TRACE.

Django also provides a simple options() method, which indicates what features the URL can provide. The default behavior uses the available view methods to indicate which HTTP methods are allowed and provide those in the Allow header of the response. If you have more features that need to be included here, such as those necessary for cross-origin resource sharing,[2] you can simply override options() to provide that information.

Decorating View Methods

The structure of these class-based views makes them somewhat interesting when it comes to decorators. On one hand, they're classes, which can't be decorated using the same decorators that are used for functions. In fact, classes can't be decorated at all prior to Python 3. On the other hand, the as_view() method returns a simple function, which can be decorated just like any other.

The simplest technique to explain is decorating the output of as_view(). Because it returns a function, it can be decorated just like any other function. So if you need to require a user to be logged in, you can simply use the standard login_required decorator, as always.

```
from django.contrib.auth.decorators import login_required

urlpatterns = patterns('',
    (r'^example/', login_required(FormView.as_view(template_name='example.html'))),
)
```

---

[2]http://prodjango.com/cors/

On the other hand, you can decorate individual methods on your class directly, if you know of things that they'll always need. Two things complicate matters more than the typical function case. First, these are instance methods, rather than simple functions, which means they accept a self argument, which isn't there on traditional function-based views. As is often the case with problems regarding decorators, the solution is another decorator, which is in this case provided by Django itself. The method_decorator can be used to wrap a normal decorator in a way that lets it ignore self and just deal with the argument it expects.

```
from django.utils.decorators import method_decorator

class FormView(View):
    @method_decorator(login_required)
    def get(request):
        # View code continues here
```

The second issue is that there are now multiple functions involved, rather than just one that can be decorated directly. You can decorate any of the functions you'd like, but an interesting fact of the dispatching process for class-based views is that dispatch() is the only method that serves the same purpose as a traditional function. All requests go through it, and it also has access to all available information about the class, the instance and the incoming request.

Therefore, this is also the best place to apply any view decorators. If you apply a decorator to dispatch(), it'll modify the behavior of every request, regardless of what other methods are used afterward. You can decorate individual methods if you have a good reason to, but it's most useful to use dispatch() and have it work the same way it does in traditional function-based views.

Using an Object As a View

As described in Chapter 2, Python provides a way to define a class in such a way that instances of it can be called as if they were functions. If defined on a class, the __call__() method will be called when the object is passed in where a function is expected. As with any other callable, such objects can also be used as Django views.

There are as many ways to use objects as views as there are ways to define objects themselves. Aside from using __call__() to receive each incoming request, what happens inside the object is up for grabs. In a typical situation, the request would be dispatched to individual methods, similar to Django's own class-based views, but you can do whatever you need.

Applied Techniques

By allowing custom objects and decorators to be used with URL patterns and views, nearly any valid Python code can customize how a URL is mapped to a view and how the view itself is executed. The following is just a taste of what's possible; the rest depends on the needs of your application.

Cross-Origin Resource Sharing (CORS)

Requests that cross from one domain to another are a security risk, because they could expose sensitive data to sites that shouldn't have access to that data. Imagine if a random blog could just make an AJAX call to your bank's website. If you were logged in and didn't have any protection in your browser, that call could send your bank account information to a blog you know nothing about and just happened to visit.

Thankfully, modern browsers do have protection against this sort of thing. By default, requests made from one site to another within your browser will be forbidden. There are legitimate uses for cross-origin requests like that, though, such as between trusted sites or when serving public data files for general use. The Cross-Origin Resource Sharing (CORS) specification allows one site to indicate which other sites can access certain resources.

CORS Decorator

With a traditional function-based view, this functionality can be added as a decorator. Here's how you could decorate a view to make it publicly available from any site that requests it:

```
@cross_origin(allow_origin=['*'])
def public_data(request):
    # Data retrieval goes here
```

The implementation is pretty straightforward, as far as decorators go:

```
def cross_origin(allow_credentials=False, allow_headers=None,
                 allow_methods=None, allow_headers=None,
                 allow_origin=None, expose_headers=None, max_age=None):
    def decorator(func):
        @functools.wraps(func)
        def wrapper(request, *args, **kwargs):
            headers = {}

            if access_control_allow_credentials:
                headers['Allow-Credentials'] = allow_credentials
            if access_control_allow_headers:
                headers['Allow-Headers'] = ', '.join(allow_headers)
            if access_control_allow_methods:
                headers['Allow-Methods'] = ', '.join(allow_methods)
            if access_control_allow_origin:
                headers['Allow-Origin'] = ' '.join(allow_origin)
            if access_control_expose_headers:
                headers['Expose-Headers'] = ', '.join(expose_headers)
            if access_control_max_age:
                headers['Max-Age'] = self.max_age

            response = func(request, *args, **kwargs)

            for name, value in headers:
                response.headers['Access-Control-%s' % name] = value

            return response
        return wrapper
    return decorator
```

There's no need to support using the decorator without arguments, because if you don't supply any arguments, it wouldn't do anything anyway. So it only supports arguments and simply has to add all the right headers when the response comes back from the decorated view. As you can see, some of them accept lists, while others accept just a single value.

CORS Mixin

This decorator could be applied to a class-based view directly, using `method_decorator`, but to make it a bit easier to configure, we could instead use a mixin. Here's how it would look on a similarly featured class-based view:

```python
class PublicData(View, CrossOrigin):
    access_control_allow_origin = ['*']

    def get(self, request):
        # Data retrieval goes here
```

The implementation gets a little more complicated than a simple decorator, but it's still pretty simple to work with:

```python
class CrossOrigin(object):
    """
    A view mixin that provides basic functionality necessary to add the necessary
    headers for Cross-Origin Resource Sharing
    """

    access_control_allow_credentials = False
    access_control_allow_headers = None
    access_control_allow_methods = None
    access_control_allow_origin = None
    access_control_expose_headers = None
    access_control_max_age = None

    def get_access_control_headers(self, request):
        headers = {}

        if self.access_control_allow_credentials:
            headers['Allow-Credentials'] = self.access_control_allow_credentials
        if self.access_control_allow_headers:
            headers['Allow-Headers'] = ', '.join(self.access_control_allow_headers)
        if self.access_control_allow_methods:
            headers['Allow-Methods'] = ', '.join(self.access_control_allow_methods)
        if self.access_control_allow_origin:
            headers['Allow-Origin'] = ' '.join(self.access_control_allow_origin)
        if self.access_control_expose_headers:
            headers['Expose-Headers'] = ', '.join(self.access_control_expose_headers)
        if self.access_control_max_age:
            headers['Max-Age'] = self.access_control_max_age

        return headers

    def dispatch(self, request, *args, **kwargs):
        response = super(CORSMixin, self).dispatch(request, *args, **kwargs)

        for name, value in self.get_access_control_headers(request):
            response.headers['Access-Control-%s' % name)] = value

        return response
```

Worth noting here is that the header functionality has been moved out into a separate method, which receives the request as an argument. This allows you to override that method in your subclass, in case you need to make changes to the CORS headers based on details of the incoming request.

For example, if you had a lot of different domains that need access to the resource, you could check the incoming request against those domains and only add that domain as an allowed origin, rather than having to include the entire list in every response. This is a prime example of how classes enable greater customization of internal details than a decorator, which tends to hide those implementations in a way that you can't modify.

Providing Both a Decorator and a Mixin

If you wanted to supply this as a reusable helper, you might even want to supply both the function decorator and the class mixin. This is easy to do by just pulling the common code out into a separate function, which can be called from each of the different approaches.

```python
def cors_headers(allow_credentials=false, allow_headers=None, allow_methods=None,
                 allow_origin=None, expose_headers=None, max_age=None):
    headers = {}

    if allow_credentials:
        headers['Access-Control-Allow-Credentials'] = allow_credentials
    if allow_headers:
        headers['Access-Control-Allow-Headers'] = ', '.join(allow_headers)
    if allow_methods:
        headers['Access-Control-Allow-Methods'] = ', '.join(allow_methods)
    if allow_origin:
        headers['Access-Control-Allow-Origin'] = ' '.join(allow_origin)
    if expose_headers:
        headers['Access-Control-Expose-Headers'] = ', '.join(expose_headers)
    if max_age:
        headers['Access-Control-Max-Age'] = self.max_age

    return response

def cross_origin(allow_credentials=false, allow_headers=None, allow_methods=None,
                 allow_origin=None, expose_headers=None, max_age=None):
    def decorator(func):
        @functools.wraps(func)
        def wrapper(request, *args, **kwargs):
            response = func(request, *args, **kwargs)
            headers = cors_headers(response, allow_credentials, allow_headers,
                                   allow_methods, allow_origin, expose_headers, max_age)
            response.headers.update(headers)
            return response
        return wrapper
    return decorator

class CrossOrigin(object):
    """
    A view mixin that provides basic functionality necessary to add the necessary
    headers for Cross-Origin Resource Sharing
    """
```

```
access_control_allow_credentials = false
access_control_allow_headers = None
access_control_allow_methods = None
access_control_allow_origin = None
access_control_expose_headers = None
access_control_max_age = None

def get_access_control_headers(self, request):
    return cors_headers(self.access_control_allow_credentials,
                        self.access_control_allow_headers,
                        self.access_control_allow_methods,
                        self.access_control_allow_origin,
                        self.access_control_expose_headers,
                        self.access_control_max_age):

def dispatch(self, request, *args, **kwargs):
    response = super(CORSMixin, self).dispatch(request, *args, **kwargs)
    headers = self.get_access_control_headers(request)
    response.headers.update(headers)
    return response
```

Now the only thing that the decorator and mixin have to do is collect arguments appropriately for each technique, leaving the details of applying the actual headers to a common function. This isn't a groundbreaking technique, but it's useful to see how decorators and mixins aren't that different after all. They're configured a bit differently, but in the end it still comes down to accepting a request and returning a response.

Now What?

URLs form the foundation of your site's architecture, defining how users access the content and services you provide. Django stays out of the way when it comes to designing your URL scheme, so you're free to build it however you like. Be sure to take the appropriate time and remember that URL configuration is still a form of site design.

Views are the real workhorses of any application, taking user input and turning it into useful output. While the whole of Python is available for views to use, Django does provide one very important tool to handle one of the most common user input tasks on the Web: forms.

CHAPTER 5

■ ■ ■

Forms

One of the key ingredients of modern Web applications is interactivity—the ability to accept input from users, which helps shape their experience. That input can be just about anything, from a simple search term to entire user-submitted novels. The key is the ability to process this input and turn it into a meaningful feature that enriches the experience for all the users of the site.

The process begins by sending an HTML form to the Web browser, where a user can fill it in and submit it back to the server. When the data arrives, it must be validated to make sure the user didn't forget any fields or enter anything inappropriate. If there was anything wrong with the submitted data, it has to be sent back to the user for corrections. Once all the data is known to be valid, the application can finally perform a meaningful task with it.

It's possible to do all this without a framework, but doing so involves a lot of duplication if multiple forms are involved. Managing forms manually also introduces a high risk of the programmer taking shortcuts in the process. It's very common to have a form skip essential validations, either from lack of time or a perceived lack of necessity. Many exploited security holes can be attributed directly to this type of negligence.

Django addresses this by providing a framework to manage those finer details. Once a form is defined, Django handles the details of generating HTML, receiving input and validating data. After that, the application can do whatever it likes with the data received. Like everything else in Django, you're also able to bypass this form handling and process things manually if necessary.

Declaring and Identifying Fields

Django's forms, like its models, use a declarative syntax where fields are assigned as attributes to the form's class definition. This is one of the most identifiable features of Django, and is used to great effect here as well. It allows a form to be declared as just a simple class while supplying a great deal of additional functionality behind the scenes.

The first difference between models and forms is how they recognize fields. Models don't actually recognize fields at all; they just check to see if an attribute has a `contribute_to_class()` method and call it, regardless of what type of object it's attached to. Forms do actually check the type of each attribute on the class to determine if it's a field, looking specifically for instances of `django.forms.fields.Field`.

Like models, forms keep a reference to all the fields that were declared, though forms do so a bit differently. There are two separate lists of fields that may be found on a form, depending on what stage it's in, each with its own purpose.

The first, `base_fields`, is a list of all the fields that were found when the metaclass executed. These are stored on the form class itself, and are available to all instances as well. Thus, this list should only be edited in extreme circumstances, as doing so would affect all future instances of the form. It's always useful as a reference when looking at a form class itself or when identifying those fields that were actually declared directly on the class.

All form instances also get a `fields` attribute, which contains those fields that will actually be used to generate the HTML for the form, as well as validate user input. Most of the time, this list will be identical to `base_fields`, since it starts as just a copy of it. Sometimes, however, a form will need to customize its fields based on some other information, so that individual instances will behave differently in different situations.

For example, a contact form may accept a User object to determine whether the user is logged in or not. If not, the form can add another field to accept the user's name.

```
from django import forms

class ContactForm(forms.Form):
    def __init__(self, user, *args, **kwargs):
        super(ContactForm, self).__init__(*args, **kwargs)
        if not user.is_authenticated():
            # Add a name field since the user doesn't have a name
            self.fields['name'] = forms.CharField(label='Full name')
```

Binding to User Input

Since forms exist specifically to accept user input, that activity must be performed before any others. It's so important that instantiated forms are considered to be in one of two states: bound or unbound. A *bound form* was given user input, which it can then use to do further work, while an *unbound form* has no data associated with it, and is generally used only to ask the user for the necessary data.

The difference between the two is made when the form is instantiated, based on whether a dictionary of data was passed in or not. This dictionary maps field names to their values, and is always the first positional argument to the form, if it's passed in. Even passing an empty dictionary will cause the form to be considered bound, though its usefulness is limited, given that without data, the form is unlikely to validate. Once a form has been instantiated, it's easy to determine whether it was bound to data by inspecting its Boolean is_bound attribute.

```
>>> from django import forms
>>> class MyForm(forms.Form):
...     title = forms.CharField()
...     age = forms.IntegerField()
...     photo = forms.ImageField()
...
>>> MyForm().is_bound
False
>>> MyForm({'title': u'New Title', 'age': u'25'}).is_bound
True
>>> MyForm({}).is_bound
True
```

Also note that all values are passed as strings. Some fields may accept other types, such as integers, but strings are the standard, and all fields know how to handle them. This is to support the most common way to instantiate a form, using the request.POST dictionary available within a view.

```
from my_app.forms import MyForm

def my_view(request):
    if request.method == 'POST':
        form = MyForm(request.POST)
    else:
        form = MyForm()
    ...
```

Sometimes a form may also accept files, which are provided a bit differently than other types of input. Files can be accessed as the FILES attribute of the incoming request object, which forms use by accepting this attribute as a second positional argument.

```
from my_app.forms import MyForm

def my_view(request):
    if request.method == 'POST':
        form = MyForm(request.POST, request.FILES)
    else:
        form = MyForm()
    ...
```

Regardless of which way it was instantiated, any instance of a form will have a data attribute, which contains a dictionary of whatever data was passed into it. In the case of an unbound form, this will be an empty dictionary. Using data on its own isn't safe, because there's no guarantee that the user-submitted data is appropriate to what the form needs, and it could in fact pose a security risk. This data must always be validated before being used.

Validating Input

Once a form has been bound to a set of incoming data, it can check the validity of that data, and should always do so before continuing. This prevents your code from making invalid assumptions about the quality of the data, and can thus prevent many security problems.

On the surface, the process of validating user input is quite simple, consisting of a single call to the form's is_valid() method. This returns a Boolean indicating whether the data was indeed valid according to the rules set by the form's fields. This alone is enough to determine whether to continue processing the form or to redisplay it for the user to correct the errors.

```
def my_view(request):
    if request.method == 'POST':
        form = MyForm(request.POST, request.FILES)
        if form.is_valid():
            # Do more work here, since the data is known to be good
    else:
        form = MyForm()
    ...
```

NEVER TRUST USER INPUT

There's an old adage in the world of Web development, which is often phrased, "User input is evil." That's a bit of an extreme, but the basic idea is that Web applications don't run in a vacuum, but are instead exposed to the outside world for a wide variety of users to interact with. Most of these users are upstanding citizens of the Web, looking only to use a site the way it was intended to be used. Others, however, would like nothing more than to bring your precious application to its knees.

Any application that takes action based on user input potentially opens itself up to some risks. Since decisions are being made based on what a user supplies, that user has a great deal of control over how the application behaves. In some cases, user input is passed directly through to database or filesystem operations, with an assumption that the input will be within some established range of known values.

Once someone comes along with malicious intent, he can use this fact to his advantage, pushing other data into the application in hopes of convincing it to do something it shouldn't, such as read content the user shouldn't have access to, write to areas that should be read-only, bring the application down so no one can use it at all or, worst of all, getting full access to the system without you even knowing it. These types of attacks are generally placed into categories, such as SQL injection, Cross-site Scripting, Cross-site Request Forgery and Form Manipulation, but one theme ties them together: they all rely on an application being too trusting of incoming data.

The solution to these types of attacks is to vigorously guard your application from malicious input, by meticulously validating everything that comes in. Django's forms have a variety of ways to control this validation, but the is_valid() method makes sure they all run, so that the application can know if the input should be used. This step should *never* be skipped, as doing so will make your application vulnerable to many of these attacks.

It's also important to realize that validation must always take place on the server, by way of form.is_valid(), regardless of what happens inside the user's Web browser. In this age of Web 2.0 and rich Web applications, much work is done in JavaScript inside the browser, and it's easy to think that this is a sufficient way to ensure the quality of incoming data, before it even arrives at the server.

However, a lot can happen between the browser and the server, and there are a great many tools freely available to help users manipulate the submitted data after it's been processed by JavaScript. HTTP is an easy protocol to work with as well, so it's trivial to bypass the browser altogether. No amount of client-side validation is sufficient to keep an application safe from attack; everything must be checked on the server.

Behind the scenes, is_valid() does even more work, by indirectly calling the form's full_clean() method, which populates two more attributes. The first, cleaned_data, is a dictionary analogous to the data attribute previously mentioned, except that its values have already been processed by the form's fields and converted to appropriate Python data types. The second is errors, a dictionary containing information about all the problems that were encountered with the incoming data.

These two attributes are somewhat tied to each other, in that no field should be identified in both attributes at the same time. That is, if a field's name is in cleaned_data, it's not in errors, and vice versa. Therefore, in an ideal situation, cleaned_data would contain data for every field, while errors would be empty.

The exact details of what data is considered valid and what errors would be returned otherwise are typically specified by each field, using its clean() method. For most forms, this is sufficient, but some may need additional validation that goes beyond a single field. To support this, Django provides a way to inject additional validation rules into a form.

Special methods may be defined on the form to assist in this process, and are named according to the fields they're associated with. For example, a method designed to validate and clean the title field would be called clean_title(). Each method defined this way is responsible for looking up its value in cleaned_data, validating it against whatever rules are appropriate for the form. If the value needs additional cleaning, the method must also replace the value in cleaned_data with an appropriately cleaned value.

Using Class-Based Views

Looking at the views shown so far, you'll notice that they tend to follow a common pattern. In fact, most form-processing views you'll run into will look a lot like this:

```
from django.shortcuts import render, redirect

def my_view(request):
    if request.method == 'POST':
```

```
        form = MyForm(request.POST, request.FILES)
        if form.is_valid():
            form.save()
            return redirect('/success/')
        return render(request, 'form.html', {'form': form})
    else:
        form = MyForm()
        return render(request, 'form.html', {'form': form})
```

As seen in Chapter 4, this can be made more manageable by handling the GET and POST cases separately in a class-based view.

```
from django.shortcuts import render, redirect
from django.views.generic.base import View

class MyView(View):
    def get(self, request):
        form = MyForm()
        return render(request, 'form.html', {'form': form})

    def post(self, request):
        form = MyForm(request.POST, request.FILES)
        if form.is_valid():
            form.save()
            return redirect('/success/')
        return render(request, 'form.html', {'form': form})
```

This is certainly an improvement, but there's still a lot of boilerplate here. You're almost always going to instantiate and validate your forms the same way, and the template rendering is identical when initially displaying the form and displaying errors. When it comes down to it, the only really interesting part about the view is where you do something with a valid form. In this case, it's just calling form.save(), but you could use it to send an email, transfer some files around, trigger a payment transaction or any number of other things.

To avoid all this duplication, Django provides another class-based view, called FormView. It abstracts away those commonalities, so you can just provide some basic details and a method named form_valid() that receives a valid form as its only argument.

```
from django.shortcuts import render, redirect
from django.views.generic.edit import FormView

class MyView(FormView):
    form_class = MyForm
    template_name = 'form.html'
    success_url = '/success/'

    def form_valid(self, form):
        form.save()
        return super(MyView, self).form_valid(form)
```

That makes things a lot simpler. In fact, you don't even have to provide form_valid(), but given that it just redirects to success_url by default, without doing anything with the form at all, you'll nearly always want to provide at least this much. There are a number of other methods you can define as well, to control various other aspects of its behavior, as needed.

- get_form_class(self)—Returns the form class to use throughout the process. By default, it simply returns the contents of the form_class attribute, which is None if you don't supply one.

- get_initial(self)—Returns a dictionary to pass into the initial argument of the form. On its own, this just returns the contents of the initial attribute of the view, which is an empty dictionary by default.

- get_form_kwargs(self)—Returns a dictionary to use as keyword arguments when instantiating the form for each request. By default, this includes the result of get_initial(), and if the request was a POST or PUT, it also adds in request.POST and request.FILES.

- get_form(self, form_class)—This returns a fully-instantiated form by passing the arguments retrieved from get_form_kwargs() into the class returned from get_form_class(). Given that you have control over all the arguments going into the form instance by way of get_form_kwargs(), this only makes sense for making modifications to the form after it's been created but before it's tested for validity.

- form_valid(self, form)—The main workhorse, this is triggered when the form has been validated, allowing you to take appropriate action. By default, this redirects the user to the result of the get_success_url() method.

- form_invalid(self, form)—A natural counterpart form_valid(), this is called when the form is considered invalid, and will be given the invalid form itself. By default, this simply re-renders the template with the form.

- get_success_url(self)—This returns the URL where the user should be sent after successful validation of the form. By default, it returns the value of the success_url attribute.

As you can see, FormView gives you a chance to customize practically every aspect of the form process. Rather than having to write a separate view for every use of a form, you can control just the parts that are specific to your needs.

If you need to work with a form for a specific model, there's another generic view that can do even more for you. Rather than having to override several of those methods to create a ModelForm instance to do what you need, Django provides a few other classes for you to work with. These all live in django.views.generic.edit, because they allow you to edit data.

- CreateView is used to help with the creation of new objects.

- UpdateView is used when editing existing objects.

- DeleteView is used for deleting existing objects.

All three views work in similar ways. To get the basic functionality, all you really need is to provide a model for them to work with. The views then handle the rest, including setting up the forms, validating user input, saving data and redirecting the user to appropriate URLs.

```
from django.views.generic import edit
from my_app.models import MyModel

class CreateObject(edit.CreateView):
    model = MyModel
```

```
class EditObject(edit.UpdateView):
    model = MyModel

class DeleteObject(edit.DeleteView):
    model = MyModel
    success_url = '/'
```

The only surprise here is that `DeleteView` actually does need a `success_url` specified, in addition to the model. Both `CreateView` and `UpdateView` result in a valid object, with data associated with it, so their default implementations can simply call the `get_absolute_url()` on the modified object.

In the case of `DeleteView`, the object being accessed no longer exists when the view is done working, so `get_absolute_url()` is not an option. Since there's no standard way to describe URLs for object lists, Django can't make any kind of guess as to where to send users. Therefore, you'll always need to declare a `success_url` in order to use `DeleteView` properly.

Custom Fields

While the fields included with Django are suitable for most tasks, not every application fits neatly into a list of situations somebody else expected to be common. For those applications where the existing fields aren't enough, it's easy to define custom fields for forms, much like how fields for models can be created. It's even easier to create form fields than model fields, since they don't have to interact with the database.

The main difference between model fields and form fields is that forms only have to deal with string input, which greatly simplifies the process. There's no need to worry about supporting multiple backends, each with its own complexities, much less all the different lookup types and relationships that add to the bulk of model fields.

As mentioned, all form fields inherit from `Field`, living at `django.forms.fields`. Because forms use this fact to distinguish fields from methods or other attributes, all custom fields must be part of this inheritance chain in order to work properly. Thankfully, `Field` provides a number of useful features that can make it much easier to implement a specific type of field.

Like many other classes, fields define a few attributes and methods to control specific behaviors, such as what widget to use and what error messages to display, as well as how to validate and clean incoming values. Any or all of them can be overridden to customize the functionality of a specific field.

Validation

Perhaps the most important behavior of a field is how it validates and cleans user input. After all, fields exist as a bridge between dangerous incoming data and a safe Python environment, so it's essential that this translation be done properly. The field's `clean()` method is primarily responsible for this, both for raising exceptions for improper data and for returning a cleaned value if the input is valid.

The method's signature is simply `clean(self, value)`, accepting the field object itself and also the incoming value. Then, if the value is deemed inappropriate according to the field's requirements, it should raise an instance of `django.forms.util.ValidationError` with a message indicating what went wrong. Otherwise, it should convert the value to whatever native Python data type is appropriate for the field and return it.

In addition to making sure error messages are as descriptive as possible, it's important to keep maintenance of error messages simple, while still allowing individual instances to override them. Django facilitates by way of a pair of attributes called `error_messages` and `default_error_messages`, as well as an argument called `error_messages`. This may seem like a tangled nest of values, but the way it works is rather simple.

A field class defines its standard error messages in a class-level attribute called `default_error_messages`. This is a dictionary mapping an easily-identifiable key to the actual error message string. Since fields will often inherit from other fields, which may define their own `default_error_messages` attributes, Django automatically combines them all into one dictionary when the field is instantiated.

In addition to using default_error_messages, Django allows individual field instances to override some of these messages by way of the error_messages argument. Any values in that dictionary will replace the default values for the keys specified, but only for that particular field instance. All other instances of the field will remain unaffected.

That means that error messages can come from three separate places: the field class itself, the field's parent classes, and the arguments used to instantiate the field. When looking to raise an exception as part of the clean() method, there needs to be a simple way to retrieve a specific error message, regardless of where it was actually defined. For this, Django populates an error_messages attribute of every field instance, which contains all the messages that were defined in all three ways. This way, clean() can simply look up a key in self.error_messages and use its value as the argument to ValidationError.

```python
from django.forms import fields, util

class LatitudeField(fields.DecimalField):
    default_error_messages = {
        'out_of_range': u'Value must be within -90 and 90.',
    }

    def clean(self, value):
        value = super(LatitudeField, self).clean(value)
        if not -90 <= value <= 90:
            raise util.ValidationError(self.error_messages['out_of_range'])
        return value

class LongitudeField(fields.DecimalField):
    default_error_messages = {
        'out_of_range': u'Value must be within -180 and 180.',
    }

    def clean(self, value):
        value = super(LatitudeField, self).clean(value)
        if not -180 <= value <= 180:
            raise util.ValidationError(self.error_messages['out_of_range'])
        return value
```

Note the use of super() here to call the clean() method of the parent DecimalField class, which first makes sure that the value is a valid decimal before bothering to check if it's a valid latitude or longitude. Since invalid values result in an exception being raised, if the call to DecimalField.clean() allows code to continue executing, then it is assured that the value is a valid decimal.

Controlling Widgets

Two other attributes defined on field classes specify which widgets are used to generate HTML for the field in certain situations. The first, widget, defines the default widget to be used when the field instance doesn't specify one explicitly. This is specified as a widget class, rather than an instance, as the widget is instantiated at the same time as the field itself.

A second attribute, called hidden_widget, controls which widget is used when the field should be output into the HTML, but not shown to the user. This shouldn't have to be overridden, as the default HiddenInput widget is sufficient for most fields. Some fields, like the MultipleChoiceField, need to specify more than one value, so a special MultipleHiddenInput is used on those cases.

In addition to specifying individual widget classes for these situations, fields can also define a widget_attrs() method to specify a set of attributes that should be added to whatever widget is used to render the field in HTML.

It receives two arguments, the usual self as well as widget, a fully-instantiated widget object that any new attributes will be attached to. Rather than attaching the attributes directly, widget_attrs() should return a dictionary of all the attributes that should be assigned to the widget. This is the technique the built-in CharField uses to assign a maxlength attribute to the HTML input field.

Defining HTML Behavior

Widgets, as mentioned in the previous section, are how fields represent themselves in a Web page as HTML. While fields themselves deal more with data validation and conversion, widgets are concerned with presenting the form and accepting user input. Each field has a widget associated with it, which handles the actual interaction with the user.

Django provides a variety of widgets, from basic text inputs to checkboxes and radio buttons, even multiple-choice list boxes. Each field provided by Django has, as its widget attribute, the widget that is most appropriate for the most common use cases for that field, but some cases may find need for a different widget. These widgets can be overridden on an individual field basis by simply supplying a different class to the field's constructor as the widget argument.

Custom Widgets

Like fields, the widgets provided with Django are useful for the most common cases, but will not fit every need. Some applications may need to provide additional information, such as a unit of measurement, to help users enter data accurately. Others may need to integrate with client-side JavaScript libraries to provide extra options, such as calendars for selecting dates. These types of added features are provided with custom widgets, which satisfy the requirements of the field they are associated with, while allowing great flexibility in HTML.

While not strictly enforced like fields, all widgets should inherit from django.forms.widgets.Widget to receive the most common functionality from the start. Then, each custom widget can override whatever attributes and methods are most appropriate for the task it needs to perform.

Rendering HTML

The most common need for a custom widget is to present a customized field display for the user, by way of HTML. For example, if an application needs a field to handle percentages, it would make it easier for users to work with that field if its widget could output a percent sign (%) after the input field. This is possible by overriding the render() method of the widget.

In addition to the normal self, the render() method receives three additional arguments: the name of the HTML element, the value currently associated with it and attrs, a dictionary of attributes that should be applied to the element. Of these, only attrs is optional, and should default to an empty dictionary if not provided.

```
>>> from django import forms
>>> class PriceInput(forms.TextInput):
...     def render(self, name, value, attrs=None):
...         return '$ %s' % super(PriceInput, self).render(name, value, attrs)
...
>>> class PercentInput(forms.TextInput):
...     def render(self, name, value, attrs=None):
...         return '%s %%' % super(PercentInput, self).render(name, value, attrs)
...
>>> class ProductEntry(forms.Form):
...     sku = forms.IntegerField(label='SKU')
...     description = forms.CharField(widget=forms.Textarea())
```

```
...        price = forms.DecimalField(decimal_places=2, widget=PriceInput())
...        tax = forms.IntegerField(widget=PercentInput())
...
>>> print ProductEntry()
<tr><th><label for="id_sku">SKU:</label></th><td><input type="text" name="sku" i
d="id_sku" /></td></tr>
<tr><th><label for="id_description">Description:</label></th><td><textarea id="i
d_description" rows="10" cols="40" name="description"></textarea></td></tr>
<tr><th><label for="id_price">Price:</label></th><td>$ <input type="text" name="
price" id="id_price" /></td></tr>
<tr><th><label for="id_tax">Tax:</label></th><td><input type="text" name="tax" i
d="id_tax" /> %</td></tr>
```

Obtaining Values from Posted Data

Since widgets are all about dealing with HTML, and values are posted to the server using a format specified by HTML, in a structure dictated by HTML elements, widgets serve the extra purpose of translating between incoming data and the fields that data maps to. This not only insulates fields from the details of how HTML inputs work, it's also the only way to manage widgets that use multiple HTML inputs, and allows widgets to fill in defaults, like None, in situations where nothing at all was submitted by the HTML input.

The widget method responsible for this task is value_from_datadict(), which takes three arguments in addition to the standard self.

- data—The dictionary provided to the form's constructor, usually request.POST

- files—The files passed to the form's constructor, using the same format as request.FILES

- name—The name of the widget, which is essentially just the name of the field plus any prefix that was added to the form

The method uses all of this information to retrieve the value submitted from the browser, make any necessary changes and return a value suitable for fields to use. This should always return a value, defaulting to None if no suitable value could be found. All Python functions return None by default, if they don't return anything else, so this rule is easily followed simply by ensuring that value_from_datadict() doesn't raise any exceptions, but for the sake of readability, it's always best to explicitly return None.

Splitting Data Across Multiple Widgets

Since widgets are a bridge between fields and HTML, they have a great deal of control over what HTML gets used, and how it reports back to the field. So much so, in fact, that it's possible to split up a single field across multiple HTML field controls. Because of where the render() and value_from_datadict() hooks are placed in the flow, this can even be done without the field having to know it's happening.

Exactly how this works depends largely on what HTML inputs the widget would use, but the general idea is simple. A field passes its value to the widget's render() method, which breaks it up into multiple HTML inputs, each containing a piece of the original value. An example of this is having a separate text box for each of the date and time components of a DateTimeField.

Then, when the widget receives the data back through its value_from_datadict() method, it assembles these pieces back together into a single value, which is then handed back to the field. At no point does the field have to deal with more than one value, regardless of what the widget does.

Unfortunately, that all requires each widget to be responsible for all the HTML markup, as well as reassembling the value when it's received. Sometimes it's just as useful to simply combine two or more existing fields, relying on *their* widgets to do the job instead. Since it's quite handy to have a utility to help with this, Django provides one.

To be accurate, Django provides two utilities: a field, MultiValueField, and a widget, MultiWidget, which are designed to work together. By themselves, they're not terribly useful in the real world. Instead, they provide a significant share of the necessary features, while allowing subclasses to fill in the details that are specific to a particular use case.

On the field side of things, MultiValueField takes care of the details when cleaning data, by validating it against each of the individual fields that make up the composite. The only two things it leaves to the subclass are the definition of which fields should be combined and how their values should be compressed into a single value suitable for use by other Python code. In Django itself, for example, the SplitDateTimeField combines a DateField with a TimeField and compresses their values to a single datetime object.

The process of defining which fields should be used is simple, and is handled in the __init__() method of the new field class. All it takes is to populate a tuple with the field instances that should be combined. Then, simply pass this tuple as the first argument to the __init__() method of the parent class, which handles the rest from there. This keeps the method definition on the specific field quite simple, typically only a few lines long.

Compressing the values generated by those multiple fields takes place in the compress() method. This takes a single value in addition to the usual self, a sequence of values that should be combined into a single native Python value. What happens within can be a bit more complicated, though, as there are a few situations to take into account.

First, there's the possibility that no value was submitted at all, for any part of the field, which would mean that the incoming data would be an empty list. By default, fields are required, in which case an exception would be thrown prior to calling compress(). If a field was declared with required=False, this is a very likely scenario, and the method should return None in this case.

In addition, it's quite possible for just part of the value to be submitted, since it's split across multiple HTML inputs. Again, if the field is required, this is handled automatically, but if the field is optional, compress() must still do some extra work to ensure that if *any* of the value is submitted, *all* of it is submitted. This is typically handled by just checking each item in the value sequence against the standard EMPTY_VALUES tuple, also located at django.forms.fields. Any portion of the field containing an empty value should then raise an exception informing the user of which portion of the field was missing a value.

Then, if all the values were submitted and were valid, compress() does its real work, returning a value suitable for use in Python when the form is being processed. The exact nature of this return value will depend entirely on the type of field being created, and how it's expected to be used. Consider the following example of a field to accept latitude and longitude coordinates as separate decimals, combining them into a simple tuple.

```python
from django.forms import fields

class LatLonField(fields.MultiValueField):

    def __init__(self, *args, **kwargs):
        flds = (LatitudeField(), LongitudeField())
        super(LatLonField, self).__init__(flds, *args, **kwargs)

    def compress(self, data_list):
        if data_list:
            if data_list[0] in fields.EMPTY_VALUES:
                raise fields.ValidationError(u'Enter a valid latitude.')
            if data_list[1] in fields.EMPTY_VALUES:
                raise fields.ValidationError(u'Enter a valid longitude.')
            return tuple(data_list)
        return None
```

With the field side of things out of the way, the next step is to create a widget that captures both of these elements separately. Since the intended display is simply two text boxes, it makes sense to make the custom widget a simple composite of two TextInput widgets, which solves the first challenge of identifying the widgets to be used. The base MultiWidget does a good job of rendering output and retrieving values from the incoming data, so the only challenge left is to convert the single compressed value into a list of values to be rendered by the individual widgets.

The counterpart to the field's compress() method is, as you might expect, the widget's decompress() method. Its signature is quite similar, taking just a single value, but its task is to split that value into as many pieces as there are widgets to render them. Ordinarily, this would be a matter of taking bits and pieces from a single value and putting them into a sequence, such as a tuple or a list. Since the LatLonField shown previously outputs its value as a tuple directly, the only thing that's left is to supply a tuple of empty values if none was provided.

```
from django.forms import fields, widgets

class LatLonWidget(widgets.MultiWidget):
    def __init__(self, attrs=None):
        wdgts = (widgets.TextInput(attrs), widgets.TextInput(attrs))
        super(LatLonWidget, self).__init__(wdgts, attrs)

    def decompress(self, value):
        return value or (None, None)

class LatLonField(fields.MultiValueField):
    widget = LatLonWidget

    # The rest of the code previously described
```

Customizing Form Markup

In addition to defining custom widgets, it's also possible to customize how forms themselves are rendered as HTML. Unlike the previous examples, the following techniques are used inside Django's template language, where it's a bit easier to make changes that are specific to an individual form.

The most obvious thing that can be customized is the actual <form> element, because Django forms don't even output that at all. This is primarily because there's no way to assume whether the form should use GET or POST, and what URL it should be sent to. Any form that needs to be submitted back to the server needs to have this specified by hand, so it's a perfect opportunity for some specialization. When using a form that includes a FileField, for example, the <form> element needs to include an attribute such as enctype="multipart/form-data".

In addition to the form's submission behavior, one common thing to configure is the presentation of the form, using Cascading Style Sheets (CSS). There are a number of ways to reference an element with CSS, but two of the most useful are by assigning an ID or a class, both of which are often placed on the <form> element itself. Since that element has to be defined, it's easy to add these extra attributes as well.

In addition, there are often uses for configuring how the form's field are displayed, depending on how the overall look of a site is achieved. Different sites may use tables, lists or even simple paragraphs to present forms, so Django tries to make it as easy as possible to accommodate these different scenarios.

When outputting a form in a template, there are a few methods available to choose which of these output formats to use. The default, as_table, wraps each field in a row, suitable for use in a standard table, while as_ul() wraps the fields in list items, and as_p() wraps them in paragraphs. None of these output any kind of element around all the fields, however; that's left to the template, so that additional attributes can be added, such as IDs and classes for CSS referencing, just like the form element.

While these three provided methods are useful for their own purposes, they're not necessarily enough for every situation. In keeping with DRY, each of them is in fact a customized wrapper around a common method, which wraps any kind of markup around all the fields in the form. This common method, _html_output(), shouldn't be called directly from outside the form, but is perfectly suitable for use by another custom method designed for a more specific purpose. It takes a number of arguments, each specifying a different aspect of the HTML output.

- normal_row—HTML to be used for a standard row. It's specified as a Python format string that will receive a dictionary, so there are a few values that can be placed here: errors, label, field and help_text. Those should be fairly self-explanatory, except that field actually contains the HTML generated by the field's widget.

- error_row—HTML used for a row consisting solely of an error message, primarily used for form-level errors that aren't tied to a specific field. It's also used for forms that are configured to show field errors on a separate row from the field itself, according to the errors_on_separate_row option described at the end of this list. It's also a Python format string, taking a single unnamed argument, the errors to be displayed.

- row_ender—Markup used to identify the end of a row. Rather than appending this to the rows, since the preceding rows must have their endings specified directly, this is used to insert any hidden fields into a last row, just before its ending. Therefore, always make sure that the following is true: normal_row.endswith(row_ender).

- help_text_html—HTML to be used when writing out help text. This markup will be placed immediately after the widget, and takes the help text as a single unnamed argument to this format string.

- errors_on_separate_row—A Boolean indicating whether field errors should be rendered using the error_row prior to rendering the field itself. This doesn't impact what values are passed to normal_row, so if the form expects errors to be on separate rows, be sure to leave errors out of that format string. Otherwise, errors will be printed twice.

Accessing Individual Fields

In addition to being able to customize a form's overall markup in Python, on the form itself, it's also quite simple to specify a form's markup directly in a template. This way, forms are as reusable as possible, while still allowing templates to have final control over the rendered markup.

Form objects are iterable, using techniques described in Chapter 2. This means that templates can simply loop over them using the for block tag, with each iteration being a field on the form, which has been bound to a value. This bound field object can then be used to display the various aspects of a field, inside whatever markup makes the most sense to a template. It has a nice selection of attributes and methods to help the process along.

- field—The original field object, with all of its associated attributes

- data—The current value bound to the field

- errors—An ErrorList (as described in the next section) containing all the errors for the field

- is_hidden—A Boolean indicating whether the default widget is a hidden input

- label_tag()—The HTML <label> element and its contents, for use with the field

- as_widget()—The default rendering of the field, using the widget defined for it

- as_text()—The field rendered using a basic TextInput instead of its own widget

- as_textarea()—The field rendered using a Textarea instead of the widget defined for it

- as_hidden()—The field rendered using a hidden input instead of any visible widget

Customizing the Display of Errors

By default, the markup used to display errors is specified by a special Python class called ErrorList, which lives at django.forms.util. This behaves just like a standard Python list, except that it has some extra methods for outputting its values as HTML. In particular, it has two methods by default, as_ul() and as_text(), which output errors as an unordered list or as unadorned text, respectively.

By creating a custom error class, as a subclass of ErrorList, it's easy to override these methods to provide custom markup when errors are displayed. This markup includes any containing elements, such as <ul>, as the entire markup will be dropped in place wherever the field's errors are displayed, whether as part of the default markup, or by accessing the field's errors attribute directly.

By default, the as_ul() method is used to render errors, though templates that wish to do further customizations can call whichever method makes the most sense for the template. In fact, it's possible to add entirely new methods and even override which method is used by default by also overriding the __unicode__() method. It's also possible for templates to simply loop through the errors in this list and wrap each one in whatever markup makes sense for the situation.

Writing a custom ErrorList subclass isn't quite enough; it also has to be passed into the form somehow to make sure it gets used. This is also quite simple: just pass the custom class into the form's constructor as the error_class argument.

In addition to displaying errors on individual fields, a form's clean() method allows errors to be shown for form-wide validation failures. Displaying this in the template requires accessing the form's non_field_errors() method.

Applied Techniques

While Django's forms are primarily designed to handle a fairly common user input requirement, they can be made to do some complicated legwork. They can be used either individually or in groups to extend the user interface even further. Nearly any form of user input can be represented using a Django form; the following is just a sample of what's available.

Pending and Resuming Forms

Forms are generally intended to receive input all at once, process that input and behave accordingly. This is something of a one-off cycle, where the only reason a form would have to be redisplayed would be to show validation errors, allowing the user to fix them and resubmit. If a user needs to stop working on a form for a time and come back later, that means starting over from scratch.

While this is generally the accepted approach, it can also be a burden for complex forms or those where the user might need to provide information that takes time to gather, such as tax information. In these situations, it would be much more useful to be able to save the form in a partially-filled state and return to it at a later point in time. That's not how forms typically work, so there's clearly some work to be done, but it's really not that hard.

Since forms are declared as classes, and there's no reason to violate that presumption, the class developed hereafter will be usable as a parent class, just like forms.Form. In fact, for all intents and purposes, it should be a drop-in replacement for the standard class, simply imbuing its subclasses with extra functionality. Consider the following form for making an offer on a house in a properties application, something that usually won't be taken lightly. By allowing the form to be pended and resumed at a later time, users can take the necessary time to review an offer before committing to such an investment.

```
from django import forms
from django_localflavor_us import forms as us_forms

from pend_form.forms import PendForm
```

```
class Offer(PendForm):
    name = forms.CharField(max_length=255)
    phone = us_forms.USPhoneNumberField()
    price = forms.IntegerField()
```

Note that, aside from the switch to `PendForm`, this is defined like any other standard Django form. The advantages of this simple change are described in the following sections, which outline a new `pend_form` application.

Storing Values for Later

In order to save a form in a partially completed state, its current values must be stored in the database somehow. They'd also have to be tied to field names, so they can be used later to re-create the form. This sounds like a job for dynamic models, which can be created automatically, based on the form's definition, to store values efficiently. However, they aren't appropriate for this use case, for a few reasons.

For one thing, form fields don't have directly equivalent model fields. Since the dynamic model would have to be filled with fields that can contain the same data as the form fields, there would have to be some way to determine a model field based on a form field. Model fields do define form fields that can be used with them, but not the other way around.

Technically, it would be possible to manually provide a mapping of form fields to model fields, so that such models could be created anyway. This would have its fair share of problems as well, since it wouldn't be able to support custom form fields. Essentially, any form field that isn't present in that mapping wouldn't have a matching model field, and the technique would fail.

Also, storing field values in model fields that are based on the form's field types would require converting those values into Python objects first, which would mean that they'd all have to be valid values. It should be possible to pend a form, even with invalid values, so that they can be corrected later. This wouldn't be at all possible if the values had to be stuffed into model fields with specific data types, which included either data validation or type-checking.

Instead, we can rely on the fact that all form data, when submitted back to the server, arrive as strings. These strings must be converted to native Python objects as part of the form validation process, so the strings themselves are the last chance to get the actual raw data from the submitted form. Better yet, since they're all strings, Django provides an easy way to store them for later use: `TextField`. A `TextField` is necessary, because different form values provide different lengths of data, some of which will likely extend beyond the 255-character limit of `CharField`.

With a reliable way to store values, the next step is to identify what other information must be stored in the database, in order to reconstitute the form. Obviously the names of the fields would be included, so the values could get put back in the right place. Also, since different forms could have different structures, with different numbers of fields, it would be best to give each field's value its own row in the database. That means there would need to be a way of keeping fields together as part of a form.

The trick here is that forms don't have a unique identifier. After all, they're not normally expected to exist outside of a specific request/response cycle, except for validation corrections, where the entire form is resubmitted as part of the new request. There's simply no built-in way to identify an instance of a form, so something different will have to be used.

One very common way of identifying complex structures like this is to create a hash based on the data. While hashes aren't guaranteed to be unique, they're close enough for most purposes, and there are some things that can be included along with a hash to get better odds of uniqueness.

In the case of a form, this hash can be taken from the complete collection of field data, so that a change in any name or value would result in a change in the hash that data would produce. Another piece of information that can be stored alongside the hash is the import path to the form, which allows for differentiation among multiple sets of data, if there are multiple forms with the same collection of fields.

Now that there are a few pieces of information to store, consider how they should relate to each other. There are essentially two levels here: the form and its values. These could be taken as two separate models, relating multiple values to a single form by way of a standard foreign key relationship. The form side would contain the form's path as well as the hash of all its values, while the value side would contain the names and values of each field, as well as a reference back to the form it belongs with.

The models.py module of the pend_form application looks like this:

```python
class PendedForm(models.Model):
    form_class = models.CharField(max_length=255)
    hash = models.CharField(max_length=32)

class PendedValue(models.Model):
    form = models.ForeignKey(PendedForm, related_name='data')
    name = models.CharField(max_length=255)
    value = models.TextField()
```

This simple structure is now capable of storing any amount of data for any form. It wouldn't be very efficient if the application needed to make complex queries on the form's data, but since it's just being used to save and restore the contents of a form all at once, it'll work quite well.

Now that there are models in place to contain the form's data, there needs to be a way to actually store that data for later retrieval. Thankfully, forms are just standard Python classes, so it's easy enough to just write an extra method that handles this task directly. Then, when the time comes to write a specific form that needs this capability, it can simply subclass the following form, rather than the usual forms.Form. This is placed in a new forms.py module in our pend_form application.

```python
try:
    from hashlib import md5
except:
    from md5 import new as md5

from django import forms

from pend_form.models import PendedForm

class PendForm(forms.Form):
    @classmethod
    def get_import_path(cls):
        return '%s.%s' % (cls.__module__, cls.__name__)

    def hash_data(self):
        content = ','.join('%s:%s' % (n, self.data[n]) for n in self.fields.keys())
        return md5(content).hexdigest()

    def pend(self):
        import_path = self.get_import_path()
        form_hash = self.hash_data()
        pended_form = PendedForm.objects.get_or_create(form_class=import_path,
                                                       hash=form_hash)
        for name in self.fields:
            pended_form.data.get_or_create(name=name, value=self.data[name])
        return form_hash
```

Note the liberal use of get_or_create() here. If an instance of a form already exists with exactly the same values, there's no sense saving the whole thing twice. Instead, it simply relies on the fact that the previous copy will be functionally identical, so it'll work for both.

Reconstituting a Form

Now that forms can be placed in the database without being fully processed, or even validated, their usefulness is still limited if they can't be retrieved later, for the user to continue working on them. The data is stored in such a way that it *can* be reassembled into a form, all that's left is to actually do so.

Since the code to do this must, by definition, be called prior to having a form instance to work with, it may seem like it must be in a module-level function. Remember that methods can be declared to be used on the class, rather than the instance, if the need arises. Since the goal here is to have all of this functionality encapsulated on a subclass, without having to worry about where all the machinery itself is written, a class method will do the trick here quite well.

What actually goes on in this new class method is a bit more interesting. In order to instantiate a form, it takes a dictionary as its first argument, which is usually just request.POST, available to all views. When loading the form later, the new request has absolutely nothing to do with the form, much less does it contain the appropriate data, so that dictionary must be constructed manually, from the data previously stored in the database.

This data may be referenced by the form hash described earlier, along with the import path of the form being used. Those two pieces of information are all that's needed to properly locate and retrieve all the field's values from the database. Since the form already knows how to get its import path, thanks to one of the methods described previously, all that's left is to provide the form's hash manually. This would most likely be captured in a URL pattern, though different applications may have different ways to go about that.

Once the hash is known, the method for resuming a form should be able to accept that, combine it with its own import path, retrieve the values from the database, populate a dictionary based on those values, instantiate a new copy of the form with those values, and return that new form for other code to use. That sounds like an awful lot of work, but it's a lot easier than it may seem.

One thing that comes to the rescue here is how Python's own dictionaries can be instantiated. The built-in dict() can accept a variety of different argument combinations, but one of the most useful is a sequence of 2-tuples, each containing the name and value of an entry in the intended dictionary. Since QuerySets return sequences already, and tools like list comprehensions and generator expressions can easily create new sequences based on them, it's quite easy to create something suitable.

Getting the import path and looking up the saved form is easy, and that object's data attribute provides easy access to all of its values. Using a generator expression, the data's name/value pairs can be easily passed into the built-in dict(), creating a dictionary that can be passed into the form object's constructor. All is made clear by the code.

```
@classmethod
def resume(cls, form_hash):
    import_path = cls.get_import_path()
    form = models.PendForm.objects.get(form_class=import_path, hash=form_hash)
    data = dict((d.name, d.value) for d in form.data.all())
    return cls(data)
```

This simple method, when called with a form's generated hash value, will return a fully-formed form object, ready to be validated and presented to the user for further review. In fact, validation and presentation will be the typical workflow in this case, giving the user a chance to see if there was anything to add or correct, before deciding to commit the form or pend it again for later.

A Full Workflow

As mentioned earlier, the normal workflow is fairly standard, with little variation across all the various forms that are in use in the wild. By allowing forms to be pended or resumed, there's an optional extra step added to the workflow, which requires some added handling in the view. Adding this new piece to the puzzle, the overall workflow looks a bit like this:

1. Display an empty form.
2. User fills in some data.
3. User clicks Submit.
4. Validate data submitted by the user.
5. Display the form with errors.
6. User clicks Pend.
7. Save form values in the database.
8. Validate data retrieved from the database.
9. Display the form with errors.
10. Process the completed form.

In order to maintain this entire workflow, the view gets a bit more complicated. There are now four separate paths that could be taken, depending on which part of the workflow is being processed at any given time. And remember, this is all just to take the necessary steps to handle the form. It doesn't take into account any of the business logic required for a specific application.

- User requests a form without any data.
- User posts data using the Pend button.
- User requests a form using a form hash.
- User posts data using the Submit button.

From there, the typical workflow steps still apply, such as checking the validity of the input data and taking the appropriate steps that are specific to the application's functionality. Once this is all rolled up together in a view, it looks something like this:

```
from django import http
from django.shortcuts import render_to_response
from django.template.context import RequestContext

from properties import models, forms

def make_offer(request, id, template_name='', form_hash=None):
    if request.method == 'POST':
        form = forms.Offer(request.POST)
        if 'pend' in request.POST:
            form_hash = form.pend()
            return http.HttpRedirect(form_hash)
        else:
            if form.is_valid():
                # This is where actual processing would take place
```

```
    else:
        if form_hash:
            form = forms.Offer.resume(form_hash)
        else:
            form = forms.Offer()


    return render_to_response(template_name, {'form': form},
                              context_instance=RequestContext(request))
```

There's a lot going on here, but very little of it has anything to do with making an offer on a house. The vast majority of that code exists solely to manage all the different states the form could be in at any given time, and would have to be repeated every time a view uses a PendForm subclass, and that's not efficient.

Making It Generic

While it's easy to see which aspects of the view are repetitive, and should thus be factored out into something reusable, it's a bit trickier to decide how to do so. The main issue is that the portion of the code that's specific to this particular view isn't just a string or a number, like has been shown in most of the previous examples, but rather a block of code.

This is something of a problem, because previous examples had shown how generic views can be used to factor out commonalities, while allowing specific differences to be specified in a URL pattern. That works well for basic data types, such as strings, numbers, sequences and dictionaries, but code is handled differently. Instead of being able to just specify the value inline in the URL pattern, this code must be defined in a separate function, which is then passed in to the pattern.

While that's certainly possible, it makes the URL configuration module a bit more cumbersome, given that there might be a number of top-level functions declared above each block of URL patterns. Lambda-style functions could be a way around this, but since they're restricted to executing simple expressions, with no loops or conditions, they'd severely limit the type of code that could be used.

One alternative is a decorator, which could be applied to a standard function, providing all of the necessary functionality in a wrapper. This way, any function can be used to contain the code that will actually process the form, with the full capabilities of Python at its disposal. That code also wouldn't have to deal with any of the boilerplate necessary to pend or resume the form, because the decorator could do all that before the view code itself even executes, simply passing in a form as an argument. Here's how the previous view could look, if a decorator was used to remove the boilerplate.

```
from pend_forms.decorators import pend_form

@pend_form
def make_offer(request, id, form):
    # This is where actual processing would take place
```

Now all that's left is to write the decorator itself, encapsulating the functionality that was removed from the previous example, wrapping it around a view that would be passed in. This would be placed in a new decorators.py module.

```
from django import http
from django.shortcuts import render_to_response
from django.template.context import RequestContext

from django.utils.functional import wraps
```

```
def pend_form(view):
    @wraps(view)
    def wrapper(request, form_class, template_name,
                form_hash=None, *args, **kwargs):
        if request.method == 'POST':
            form = form_class(request.POST)
            if 'pend' in request.POST:
                form_hash = form.pend()
                return http.HttpRedirect(form_hash)
            else:
                if form.is_valid():
                    return view(request, form=form, *args, **kwargs)
        else:
            if form_hash:
                form = form_class.resume(form_hash)
            else:
                form = form_class()

        return render_to_response(template_name, {'form': form},
                                  context_instance=RequestContext(request))
    return wrapper
```

Now, all that's necessary is to set up a URL configuration that provides both a form class and a template name. This decorator will handle the rest, only calling the view when the form has been completed and submitted for processing.

A Class-Based Approach

Now that you've seen how this could be done with traditional, function-based views, remember that Django's new class-based views offer a different approach to many problems, and this is no exception. Earlier in this chapter, you saw how the FormView class provides most of what you need to work with forms, and we can extend that to work with our pending functionality as well. In fact, because we can add new methods to the view class, it's no longer necessary to provide a custom Form subclass. It can be done using any stock form you have in your code. Let's start by retrieving a previously pended form. Some of the utility methods that were previously placed on the Form subclass can be reused here intact, but we also need a way to pass the existing values into the new form, which is a perfect task for get_form_kwargs().

```
from django.views.generic.edit import FormView
from pend_form.models import PendedValue

class PendFormView(FormView):
    form_hash_name = 'form_hash'

    def get_form_kwargs(self):
        """
        Returns a dictionary of arguments to pass into the form instantiation.
        If resuming a pended form, this will retrieve data from the database.
        """
        form_hash = self.kwargs.get(self.form_hash_name)
```

```
        if form_hash:
            import_path = self.get_import_path(self.get_form_class())
            return {'data': self.get_pended_data(import_path, form_hash)}
        else:
            return super(PendFormView, self).get_form_kwargs()

    # Utility methods

    def get_import_path(self, form_class):
        return '%s.%s' % (form_class.__module__, form_class.__name__)

    def get_pended_data(self, import_path, form_hash):
        data = PendedValue.objects.filter(import_path=import_path, form_hash=form_hash)
        return dict((d.name, d.value) for d in data)
```

Since the purpose of get_form_kwargs() is to supply arguments to the instantiation of the form, all we really need to do here is retrieve the appropriate values and return them instead of the default values. This will suffice to fill a populated form if a form hash is provided in the URL.

Notice also that form_hash_name is included as a class-level attribute. This allows users of this view to override what argument indicates that the form is being pended. All you need to do is supply it as a class attribute, and Django will allow it to be customized, falling back to your defined value as a default.

The next stage will allow users to actually save form values for later. As before, this will need to store the form and its values in the database, along with a hash of that information for later retrieval. In addition to some additional utilities, the bulk of the work must be done in the post() method, because that's our entry point when the form is submitted.

The raw functionality of saving the form involves quite a few pieces, some of which can be reused from the previous steps. Here's what's needed for saving forms for later, so we can discuss it before showing all the code together.

```
from django.views.generic.edit import FormView
from pend_form.models import PendedForm, PendedValue

class PendFormView(FormView):
    pend_button_name = 'pend'

    def post(self, request, *args, **kwargs):
        """
        Handles POST requests with form data. If the form was pended, it doesn't follow
        the normal flow, but saves the values for later instead.
        """
        if self.pend_button_name in self.request.POST:
            form_class = self.get_form_class()
            form = self.get_form(form_class)
            self.form_pended(form)
        else:
            super(PendFormView, self).post(request, *args, **kwargs)

    # Custom methods follow

    def get_import_path(self, form_class):
        return '%s.%s' % (form_class.__module__, form_class.__name__)
```

```
    def get_form_hash(self, form):
        content = ','.join('%s:%s' % (n, form.data[n]) for n in form.fields.keys())
        return md5(content).hexdigest()

    def form_pended(self, form):
        import_path = self.get_import_path(self.get_form_class())
        form_hash = self.get_form_hash(form)
        pended_form = PendedForm.objects.get_or_create(form_class=import_path,
                                                       hash=form_hash)
        for name in form.fields.keys():
            pended_form.data.get_or_create(name=name, value=form.data[name])
        return form_hash
```

The post() method normally dispatches between the form_valid() and form_invalid() methods, but since a pended form isn't necessarily valid or invalid, it needs to be overridden to provide a third dispatch option. That third dispatch is handled by form_pended(), named to coincide with Django's own form validity methods. It does the work of saving the form and its associated data, reusing some utilities from Django as well as the previous iteration for displaying the pended form.

And here's what it all looks like together:

```
from django.views.generic.edit import FormView
from pend_form.models import PendedForm, PendedValue

class PendFormView(FormView):
    form_hash_name = 'form_hash'
    pend_button_name = 'pend'

    def get_form_kwargs(self):
        """
        Returns a dictionary of arguments to pass into the form instantiation.
        If resuming a pended form, this will retrieve data from the database.
        """
        form_hash = self.kwargs.get(self.form_hash_name)
        if form_hash:
            import_path = self.get_import_path(self.get_form_class())
            return {'data': self.get_pended_data(import_path, form_hash)}
        else:
            return super(PendFormView, self).get_form_kwargs()

    def post(self, request, *args, **kwargs):
        """
        Handles POST requests with form data. If the form was pended, it doesn't follow
        the normal flow, but saves the values for later instead.
        """
        if self.pend_button_name in self.request.POST:
            form_class = self.get_form_class()
            form = self.get_form(form_class)
            self.form_pended(form)
        else:
            super(PendFormView, self).post(request, *args, **kwargs)
```

```
# Custom methods follow

def get_import_path(self, form_class):
    return '{0}.{1}'.format(form_class.__module__, form_class.__name__)

def get_form_hash(self, form):
    content = ','.join('{0}:{1}'.format(n, form.data[n]) for n in form.fields.keys())
    return md5(content).hexdigest()

def form_pended(self, form):
    import_path = self.get_import_path(self.get_form_class())
    form_hash = self.get_form_hash(form)
    pended_form = PendedForm.objects.get_or_create(form_class=import_path,
                                                   hash=form_hash)
    for name in form.fields.keys():
        pended_form.data.get_or_create(name=name, value=form.data[name])
    return form_hash

def get_pended_data(self, import_path, form_hash):
    data = PendedValue.objects.filter(import_path=import_path, form_hash=form_hash)
    return dict((d.name, d.value) for d in data)
```

Now you can use this like you would any other class-based view. All you need is to provide it a form class, as well as override any of the default values specified here or in FormView itself. Templates, button names and URL structures are customizable by simply subclassing the PendFormView and working from there. The only thing you'll need to do beyond that is to add a button to your template to allow your users to pend the form.

Now What?

In order to be truly useful in the real world, forms must be presented to users as part of an HTML page. Rather than trying to generate that HTML content directly inside Python code, Django provides templates as a more designer-friendly alternative.

CHAPTER 6

■ ■ ■

Templates

While Chapter 2 made it clear that Django is built entirely on Python, and standard Python rules apply, templates are the exception to the rule. Templates are Django's way of generating text-based output, such as HTML or emails, where the people editing those documents may not have any experience with Python. Therefore, templates are designed to avoid using Python directly, instead favoring an extensible, easy-to-use custom language built just for Django.

By disallowing arbitrary Python expressions, templates are certainly restricted in some ways, but there are two things to keep in mind. First, the template system is backed by Python, just like everything else in Django, so it's always possible to add Python-level code for specific features. It's just bad form to include the actual Python code in the template itself, so Django provides other means for plugging in that extra code.

More importantly, drawing a clear line between templates and the Python code that powers them allows two separate groups of people, with different backgrounds and skill sets, to work together. For many hobbyist projects, this probably sounds like a waste, since the only people working on the site are developers. In many commercial environments, however, developers are often a separate group of people from those tasked with maintaining the site's content and visual structure.

By clearly separating the tasks of development and template editing, it's easy to set up an environment where developers work on the things that they're really needed for, while content editors and designers can work on things that don't really require development experience. Django's templates are fairly simple in nature, and easy to pick up by most anyone, even those without any programming experience.

The basic details of what the template syntax looks like and the included tags and filters are well described elsewhere. Instead of focusing on those higher-level details, this chapter will cover how templates are loaded, parsed and rendered, how variables are managed within a template and how new tags and filters can be created. Essentially, it's all about what developers can do to make life as easy as possible for their content editing counterparts.

What Makes a Template

Even though templates aren't written in Python directly, they're backed by Python, making all the good stuff possible. When a template's code is read in from a file or other source, it's compiled into a collection of Python objects, which are then responsible for rendering it later. Exactly how these objects work can be ignored for basic template usage, but as with anything else, a proper understanding unlocks a world of possibilities.

Taking a peek inside the `django.template` package, the `Template` class stands out as the starting point for template operations, and rightly so. When a template is loaded, its content is passed to a new instance of `Template`, along with some optional information about where the template itself came from. There are three arguments passed in to new `Template` objects, on which everything is based.

- `template_string`—The only required argument, this contains the actual content of the template, as read in from a file. The great thing here is that `Template` accepts a string, not a filename or an open file object. By accepting just a string—either a Unicode string or a regular string encoded in UTF-8—it's possible to set up templates from any source. Some interesting uses of this can be found in this chapter's Applied Techniques.

- `origin`—An object representing where the template came from, such as a template loader or just a raw string. It's only used when the `TEMPLATE_DEBUG` setting is `True`, and can often be left out without penalty, but it's always best to include it for development situations, where it can help debug problems involving multiple template loaders.

- `name`—The name of the template, as passed to whatever loader requested it, if any. This is often just a relative path to the template, but could theoretically be anything that makes sense in a particular situation. After all, what Django really cares about is the `template_string`; the rest is just useful when debugging problems.

The actual code for `Template` is fairly minimal, deferring most of its work to a utility function called `compile_string()`, which parses the raw text, compiling it into a sequence of nodes. These nodes are just Python objects, each configured for a specific part of the template. Taken together, they represent the entire template, from start to finish, in a way that can be more easily and efficiently rendered.

These nodes are attached to the template as an attribute called `nodelist`. When rendering the template with data, it simply iterates over this list, rendering each node individually. This keeps the `Template` code very minimal, while allowing maximum flexibility. After all, if each individual theme is responsible for rendering itself, it has the full power of Python at its disposal. Therefore, creating or customizing template nodes is a simple matter of writing some real Python code.

Exceptions

All of this assumes that the template works correctly all the way through. When working with templates, there are a number of things that can go wrong, and thus a few different exceptions that could be raised. While the following exceptions are handled automatically in a way that works for most cases, it's possible to catch these instead and handle them separately.

- `django.template.TemplateSyntaxError`—The template code doesn't validate as proper syntax, usually due to the use of an invalid tag name. This is raised immediately when trying to instantiate a `Template` object.

- `django.template.TemplateDoesNotExist`—The requested template couldn't be loaded by any of the known template loaders. This is issued by the template loading functions described in the "Retrieving Templates" section of this chapter.

- `django.template.TemplateEncodingError`—The template string provided couldn't be forced to a Unicode string by the `Template` object. Template strings must either be a Unicode string already, or be encoded in UTF-8; any other encoding must be converted to one of those two types prior to being passed to a new `Template`. This will be raised immediately when trying to construct a new `Template` object.

- `django.template.VariableDoesNotExist`—A specified variable name couldn't be resolved in the current context. See the "Context" section later in this chapter for details on this process and what situations will cause this exception to be raised.

- `django.template.InvalidTemplateLibrary`—A template tag specified some invalid parameters to one of the tag library registration functions. A single tag issuing such an error will cause the entire tag library to stop loading, and none of the tags will be available to the template. This is raised when using the {% load %} template tag.

The Process at Large

Once a string is obtained from a loader, it must be converted from a single string to a set of Python objects that can be rendered. This happens automatically, and no intervention is necessary for most cases, but as with most of Django, an understanding of these internals can be quite useful. The following steps explain how a template is processed. All the classes involved live at `django.template`.

1. A new `Template` object accepts the raw string of the template's contents, forming the object that will be used later.

2. A `Lexer` object also receives the raw template string, to begin processing the template contents.

3. `Lexer.tokenize()` uses a regular expression to split the template into individual components, called tokens.

4. These tokens populate a new `Parser` object.

5. `Parser.parse()` goes through the available tokens, creating nodes along the way.

6. For each block tag, `Parser.parse()` calls an external function that understands the tag's syntax and returns a compiled `Node` for that tag.

7. The list of compiled nodes is stored on the `Template` object as its `nodelist` attribute.

Upon completion, you're left with a `Template` object that contains references to Python code, rather than the raw string that started the process. That original string is discarded after the node list is created, because those nodes contain all the necessary functionality to render the template. The `Lexer`, `Parser`, and all the `Token` objects are also discarded once the process completes, but they can be very useful along the way.

Content Tokens

The `Lexer` object is responsible for making a first pass through the template's contents, identifying different components that are present. In addition to the template string itself, `Lexer` also accepts an `origin`, which indicates where the template came from. This processing is done by the `Lexer.tokenize()` method, which returns a list of `Token` objects. This could be seen as processing the template's syntax, but not its semantics: individual components are identified, but they don't yet carry much meaning.

Tokens contain all the information necessary to create nodes, but tokens themselves are relatively simple. They have just two attributes: `token_type` and `contents`. The value for `Token.token_type` will be one of four constants defined in `django.template`, while its `contents` will be defined by the type of token it is.

*   `TOKEN_VAR`—Variable tags, using the `{{ var }}` syntax, are placeholders for data that won't be provided until the template is rendered. The `contents` attribute contains the full variable reference string, unparsed.

*   `TOKEN_BLOCK`—Block tags—commonly called "template tags"—use the `{% name %}` syntax and are populated by a Python object that can execute custom code during template rendering. The `contents` attribute contains the full contents of the tag, including the tag's name and all its arguments.

*   `TOKEN_COMMENT`—Comment tags use a `{# comment #}` syntax and are essentially ignored by the template engine. Tokens are generated for them as part of the lexing process, but their `contents` are empty and they don't become nodes later in the process.

*   `TOKEN_TEXT`—Text tokens are generated for all other content in the template, storing the text in `contents`.

A Lexer always gets created and utilized automatically during standard template processing, but can also be used directly. This is a useful way to inspect and analyze templates without the overhead of compiling them completely. To illustrate, consider the following example, which parses a simple one-line template into a series of tokens. Note that the token_type is printed only by value; it's far more useful to compare this value to the constants named previously.

```
>>> from django.template import Lexer
>>> template = 'This is {# only #}{{ a }}{% test %}'
>>> for token in Lexer(template, 'shell').tokenize():
...     print '%s: %s' % (token.token_type, token.contents)
...
0: This is
3: only
1: a
2: test
```

Parsing Tokens into Nodes

Once a Lexer has split the template string into a list of tokens, those tokens are passed to a Parser, which examines them in more detail. This is the semantic side of template processing, where each token is given meaning by attaching a corresponding Node object to the template. These nodes vary greatly in complexity; comment tokens don't produce nodes at all, text nodes have very simple nodes and block tags could have nodes that encompass the whole remainder of the template.

The Parser object itself is a bit more complicated than Lexer, because it's responsible for more of the process. Its parse() method has to work its way through the list of tokens, identifying which tokens require nodes and which type of nodes to create along the way. Each token is retrieved and removed from the list using Parser.next_token(). That token is then used to determine what type of node to create.

For text and variable tokens, Django supplies standard nodes that are used for all instances. These are TextNode and VariableNode, respectively, and they are also available at django.template. Comment tokens are simply ignored, with no node generated at all. Block tokens go through the template tag library, matching the name of the tag with a node compilation function.

These compilation functions, described in the "Template Tags" portion of the "Adding Features for Templates" section later in this chapter, are each responsible for parsing a token's contents and returning a Node object. Each function receives two arguments: the Parser object and the current token. Having access to the Parser object, node compilation functions can access a few additional methods to help control how much of the template that node has access to.

- parse(parse_until=None)—This is the same method that gets called when the template is first processed, and it can also be called from within a node. By supplying a tag name for the parse_until argument, this method will return just those nodes up to that tag name. This is how tags such as block, if and for wrap around additional content between the opening and closing tags. Note that this returns fully compiled nodes.

- next_token()—This retrieves and returns one token from the list. It also removes that token, so that future nodes don't receive any tokens that have already been processed. Note that this returns a token that has not yet been compiled into a node.

- skip_past(endtag)—This method is similar to parse(), accepting a tag that marks the end of where the template should be processed. The main difference is that skip_past() doesn't parse any of the tokens into nodes along the way, nor does it return any of the tokens that were found. It simply advances the template to beyond the end tag, ignoring anything in between.

Template Nodes

While it may seem like a complicated concept, template nodes are fairly simple. All template nodes extend the basic Node class, located at django.template. In addition to an __init__() method to customize the node's behavior, nodes have just a few methods that need to be included.

First, to maintain a common structure across all objects in a template, every template node is iterable, yielding all nodes that are contained within the node in question, rather than rendering their contents. This allows an easy way to get at all the nodes in a template.

By default, Node simply yields itself, which works well for simple template tags that just render a small snippet of text. For more complicated tags that encapsulate other content, this __iter__() should return all the nodes that were contained within it.

In addition, nodes must also provide a method called get_nodes_by_type(), though the default usually works well enough for most nodes. This method takes a single argument, nodetype, the class of node to retrieve. The node where the method was called will be checked to see if it's an instance of that class, as well as any other nodes within it. All nodes found that are indeed instances of the specified type will be returned in a list, or an empty list will be returned if none were found.

The most important method on a node is render(), which is used to output the final text. Since rendering to text requires the data that was passed to the template, this method accepts a single argument, a context object as described in the upcoming "Context" section.

Rendering Templates

Since a template is really just a collection of compiled instructions, getting those instructions to produce output text requires a separate step. Templates can be rendered using the simple render() method, which takes a context object as its only argument.

The render() method returns a string, containing the fully-rendered output, based on the compiled nodes and the context variables. This output will often be HTML, but can be anything, since Django templates are designed to work with any text-based format. The bulk of the work of rendering gets delegated to the individual nodes themselves, with the template just iterating over all the nodes, calling render() on each in turn.

By offloading this work onto each node itself, the overall template code can be less complex, while also maximizing the flexibility of the template system in general. Since each node is fully responsible for its behavior, the possibilities are nearly limitless.

Context

A template itself is mostly just a bunch of static content, logic, and placeholders for data to be filled in later. Without having data to fill in the blanks, it's relatively useless to a Web application. On the surface, it seems like a standard Python dictionary would suffice for this, since template variables are just names, which can be mapped to values. In fact, Django will even allow a dictionary to be used in certain cases.

One drawback of this approach is that there are some situations where a template tag might need to alter some data, and have that alteration persist for only a specific portion of the template. For example, when looping through a list, each item in the list should be available for use by other tags, but once the loop completes, that variable should no longer be accessible to the rest of the template. Beyond that, if a loop defines a variable that already had a value, that existing value should be restored once the loop finishes executing.

CONTEXTS VS. NAMESPACES

In Python, variables are assigned to namespaces, where they can later be retrieved by name, making template contexts very similar. There are also some notable differences that may cause some confusion.

Python allows namespaces to be nested, but only inside a defined class or function. In these nested namespaces, new variables aren't accessible to the other namespaces that enclose them. Other types of code blocks, such as conditionals and loops, share the namespace with whatever code surrounds them, so new variable assignments persist after the block finishes executing. This works well because namespaces are based on where the code is written, rather than where it executes, so the programmer can easily make sure that there aren't any conflicts with related names.

When writing a template tag, there is no way of knowing what variables will be defined in the template where the tag gets used. If it adds any new variables to the context, those could very well overwrite something else that was already set in the template. To overcome this, templates offer push() and pop() methods to allow tags to manually create a new nesting level and remove it when finished with it.

This makes templates work a bit differently from Python code in this respect, since blocks like loops essentially create a new namespace for the duration of their execution, removing it when finished. These differences may be a bit confusing at first to programmers, but designers working just with templates will only have one behavior to get used to.

To accomplish all this, Django implements its data mapping as a special Context object, which behaves much like a standard dictionary, but with some extra features. Most notably, it encapsulates a list of dictionaries internally, each of which represents a certain layer in the data map. This way, it can function like a stack as well, with the ability to push() new values onto it and pop() a layer off when no longer needed.

Neither push() nor pop() take any arguments. Instead, they simply add or remove a dictionary at the front of the list, adjusting which dictionary will be used first when looking up variables, as described next. This functionality prevents a standard dictionary from being used in most cases; it'll work fine as long as the template is simple, but as soon as one of these tags is encountered, it'll raise an AttributeError because it's missing these extra methods.

Simple Variable Resolution

Looking up data in the context is one of the most basic operations, though there's a lot that happens when a variable is referenced in a template. First, when using the standard {{ var }} syntax, Django automatically checks the context dictionaries in order from the one added most recently to the one added first. This lookup can also be performed manually on the context itself, using standard dictionary lookup syntax, which works just as well for retrieving values as setting them.

If the given name doesn't exist in the topmost dictionary, the context falls back to the next dictionary in line, checks for the name again and the process continues. Often, the phrase "current context" is used to describe the values that are available to a template tag at any specific point in time. Even though a template will use the same context object throughout the rendering process, the current context at any given point will change depending on what tags are in use and what values are retrieved by those tags.

```
>>> from django.template.context import Context
>>> c = Context({'a': 1, 'b': 2})
>>> c['a'], c['b']
(1, 2)
>>> c.push()
```

```
>>> c['a'], c['b']
(1, 2)
>>> c['b'] = 3
>>> c['a'], c['b']
(1, 3)
>>> c.pop()
{'b': 3}
>>> c['a'], c['b]
(1, 2)
```

If it gets through all available dictionaries without finding anything, it raises a KeyError as a standard dictionary would. That KeyError is normally handled by Django directly, replacing the variable reference with a constant value defined in the site's settings. By default, the TEMPLATE_STRING_IF_INVALID setting is set to an empty string, but this may be overridden by any site that wishes to display something different for this case.

Complex Variable Lookup

In addition to simple name lookups, variables can also contain references to certain portions of an object, using a period to separate one layer from the next. This allows a variable node to reference not just an object, but perhaps an attribute of that object, a method call or an entry in a dictionary or a list. This is also nested, so each time a dot resolves a new variable, another dot can resolve the next layer deep, such as {{ request.META.host }}.

This is handled using a separate class, appropriately named Variable. It's instantiated with a single argument, the string to be used as the variable's path, including any periods separating portions of the path. Once instantiated, it provides a single method, resolve(), which is used to perform all the necessary steps of retrieving the requested value. This method takes a single argument, the context where the variable should be found.

If the variable was declared with a literal value, such as a number or a quoted string, rather than a named variable, that value will always be returned directly, without even referencing the provided context. Otherwise, this resolves the first portion of the variable using the simple lookup described previously. If that part is found, it continues on to the next portion, and so on.

Each step in the chain after the first is based on the object that was retrieved in the step before it. When determining what to get at each stage, resolve() goes through a few different stages, with an error at each stage causing the lookup to continue on to the next stage.

- *Dictionary lookup*—The name provided is used as a dictionary key.

- *Attribute lookup*—The name is used in the standard getattr() method.

- *Method call*—If the attribute lookup retrieved a callable, such as a function, that callable is executed without any arguments. If this succeeds, the return value is used, but if the function requires any arguments, it will be skipped. Also, if the function has an alters_data attribute set to True, the function will be skipped, as a security precaution.

- *List-index lookup*—The variable name is coerced to an integer, if possible, and used as an index lookup to see if the value is present in a list.

```
>>> from django.template import Variable
>>> c = Context({'var': [1, 2, {'spam': u'eggs'}]})
>>> var = Variable('var')
>>> zero = Variable('var.0')
>>> one = Variable('var.1')
>>> spam = Variable('var.2.spam')
```

```
>>> var.resolve(c)
[1, 2, {'spam': u'eggs'}]
>>> zero.resolve(c)
1
>>> one.resolve(c)
2
>>> spam.resolve(c)
u'eggs'
```

Since this provides a much more robust and feature-rich way to access variables, it's always best to use `Variable` when a node needs to be able to access data from a template. This will ensure that template authors have as much flexibility as possible when referencing variables, even in custom tags.

Including Aspects of the Request

It's often necessary to include certain attributes from the incoming HTTP request, or at least to look up some other useful information based on those attributes, and include them in the template context. There's no way for Django to magically get the request from the view into the template system, so it has to be passed in manually.

Since `Context` on its own only accepts a dictionary as an argument, a different object is necessary to make this happen. `RequestContext`, also located at `django.template.context`, accepts a request object as its first argument, while the normal dictionary is pushed back to the second argument instead. Aspects of the request can then be retrieved when preparing the context for use by the template.

It's always best to use `RequestContext` whenever rendering a template as part of an HTTP cycle. Django's own generic views use it consistently, and most third-party applications also use it reliably. Failing to use `RequestContext` may result in templates not having access to necessary data, which can cause the template to render incorrectly.

For many sites, templates might get rendered as part of an automated process, such as a nightly job to send out billing notification emails. In these situations, there is no HTTP request coming in, so `RequestContext` is inappropriate. Simply using a standard `Context` will be sufficient in these cases.

Once a `RequestContext` is instantiated with a request, it has to populate context variables based on attributes of that request. It doesn't do this arbitrarily, but rather runs through code specified by another hook in Django.

Retrieving Templates

So far, all that's been illustrated is how to work with templates once they already exist. In the real world, templates will have to be loaded on demand, according to the needs of a particular view, so there's clearly more work to be done.

One particular requirement of retrieving templates is that they be referenced by name only, so that they can be loaded from different locations between development and production environments, without changing the code for any of the views. Chapter 8 shows how to write your own template loader, further increasing the available options. To handle this abstraction, Django provides two utility functions that should be used when retrieving templates.

django.template.loader.get_template(template_name)

Most of the time, a view knows about exactly one template, so only one name is given. The `get_template()` function takes the name of the requested template and returns a fully instantiated `Template` object. Then, that template can be rendered according to the needs of the view.

Behind the scenes, `get_template()` checks each template loader for the presence of a template with the given name, then returns the first one it finds. If no template was found matching the specified name, it raises a `TemplateDoesNotExist` exception.

django.template.loader.select_template(template_name_list)

Sometimes, it's necessary to retrieve a template using one of a few different names. This is often the case when an application would like to provide some kind of default template every time a view is accessed, while allowing a different template to be loaded in certain cases.

Consider a real estate site, where every property listing is expected to look the same. Naturally, the view for the property listing would simply use the same standard template for every listing in the database. If, however, a property comes along that has special requirements for its listing, such as additional buyer incentives or a special notice about an urgent need to close quickly, the standard template might not have a place for that. That information might also need to be rearranged on the page for a particular listing.

To handle these cases, select_template() takes a list of template names, rather than just a single value. For each name in the list, it calls get_template() to try to retrieve it, and if that fails, it simply moves on to the next name in the list. That way, a more specific name can be supplied first—often based on an object's ID or slug—followed by a more generic fallback.

```
>>> from django.template import loader
>>> t = loader.get_template('property/listing.html')
>>> t.name
'property/listing.html'>>> loader.get_template('property/listing_123.html')
Traceback (most recent call last):
  ...
django.template.TemplateDoesNotExist: property/listing_123.html
>>> t = loader.select_template(['property/listing_123.html',
                                'property/listing.html'])
>>> t.name
'property/listing.html'
```

In a real application, the number included in the most specific template name would be supplied by something dynamic, such as the URL being requested. That way, new property listings would use the generic template by default, but customizing an individual listing is as simple as dropping in a new template using the more specific name.

Shortcuts to Load and Render Templates

While it's definitely nice to have full control over how templates get loaded and rendered, the common flow is to just load the template, render it with a given context, and access the resulting string. This involves a few steps, which can easily get repetitive, so Django provides a couple ways to make the process simpler.

render_to_string(template_name, dictionary=None, context_instance=None)

Living at django.templates.loader, this simple function takes a few arguments and returns a string resulting from the template rendering. A template name is retrieved according to the name provided, and is then immediately rendered by passing the given dictionary into the provided context.

If the dictionary isn't provided, an empty dictionary is used instead, while if no context is provided, Django will simply use a Context. Most of the time, it's most appropriate to use RequestContext, so that all context processors get applied as well. Since Django can't magically find the request being used, a RequestContext must always be first instantiated with the request, then passed in as the context_instance.

render_to_response(template_name, dictionary=None, context_instance=None, content_type=None)

Living at `django.shortcuts`, this function works almost identically to `render_to_string()`, except that it uses the resulting string to populate an `HttpResponse` object, which is covered in detail in the next chapter. The only other difference is that this accepts an optional `mimetype`, which will be used when populating the `HttpResponse`.

Adding Features for Templates

Perhaps the most powerful feature of Django's templates is the ease with which new features can be added to them, without having to modify the framework itself. Each application can provide its own set of new features, rather than expecting site developers to provide their own.

Django's own template features can be split into two types, variables and tags, and custom add-ons fit right into those two areas. Variables can't really be added in code, since they're controlled by the template's context, but variable filters are a way for applications to allow variables to be modified easily. Tags, on the other hand, can do just about anything, from adding or modifying variables in the context to branching based on variables to injecting other templates.

Setting Up the Package

In order to make things easier for template authors, Django requires your template features to live at a specific package structure within an application. The {% load %} tag uses this structure to locate a specific module among all the installed applications, without the need for complex configurations that would make life more difficult for template designers.

Any application can supply new template features by creating a `templatetags` package within the application's main package. This new package can contain any number of modules, each containing a group of features that relate to each other. For example, a mail application could provide features that format text, perform basic math and show relationships between messages. The package structure would look something like this:

```
mail/
    __init__.py
    forms.py
    models.py
    urls.py
    views.py
    templatetags/
        __init__.py
        text.py
        math.py
        relationships.py
```

When writing templates for this application—or any other application you use in your site—the {% load %} tag makes those features available, accepting the names of the modules to load. These modules can come from any application in your INSTALLED_APPS setting. Django first looks for a `templatetags` package in each application, then looks for the module named in the {% load %} tag.

```
{% load text math relationships %}
```

Variable Filters

When variables are used in templates, they're normally just shown exactly as they were passed into the context by the current view. Sometimes, it's necessary to format or otherwise modify some of those values to suit the needs of a particular page. These types of presentational details are best placed in the template, so the view can just pass the raw values through, without regard to what the templates might do with them.

Django provides a number of these filters in its core distribution, intending to handle many of the most common situations you're likely to encounter. Full documentation is available online,[1] but here are a few of the most common filters:

- `capfirst`—Returns a string with the first letter capitalized

- `length`—Returns the number of items in a given sequence

- `date`—Formats a date using a string as an argument

Filters are just Python functions that take the variable's value as input, and return the modified value as a return value. This is really as simple as it sounds, though there is still a good bit of flexibility. Here's what a simple filter function might look like, for displaying the first few characters of a variable, used as `{{ var_name|first:3 }}`.

```python
from django.template import Library
from django.template.defaultfilters import stringfilter

register = Library()

@register.filter
@stringfilter
def first(value, count=1):
    """
    Returns the first portion of a string, according to the count provided.
    """
    return value[:count]
```

Accepting a Value

The first argument is the variable's value, and is always passed in, so it should always be required by the filter function. This value is typically the variable that was passed into the template's context, but filters can be chained together, so this value may actually be the result of another filter having already executed. Filters should therefore be made as generic as possible, accepting a wide range of input and handling it as gracefully as possible.

■ **Tip** This notion of "be liberal in what you accept," has been long considered a best practice for interoperable systems. It has been documented as far back as 1980, during the formation of technologies that today's Web is built on. The counterpart is to be "conservative in what you send," which recommends in this case that filters should always return the same data type.

---

[1] `http://prodjango.com/tags/`

Since the value could contain data from anything the view provides, or the result from any previous filters, care should be taken when making assumptions about its type. It will often be a string, but could be a number, model instance or any number of other native Python types.

Most filters are designed to work with strings, so Django also provides a useful shortcut for dealing with those. It's not guaranteed that the input will be a string, so string-based filters would always need to start by coercing the value to a string before continuing. There's already a decorator for this process, called `stringfilter`, which is located at `django.template.defaultfilters`. This automatically coerces the incoming value to a string, so the filter itself doesn't have to.

It's also important to make sure that no changes are made to this object directly. In the event that the input is a mutable object, such as a list or a dictionary, any changes made within the filter will also be reflected in any future uses of that variable in the template. If there are any changes to be made, such as prefixing or reorganizing items, it's essential to make a copy first, so those changes are reflected only in the filter itself.

Accepting an Argument

In addition to receiving the variable itself, it's also possible for a filter to accept an argument to customize its use. The only change necessary to accept an argument is to define an additional argument on the function. It's also easy to make an argument optional, simply by providing a default value in the function's definition.

Like the variable itself, this can also be of any type, since it can either be specified as a literal or supplied through another variable. There isn't any provided decorator for coercing this value to a string, as numbers are very common as filter arguments. Whatever argument your filter expects, just make sure to explicitly coerce it to the type it needs, and always catch any exceptions that might occur during that coercion.

Returning a Value

The vast majority of the time, a filter should return a string, since it's expected to be sent into the output of the rendered template. There is definite use for filters that return other types of data, such as a filter that averages the numbers in a list, returning the result as a number, but those are far less common, and should be well-documented in case other filters are chained with them, to avoid unexpected results.

More important is the fact that filters should *always* return a value. If anything goes wrong during the filter's processing, no exceptions should be raised. This also means that if the filter calls some other function that might raise an exception, the exception should be handled by the filter so it doesn't raise up beyond that. In the event of any of these problems, the filter should either return the original input or an empty string; which one to use will depend on the purposes of the filter in question.

Registering As a Filter

Once the function is all written up, it's registered with Django by using the `Library` class provided at `django.template`. Once instantiated, `Library` has a `filter()` method that can be used as a decorator, which, when applied to the filter function, automatically registers it with Django. That's all that's necessary on the code side.

This doesn't make it globally available to all templates by default, but rather just tells Django that the application provides it. Any template that would like to use it must still load the application's template features using the {% load %} tag.

Template Tags

Filters serve a very useful and practical purpose, but since they can only receive up to two values—the variable and an argument—and can only return one value, it's easy to see how quickly an application can outgrow them. Getting more functionality requires the use of template tags, which allow just about anything.

Like filters, Django provides a number of tags in its core distribution, which are documented online. Some of the more common tags are listed here, along with a brief description of their functionality.

- for—Allows a template to loop over the items in a sequence
- filter—Applies a template filter, such as those described previously, to all the content contained within the tag
- now—Prints out the current time, using some optional arguments to format it

Template tags are implemented as a pairing of a function and a Node class, with the former configuring the latter. The node is just like the nodes described earlier, representing the compiled structure of the template tag. The function, on the other hand, is used to accept the various allowable syntax options for the tag and to instantiate the node accordingly.

A Simple Tag

The simplest form of tag only exists in and of itself, typically to inject additional content into the page, based on some arguments. The node for this case is extremely simple, just taking and storing those arguments and formatting them into a string during rendering. Here's how it would look if the filter from the previous section were instead implemented as a tag. In the template, this would look like {% first var_name 3 %}.

```python
from django.template import Library, Node, Variable

register = Library()

class FirstNode(Node):
    def __init__(self, var, count):
        self.var = var
        self.count = count

    def render(self, context):
        value = self.var.resolve(context)
        return value[:self.count]
```

The function to compile it, on the other hand, is a bit more complicated. Tag functions, unlike filter functions, always take two arguments: the template parser object, and a token representing the text contained within the tag. It's up to the compilation function to extract the necessary bits of information from these two objects.

For a simple tag like this, it's not necessary to worry about the parser object, but the token is still necessary in order to get the argument, if one was specified.

The most important thing to know about the token is the split_contents() method, which intelligently breaks apart a tag's declaration into individual components, including the tag's name and its arguments.

It correctly handles variable references, quoted strings and numbers, though it doesn't do any variable resolution, and leaves the quotes around quoted strings.

In order to get the two necessary bits of information out of our template tag, token.split_contents() is used to extract them from the declared string. Then, these can be coerced to the correct types and used to instantiate the node described previously.

```python
@register.tag
def first(parser, token):
    var, count = token.split_contents()[1:]
    return FirstNode(Variable(var), int(count))
```

A Shortcut for Simple Tags

Thankfully, there's a shortcut that makes this process a whole lot easier. The Library object contains another decorator method, simple_tag(), which handles simpler cases like this. Behind the scenes, it handles the parsing and resolution of arguments, and even the creation of the node class, so all that's left for the template tag is a single function that looks quite similar to a variable filter.

```
from django.template import Library

register = Library()

@register.simple_tag
def first(value, count):
    return value[:count]
```

This is still of limited use, but there are many such situations where a simpler tag is necessary, and the shortcut can become quite a time-saver. For more advanced needs, manually creating the node offers much more power and flexibility.

Adding Features to All Templates

Django doesn't automatically load all applications' template filters and tags by default; instead, it uses just a default set for all templates. For those templates that need to access a specific application's template features and using the {% load %} tag is too much overhead, there's also an option where an application can be added to the default set of tags for all templates.

Also living at django.template, the add_to_builtins() function takes the name of the application to be included by default. Specifically, this is the app_label for that application, as described in Chapter 3. Once an application is supplied to this function, all of its tags and filters will be made available to all templates. This can be called anywhere that will be executed when the application loads, such as its __init__.py module.

This should be used sparingly, as it does incur some added overhead for even those templates that don't use any of that application's features. In some cases, however, it's necessary to override the behavior of default filters or tags, and add_to_builtins() provides that option. Keep in mind that more than one application can do this, so there's still no guarantee *which* application's version of a particular feature will be used. Django will simply overwrite them as they're encountered, so the last application to load is what will be used. Use it with care.

Applied Techniques

Django templates are designed to make things as easy as possible for the people who have to write templates on a regular basis. Advanced techniques are used to reinforce this idea, simplifying tasks that might otherwise be too complex to perform in a template. An application will often have its own unique template needs and should provide tags and filters to satisfy them. Even better is to provide features that can be reused by other applications if necessary.

Embedding Another Template Engine

While Django's template engine is suitable for most common cases, its limitations may cause frustration in situations where more power or flexibility is needed. Template tags extend Django's functionality, but only by involving programmers to write them for each individual need.

Another template engine with a different design philosophy might be more suitable to some of these needs. By allowing template designers to switch to an alternative engine for portions of templates, additional functionality is exposed without requiring additional programming. Tags can still simplify common tasks, but switching template engines can be an easy way to support corner cases.

One such alternative template engine is Jinja,[2] which has a syntax fairly similar to Django. There are fundamental differences in the design philosophies, making Jinja a better choice for situations where the output requires complex conditions and logic. These aspects make it a perfect candidate for embedding within Django templates.

To illustrate this, consider a template that needs to calculate a composite value to display in a template. This feature isn't available in Django, so it would ordinarily require a custom template tag or a view that calculated the value before sending it to the template.

```
{% load jinja %}

{% for property in object_list %}
Address: {{ property.address }}
Internal area: {{ property.square_feet }} square feet
Lot size: {{ property.lot_width }}' by {{ property.lot_depth }}'

{% jinja %}
Lot area: {{ property.lot_width * property.lot_depth / 43560 }} acres
{% endjinja %}
{% endfor %}
```

Django will automatically process everything up to the `jinja` tag, passing all remaining tokens to the Jinja compilation function along with the `Parser` object. The parser and tokens can be used to extract the content written between the `jinja` and `endjinja` tags. This then needs to be converted back into string content before being passed to Jinja for rendering.

Converting a Token to a String

Before diving into the full compilation function, first notice that tokens must be converted back into strings for Jinja to process them. Jinja uses a fairly similar syntax for its templates, so Django's Lexer accurately identifies variable, block and comment tags. Though Jinja also creates tokens for those tags, tokens from the two template engines aren't compatible with each other, so they must be converted back to strings. Jinja can then process them as it would any template from any source.

To accomplish this conversion, the node compilation function will rely on a separate function, which takes a token and returns a string. It works on the fact that `django.template` also contains constants for the beginning and ending portions of these tags. With this information and the structure of tokens, a suitable string can be created from a given token.

```
from django import template

def string_from_token(token):
    """
    Converts a lexer token back into a string for use with Jinja.
    """
    if token.token_type == template.TOKEN_TEXT:
        return token.contents
```

[2]http://prodjango.com/jinja/

```
    elif token.token_type == template.TOKEN_VAR:
        return '%s %s %s' % (
            template.VARIABLE_TAG_START,
            token.contents,
            template.VARIABLE_TAG_END,
        )

    elif token.token_type == template.TOKEN_BLOCK:
        return '%s %s %s' % (
            template.BLOCK_TAG_START,
            token.contents,
            template.BLOCK_TAG_END,
        )

    elif token.token_type == template.TOKEN_COMMENT:
        return u'' # Django doesn't store the content of comments
```

This won't produce an exact replica of the original template string. Some whitespace gets removed during Django's Lexer processing and comments lose their contents entirely. All functional aspects of the tags are retained, so the template will still work as advertised, but know that some minor formatting issues may arise as the result of this technique.

Compiling to a Node

With a function in place to reproduce strings for the tokens within the jinja block, the next step is to generate a Node that will be used to render the content along with the rest of the template. When gathering up the content between an opening tag and its closing tag, compilation functions often make use of the Parser.parse() method, passing in the name of the end tag, which will return a list of Node objects representing the inner content.

Since Jinja tags can't be processed using Django's node functions, Parser.parse() will cause problems due to incorrect syntax. Instead, the Jinja compilation function must access the tokens directly, which can then be converted back to strings. There are no provided functions to do this entirely, but combining Parser.next_token() with some extra logic will work quite well.

The compilation function can loop over the available tokens, calling Parser.next_token() each time. This loop will execute until either an endjinja block token is found or there are no more tokens in the template. Once a token is obtained from the parser, it can be converted to a string and added to an internal template string that can be used to populate a JinjaNode.

```
import jinja2
from django import template
from django.base import TemplateSyntaxError

register = template.Library()

def jinja(parser, token):
    """
    Define a block that gets rendered by Jinja, rather than Django's templates.
    """
    bits = token.contents.split()
    if len(bits) != 1:
        raise TemplateSyntaxError("'%s' tag doesn't take any arguments." % bits[0])
```

```
        # Manually collect tokens for the tag's content, so Django's template
        # parser doesn't try to make sense of it.
        contents = []
        while 1:
            try:
                token = parser.next_token()
            except IndexError:
                # Reached the end of the template without finding the end tag
                raise TemplateSyntaxError("'endjinja' tag is required.")
            if token.token_type == template.TOKEN_BLOCK and \
                token.contents == 'endjinja':
                break
            contents.append(string_from_token(token))
        contents = ''.join(contents)

    return JinjaNode(jinja2.Template(contents))
jinja = register.tag(jinja)
```

■ **Caution**   By not using the parser's `parse()` method, you won't be able to use any other Django tags inside of the
`{% jinja %}` tag. That's not a problem here, since the contents are processed by Jinja instead, but using this technique
without a good reason can cause problems with other types of tags.

Preparing the Jinja Template

Once the compilation function retrieves the Jinja template contents from the Django template tokens, a `JinjaNode` is
created to access that template. Jinja provides its own `Template` object that compiles content into tangible objects, so
it makes sense to use it when a `JinjaNode` is created.

   Then, when it comes time to render the `JinjaNode`, all it takes is to render the compiled Jinja template and return
that output back to Django's template. This task is trickier than it may seem on the surface, because Django's `Context`
objects, which contain variables that should be passed to Jinja, don't behave entirely like Python dictionaries. They
support the common dictionary-style syntax for accessing keys, but internally, their structure is quite different from
what Jinja expects.

   To pass a nested `Context` object to the Jinja template properly, it must first be flattened to a single, standard
Python dictionary. This can be done fairly easily, simply by looping through the individual dictionaries stored in
the context and assigning them to a new dictionary, maintaining the precedence that Django itself uses: the first
appearance of a particular key takes priority over any other instances of that same key. Only if a key doesn't exist in
the new Jinja context dictionary should it be added, so that no existing values get overwritten in the process.

   Once the dictionary is available, that data can be passed to Jinja's own `Template.render()` method. The result
from that method is the properly rendered content that can be returned from the `JinjaNode.render()`, placing that
content in the page.

```
import jinja2

class JinjaNode(template.Node):
    def __init__(self, template):
        self.template = template
```

```
def render(self, django_context):
    # Jinja can't use Django's Context objects, so we have to
    # flatten it out to a single dictionary before using it.
    jinja_context = {}
    for layer in django_context:
        for key, value in layer.items():
            if key not in jinja_context:
                jinja_context[key] = value
    return self.template.render(jinja_context)
```

Enabling User-Submitted Themes

Earlier in this chapter, we discovered that templates can be loaded from any source, as long as there's an appropriate loader that knows how to retrieve them. One shortcoming of that approach is that it's only valid for loading templates for everybody; there's no way of associating templates with a specific user.

That's not really a failure in any way, since most applications would need it to work exactly as it does. Also, user information is only available once a request comes in, so there wouldn't be any way to access it in a generic fashion. Every tool has its time, and there are certainly times where it's useful to have templates tied to users.

Consider a site where users are encouraged to customize their own experience, by supplying custom themes that will be used while they're logged in. This gives users a great deal of control over how they engage in the site, and can pull them further into the experience. This can be enhanced still further if they're given the opportunity for their own custom themes to be made available for others to use. This idea isn't good for all sites, but for heavily community-oriented sites, especially those in artistic circles, it can be a great boost to the user experience.

A WORD ABOUT ADVERTISING

Many sites on the Web today are funded at least in part by advertisements placed on their various pages. This advertising only works if it's actually shown to users, so they have a chance to click on ads and buy products or services. By introducing user-editable themes to a site, users have a perfect opportunity to remove any ads a site may rely on, so it's important to carefully consider whether this is right for your site.

Any themes that a site's staff approves for the use of the site's general audience can be checked first to ensure that they don't cause any harm to the advertising on the site, or to the site's own branding. This is a great way to enforce at least some quality control on the process. The problem is that users can create themes to behave however they like, prior to submitting them for approval, and may use them on their own through the site, removing ads from their own experiences.

One way to minimize the impact of this problem is to offer paid site memberships, with one of the benefits being the ability to create custom themes. This way, unpaid users will always see advertising as a way of funding their use of the site, while paid users are offsetting their lack of advertising with an annual fee.

In fact, if your site adopts this model, it's best to remove ads for paid users altogether, regardless of what theme they're using. Nobody likes paying for the use of a site, only to still be presented with advertising designed to bring further revenue to that same site.

On the surface, it may seem like this is a perfect job for Cascading Style Sheets (CSS). CSS is all about the presentation of Web sites, but it's always limited by the ordering of content on a page. For example, markup placed higher in the document is difficult to place at the bottom of a page, and vice versa. By allowing users to edit the template that determines those positions, it's easy to unlock many more possibilities.

Using Django templates poses some technical and security challenges that must be overcome, and solving these challenges exposes a number of interesting ways to use templates. First, consider the problems that need to be solved.

- If templates are to be edited, they should be stored in the database.

- Templates need to be tied to a specific user, to restrict them from editing everything, and also for assigning credit to the proper authors when themes get promoted.

- Users can't have access to the full range of the Django template language. That's a security risk that would expose way too much information to just anyone.

- Themes must be approved by staff members prior to being made available for use by everyone.

- Once themes are submitted for approval, and after they've been approved, users shouldn't be able to make any changes.

- A user's personal theme—whether personally created or selected from the work of others—should be used on all portions of the site.

- In addition to the template itself, each theme should have a CSS file associated with it, to better style other aspects of the site.

That's quite a list of things that need to be covered, and individual sites may have even more requirements. It's not quite as bad as it may seem on the surface, as Django already has many things in place to make those problems easy to solve.

Setting Up the Models

The first order of business is to make a place for templates to be stored in the database. In standard Django fashion, this is done with a model, with fields for the various properties of the template. For this application, a theme consists of a few various pieces of information:

- A block of text to be used as the content of the template

- A URL to a CSS file

- A user who created it

- A title, so other users can easily reference it, should it be made available for everyone

- An indication of whether it's the site-wide default, so that users who haven't yet selected a theme still have one to use

Most of this information will only be used by the theme object itself, as only the main block of text will be passed in to the template. It's easy to think of a theme as a template in its own right, where it's simultaneously a set of data that gets stored in the database and a set of instructions that are used to render HTML. Python provides a way to make that notion explicit and offers a simple way to deal with themes.

By using multiple inheritance, it's possible for a theme to be both a model and a template, behaving in whichever way is necessary for the task at hand. The class inherits from `django.db.models.Model` and `django.template.Template`, and `__init__()` is overridden to initialize both sides separately:

```
from django.db import models
from django import template
from django.contrib.auth.models import User
```

149

```
from themes.managers import ThemeManager

class Theme(models.Model, template.Template):
    EDITING, PENDING, APPROVED = range(3)
    STATUS_CHOICES = (
        (EDITING, u'Editing'),
        (PENDING, u'Pending Approval'),
        (APPROVED, u'Approved'),
    )
    author = models.ForeignKey(User, related_name='authored_themes')
    title = models.CharField(max_length=255)
    template_string = models.TextField()
    css = models.URLField(null=True, blank=True)
    status = models.SmallIntegerField(choices=STATUS_CHOICES, default=EDITING)
    is_default = models.BooleanField()

    objects = ThemeManager()

    def __init__(self, *args, **kwargs):
        # super() won't work here, because the two __init__()
        # method signatures accept different sets of arguments
        models.Model.__init__(self, *args, **kwargs)
        template.Template.__init__(self, self.template_string,
                                   origin=repr(self), name=unicode(self))

    def save(self):
        if self.is_default:
            # Since only one theme can be the site-wide default, any new model that
            # is defined as default must remove the default setting from any other
            # theme before committing to the database.
            self.objects.all().update(is_default=False)
        super(Theme, self).save()

    def __unicode__(self):
        return self.title
```

That's enough to get the themes themselves stored in the database, but it still doesn't cover how a user can select a theme to use while browsing the site. Ordinarily, that would be set up as a ForeignKey on the model that references Theme, but since the User model is outside our control, something else will need to be done.

One way to store user-centric information, such as preferences, is to add a custom user model. Django's official documentation[3] covers this in detail, but the basic idea is that you can provide your own model to use in place of Django's own user model. Your custom model can contain additional fields for anything user-related, including selected themes. A site can only have one custom user model, though, and it makes little sense to hijack that feature solely for the purpose of supporting themes. Instead, we can use a ManyToManyField to connect it to the User model.

```
class Theme(models.Model):
    ...  # All the other fields shown above
    users = models.ManyToManyField(User, through='SelectedTheme')
    ...  # All the other methods shown above
```

---

[3] http://prodjango.com/custom-user/

```
class SelectedTheme(models.Model):
    user = models.OneToOneField(User)
    theme = models.ForeignKey(Theme)
```

By using a `OneToOneField`, we can ensure that each user only appears once in the intermediary table. That way, each user can only have one selected theme. There are also some utility functions that can help manage this behavior a bit. There are actually two different methods that would be useful here, both for getting themes based on the user. One is for retrieving a user's selected theme, while the other is for retrieving the themes a user has created.

```
from django.db import models
from django.conf import settings

class ThemeManager(models.Manager):
    def by_author(self, user):
        """
        A convenience method for retrieving the themes a user has authored.
        Since the only time we'll be retrieving themes by author is when
        they're being edited, this also limits the query to those themes
        that haven't yet been submitted for review.
        """
        return self.filter(author=self, status=self.model.EDITING)

    def get_current_theme(self, user):
        return SelectedTheme.objects.get(user=user).theme
```

With this manager in place, it's easy to retrieve themes for a specific user, both those that user can edit, and the one that user should use when browsing the site. Having these shortcuts in place helps make views simpler, allowing them to focus on the business they really have to do. The whole point of a site-wide theme is that it's used for *every* view, so clearly something else needs to be done to accommodate that.

Supporting Site-Wide Themes

Individual views have enough to worry about, and shouldn't be responsible for managing themes. Instead, there needs to be a way to retrieve a user's selected theme—or the default—and have that automatically applied to whatever template a view uses. Ideally, all this should happen without any changes to the views, so there's little extra work that needs to be done.

This is a job best suited for a context processor, a concept described earlier in this chapter. By using a context processor, every view that uses `RequestContext` will automatically have access to the proper theme. This makes the ordinarily good advice of always using `RequestContext` now an absolute requirement. As will be seen in the next section, templates will explicitly rely on the theme being available, and failing to use `RequestContext` will violate that assumption.

The context processor required for this process is fairly straightforward, but it has to provide a few specific features. It must determine whether the current user is logged in or not, identify the user's selected theme, fall back to a default theme if no theme is selected or if the user isn't logged in, and it must return the proper theme so that it may be added to the template's context. This code would be placed in a module called `context_processors.py`, in keeping with the conventions used within Django itself.

```
from django.conf import settings

from themes.models import Theme

def theme(request):
    if hasattr(request, 'user') and request.user.is_authenticated():
        # A valid user is logged in, so use the manager method
        theme = Theme.objects.get_current_theme(request.user)
    else:
        # The user isn't logged in, so fall back to the default
        theme = Theme.objects.get(is_default=True)
    name = getattr(settings, 'THEME_CONTEXT_NAME', 'theme')
    return {name: theme}
```

Note the use of hasattr() here in the test to see whether a user is logged in. That may seem unnecessary, but by adding that simple condition to the test, it allows this context processor to be used with no middleware requirements. Otherwise, it would always require django.contrib.auth.middleware.AuthenticationMiddleware, which places the user attribute on the request. If that middleware isn't in use, every user will simply receive the default theme.

Also, note that the name of the context variable is driven by another new setting, this time called THEME_CONTEXT_NAME. This defaults to 'theme', so that it's not necessary to supply a name explicitly unless that causes a clash with some other feature. This is a bit of a recurring theme (pun intended), because with an application that has to interact with a good deal outside of itself, such as user models and template contexts, it's important to make sure conflicts are kept to a minimum.

With this file in place, the only thing left is to add 'themes.context_processors.theme' to the TEMPLATE_CONTEXT_PROCESSORS setting to make sure it gets applied to all the templates. Once the theme is made available to the template, it's still necessary to make sure the template can access it and make use of it.

Setting Up Templates to Use Themes

The end goal of themes is to reorder the components of a page, so it's important to identify what a "component" is. In terms of Django templates, this would mean a block of markup, identified by the {% block %} template tag. Each component of a page could be defined in a separate block, separating each bit into its own space.

With Django's template inheritance, it's possible to define blocks in one template that will be filled in with content from another template. This way, a page-specific template can define what goes in each block, while a base template can specify where those blocks are rendered, and what other markup gets placed around them. This would be an excellent way to reorder significant portions of a page, as long as there's a way to dynamically specify where the base template places all the blocks.

Django supports template inheritance through the {% extends %} tag, which takes a single argument to identify the base template to extend. Typically, this is a hard-coded name of the template to use as a base. It can also take a context variable, containing a string to use as this base template. If that context variable points to a template instance, Django will use that instead of bothering to look up a template anywhere else.

Taking advantage of this in a template is easy; just put {% extends theme %} at the top of the template. If you've specified a THEME_CONTEXT_NAME explicitly for your site, make sure to change theme to whatever you've entered for that setting. That still only covers part of it. It's still necessary to get the templates to make use of the blocks defined in the theme.

There's no universal way to do this, since each site will have its own template inheritance setup, and its own set of blocks that every page will need to fill in. Typically, these blocks would be used for things like page title, navigation, page content and footers, but different sites may have different needs.

In addition, a site may have more blocks that can't be rearranged, but are instead defined inside of other blocks. These wouldn't be taken into consideration for our purposes at the moment, since themes are only concerned with blocks that can be moved around. Consider an application with the following blocks that can be customized:

- `logo`—The site's logo, as an image
- `title`—The title of the current page
- `search`—A search box, possibly with advanced options
- `navigation`—A collection of links or other interface used for getting around the site
- `sidebar`—A bit of content related to the current page
- `content`—The flesh of the current page, whether that be a product listing, press release, search results or contact form
- `footer`—A copyright disclaimer, along with a few links for job openings, investor relations and contact information

Every theme must define all of these blocks in order to make sure the whole site gets displayed, so it's important to outline them explicitly. Every template on the site needs to define content to be placed into these blocks, so that there's always something to put in the right places. Many of those blocks aren't specified to any particular page, so template inheritance comes to the rescue here as well.

By placing another template layer between the theme and the individual page, some blocks can be populated automatically for all pages, while others are left for individual pages to fill in. The individual page template still has final authority, with the ability to override *any* block with new content, if necessary. That just leaves the issue of making sure that templates do in fact define all the blocks required by the site's inheritance scheme.

Validating and Securing Themes

Any time a site accepts input from users, it must be scrutinized to make sure that it fulfills a certain set of requirements and stays within acceptable limits. Themes are no exception there, but user-editable templates also represent a very real security risk. Django takes steps to ensure that templates can't execute any common functions that make changes to the database, but there are a number of other things a template can do.

By default, only Django's own data-altering methods are secured from templates by using the `alters_data` attribute. Any application's models may define other methods that make changes to the database, and if those aren't marked with `alters_data`, they're fair game for use in templates. Even read-only access, if not kept in check, can be a problem. A theme is used on every page, and many pages will have access to a wide array of objects through model relationships.

There are so many ways to access things that should be kept private that no blacklist approach can ever hope to be complete. Instead, a whitelist approach is necessary, where themes are only allowed to use a small subset of features provided by Django's template system. The trick is determining the right way to approach a problem like this.

On the surface, it may seem like regular expressions are the way to go. After all, Django itself uses a regular expression to parse templates and break them up into nodes, so surely it would be trivial to write a more limited expression to secure templates. That may be true for now, but remember that Django is constantly improving, and the future may bring new syntax to templates.

However unlikely that may be, if it does happen, no amount of careful crafting of our regular expression can predict what new syntax might be included in the future. Anything that slips past this protection has the potential to harm the site or divulge confidential information. That's a lot to pin on the hope that the template syntax will remain constant.

Instead, we'll rely on Django's own regular expression to compile the template into a list of nodes, just like normal. Then, once it's been compiled to a nodelist, it's easy to peek at those nodes to make sure they're all doing the right thing. Using this, forms can easily verify that the template defines all the right blocks and nothing else. Theme templates must:

- Inherit from the template referenced by the THEME_EXTENDS setting.

- Provide one block with the name referenced by a THEME_CONTAINER_BLOCK setting.

- Populate that block with all the blocks referenced in the THEME_BLOCKS setting.

- Provide no content in any of the THEME_BLOCKS blocks.

- Provide no other blocks than those mentioned in the THEME_BLOCKS setting.

- Contain no other tags whatsoever, only text.

```python
from django import forms
from django import template
from django.template.loader_tags import BlockNode, ExtendsNode
from django.conf import settings
from theme import models

class ThemeForm(forms.ModelForm):
    title = forms.CharField()
    body = forms.CharField(widget=forms.Textarea)

    def clean_body(self):
        try:
            tpl = template.Template(self.cleaned_data['body'])
        except template.TemplateSyntaxError as e:
            # The template is invalid, which is an input error.
            raise forms.ValidationError(unicode(e))

        if [type(n) for n in tpl.nodelist] != [ExtendsNode] or \
            tpl.nodelist[0].parent_name != settings.THEME_EXTENDS:
                # No 'extends' tag was found
                error_msg = u"Template must extend '%s'" % settings.THEME_EXTENDS
                raise forms.ValidationError(error_msg)

        if [type(n) for n in tpl.nodelist[0].nodelist] != [BlockNode] or \
            tpl.nodelist[0].nodelist[0].name != settings.THEME_CONTAINER_BLOCK:
                # Didn't find exactly one block tag with the required name
                error_msg = u"Theme needs exactly one '%s' block" % \
                            settings.THEME_CONTAINER_BLOCK
                raise forms.ValidationError(error_msg)

        required_blocks = list(settings.THEME_BLOCKS[:])
        for node in tpl.nodelist[0].nodelist[0].nodelist:
            if type(node) is BlockNode:
                if node.name not in required_blocks:
                    error_msg = u"'%s' is not valid for themes." % node.name)
                    raise forms.ValidationError(error_msg)
```

```
                required_blocks.remove(node.name)
                if node.nodelist:
                    error_msg = u"'%s' block must be empty." % node.name)
                    raise forms.ValidationError(error_msg)
            elif type(node) is template.TextNode:
                # Text nodes between blocks are acceptable.
                pass
            else:
                # All other tags, including variables, are invalid.
                error_msg = u"Only 'extends', 'block' and plain text are allowed."
                raise forms.ValidationError(error_msg)

        if required_blocks:
            # Some blocks were missing from the template.
            blocks = ', '.join(map(repr, required_blocks))
            error_msg =  u"The following blocks must be defined: %s" % blocks
            raise forms.ValidationError(error_msg)

    class Meta:
        model = models.Theme
```

An Example Theme

Even with an application in place, it may be difficult to understand how a theme would be written to work with the site. Consider a site using this themes application with the following settings:

```
THEME_EXTENDS = 'base.html'
THEME_CONTEXT_NAME = 'theme'
THEME_CONTAINER_BLOCK = 'theme'
THEME_BLOCKS = (
    'title',
    'sidebar',
    'links',
)
```

The base.html template at the root of the inheritance chain might look like this:

```
<html>
<head>
<title>{% block title %}{% endblock %}</title>
<link rel="stylesheet" type="text/css" href="/style.css"/>
</head>
<body>{% block theme %}{% endblock %}</body>
</html>
```

A theme can then be written to fill in the application's requirements: extend from base.html, provide a theme block and fill it with empty title, sidebar and links blocks. Unlike the other templates, this code would be stored in the database, as an instance of the Theme model.

```
{% extends 'base.html' %}

{% block theme %}
<h1>{% block title %}{% endblock %}</h1>
<ul id="links">{% block links %}{% endblock %}</ul>
<div id="content">{% block content %}{% endblock %}</div>
{% endblock %}
```

Now, individual templates for the rest of the site can be written to extend from the theme variable and fill in the title, sidebar and links blocks. Consider the template for the root of a real estate site:

```
{% extends theme %}

{% block title %}Acme Real Estate{% endblock %}

{% block links %}
<li><a href="{% url home_page %}">Home</a></li>
<li><a href="{% url property_list %}">Properties</a></li>
<li><a href="{% url about_page %}">About</a></li>
{% endblock %}

{% block content %}
<p>Welcome to Acme Real Estate!</p>
{% endblock %}
```

With all of these templates in place, loading up the root of the site will yield a full HTML document like the following:

```
<html>
<head>
<title>Acme Real Estate</title>
<link rel="stylesheet" type="text/css" href="/style.css"/>
</head>
<body>
<h1>Acme Real Estate</h1>
<ul id="links">
<li><a href="/">Home</a></li>
<li><a href="/properties/">Properties</a></li>
<li><a href="/about/">About</a></li>
</ul>
<div id="content">
<p>Welcome to Acme Real Estate!</p>
</div>
</body>
</html>
```

Now What?

Views and templates combine to determine what content should be sent to users, but it still has to make its way to the browser. Django speaks HTTP fluently, so there are a number of ways to customize that journey.

CHAPTER 7

■ ■ ■

Handling HTTP

The Hypertext Transfer Protocol (HTTP) is the fundamental language for communication over the Web. It's spoken by both Web servers and Web browsers, along with a variety of specialty tools for dealing with the Web.

The Python community has done a tremendous amount of work to standardize the behavior of applications that interact with HTTP, culminating in PEP-333,[1] the Web Server Gateway Interface (WSGI). Since Django follows the WSGI specification, many of the details listed in this chapter are a direct result of compliance with PEP-333.

Requests and Responses

Because HTTP is a stateless protocol, at its heart is the notion of a request and a response. Clients issue a request to the server, which returns a response containing the information requested by the client or an error indicating why the request couldn't be fulfilled.

While requests and responses follow a detailed specification, Django provides a pair of Python objects that are designed to make the protocol much easier to deal with in your own code. A basic working knowledge of the protocol is useful, but most of the details are handled behind the scenes. These objects are described in this section, along with notes indicating the relevant portions of the specification that should be referenced.

HttpRequest

As described in Chapter 4, every Django view receives, as its first argument, an object representing the incoming HTTP request. This object is an instance of the HttpRequest class, which encapsulates a variety of details concerning the request, as well as some utility methods for performing useful functions.

The base HttpRequest class lives at django.http, but individual server connectors will define a subclass with additional attributes or overridden methods that are specific to the Web server being utilized. Any overridden methods or attributes should behave as documented here, and any additional information will be best documented in the code for the server interface itself.

HttpRequest.method

The HTTP specification outlines a variety of *verbs* that can be used to describe the type of request being performed. This is typically referred to as its *method*, with different request methods having specific expectations of how they should be handled. In Django, the method being used for the request is represented as the method attribute of the HttpRequest object. It will be included as a standard string, with the method name in all uppercase letters.

---

[1]http://prodjango.com/pep-333/

Each method describes what the server should do with the resource identified by the URL. Most Web applications will only implement GET and POST, but a few others are worth explaining here as well. Further details on these—and others not listed here—can be found in the HTTP specification,[2] as well as many other resources on the Web.

- DELETE—Requests that the resource be deleted. Web browsers don't implement this method, so its use is limited to Web service applications. In typical Web browser applications, such operations are done with a POST request, since GET requests aren't allowed to have side effects, such as removal of the resource.

- GET—Retrieves the resource specified by the URL. This is, by far, the most common type of request made on the Web, as every standard retrieval of a Web page is done with a GET request. As noted in the "Safe Methods" section, GET requests are assumed to have no side effects on the server; they should retrieve the specified resource and do nothing else.

- HEAD—Retrieves some information about the resource without getting the entire contents. Specifically, the response to a HEAD request should return exactly the same headers as a GET request, only without anything in the body of the response. Web browsers don't implement this method, but since the server-side operation is essentially just a GET request without a response body, it is rarely missed. In Web service applications, a HEAD request can be a low-bandwidth way to retrieve information about a resource, such as whether it exists, when it was last updated or the size of its content.

- POST—Requests that the attached data be stored in some way related to the resource specified by the URL. This could mean comments on a blog post or news article, answers to a question, replies to a Web-based email or any number of other related situations.

  This definition is only valid in Web service environments, where a differentiation can be made between PUT and POST. In standard Web browsers, only GET and POST are reliably available, so POST is used for any situation that modifies information on the server. Using POST to submit data from a form is little more than a footnote in the official HTTP specification, but is the most popular use of the method.

- PUT—Requests that the attached data be stored at the resource specified by the URL. This could be seen as a "create" or "replace" operation, depending on whether the resource already exists. This method isn't traditionally available in Web browsers, though, so its use is limited to Web service applications. In a standard Web browser, the operation specified by PUT is done with a POST request instead.

"Safe" Methods

As alluded to in the previous section, there is an important distinction to be made among various types of HTTP requests. The specification refers to GET and HEAD as "safe" methods, which only retrieve the resource specified by the URL, without making any changes on the server at all. To be explicit, a view that processes a GET or HEAD request shouldn't make any changes except those that are incidental to retrieving the page.

The goal of safe methods is to allow the same request to be made more than once and at various times, without any adverse effects. This assumption allows GET requests to be used by bookmarks and browser histories without a warning to the user when the request is made more than once. An example of an allowed change is updating a count that indicates how many times the page was viewed.

---

[2]`http://prodjango.com/http-methods/`

"Idempotent" Methods

In addition to safe methods, the HTTP specification describes PUT and DELETE as "idempotent," meaning that, even though they are intended to make changes on the server, those changes are reliable enough that calling the same request with the same body multiple times will always make the same changes.

In the case of PUT, the resource would be created the first time the request is performed, and each subsequent request would simply replace the resource with the same data that was originally submitted, thus leaving it the same. For DELETE, each subsequent request after the resource was originally deleted would result in an error, indicating that the resource isn't present, thus leaving the state of the resource the same each time. On the other hand, POST is expected to make changes or additions on each request. To represent this situation, Web browsers present a message when a POST request is performed more than once, warning the user that subsequent requests could cause problems.

HttpRequest.path

This attribute contains the complete path that was requested, without any query-string parameters attached. This can be used to identify the resource being requested, without relying on which view will be called or how it will behave.

Accessing Submitted Data

Any time a request comes in, it can potentially be accompanied by a variety of data provided by the Web browser. Processing this information is key to making a Web site dynamic and interactive, so Django makes it easy and flexible. Just as there are many ways to submit data to a Web server, there are as many ways to access that data once it arrives.

Data that comes in using the standard query-string format[3] sent by most browsers is automatically parsed into a special type of dictionary class called `QueryDict`. This is an immutable subclass of `MultiValueDict`, which means that it functions mostly like a dictionary, but with a few added options for handling multiple values for each key in the dictionary.

The most significant detail of `QueryDict` is that it's instantiated with a query-string from an incoming request. For more information on the details of how to access values in a `QueryDict`, see the details for `MultiValueDict` in Chapter 9.

HttpRequest.GET

If the request came in with the GET method, its `GET` attribute will be a `QueryDict` containing all the values that were included in the query-string portion of the URL. Of course, while there's no technical restriction on when `GET` can be used to get parameters out of a URL, the goal of clean URLs limits the situations where it's most advantageous.

In particular, it's important to separate parameters that identify a resource from those that customize how the resource is retrieved. This is a subtle, but important, distinction. Consider the following examples:

- `/book/pro-django/chapter07/`

- `/news/2008/jun/15/website-launched/`

- `/report/2008/expenses/?ordering=category`

As you can see, most of the data sent to the view for GET requests should be placed in the URL itself, rather than the query-string. This will help search engines index them more efficiently, while also making it easier for users to remember them and communicate them with others. As with many other principles, this isn't an absolute rule, so keep query-strings and the `GET` attribute in your toolbox, but use them with care.

---

[3]`http://prodjango.com/query-string/`

HttpRequest.POST

If the request comes in with a PUT or POST method using a standard HTML form, this will be a QueryDict containing all the values submitted with the form. The POST attribute will be populated for all standard forms, regardless of the encoding type, with or without files.

However, the HTTP specification allows these requests to supply data in any format, so if the incoming data doesn't fit the format of a query-string, HttpRequest.POST will be empty, and the data will have to be read in directly through HttpRequest.raw_post_data.

HttpRequest.FILES

If an incoming PUT or POST request includes any uploaded files, those files will be stored away in the FILES attribute, which is also a QueryDict, with each value being a django.core.files.uploadedfile.UploadedFile object. This is a subclass of the File object described later, in Chapter 9, providing a few extra attributes specific to uploaded files.

- content_type—The Content-Type associated with the file, if any was provided. Web browsers typically assign this based on the last part of the filename, though a Web service call could specify this more accurately based on the actual type of content.

- charset—The character set that was specified for the uploaded file's content.

HttpRequest.raw_post_data

Any time a request comes in with data in the body of the request, as is done for PUT and POST, the raw_post_data attribute provides access to this content, without any parsing. This isn't typically necessary for most Web sites, as the GET and POST attributes are more appropriate for the most common types of requests. Web services may accept data in any format, and many use XML as a primary means of data transfer.

HttpRequest.META

When a request comes in, there is a significant amount of information related to the request that doesn't come through in a query-string and isn't available in the GET or POST attributes on the request. Instead, data regarding where the request came from and how it got to the server is stored in the request's META attribute. Details of which values are available in META can be found in PEP-333.

In addition, each request is accompanied by a number of headers, which describe various options the client would like to make known. Exactly what these types of headers can contain is specified in the HTTP specification,[4] but they typically control things like a preferred language, allowable content-types and information about the Web browser.

These headers are also stored in META, but in a form slightly altered from how they came in originally. All HTTP header names become uppercase, are prefixed with HTTP_ and have all of their dashes replaced with underscores.

- Host becomes HTTP_HOST.

- Referer becomes HTTP_REFERER.

- X-Forwarded-For becomes HTTP_X_FORWARDED_FOR.

---

[4] http://prodjango.com/http-headers/

HttpRequest.COOKIES

Since each HTTP request is a fresh connection between the client and the server, cookies are used as a way to identify clients that make multiple requests. In a nutshell, cookies are little more than a way to send a name and associated value to a Web browser, which that browser will then send back each time it makes a new request to the Web site.

While cookies are set during the response phase of the process, as documented under HttpResponse, the task of reading cookies from an incoming request is quite simple. The COOKIES attribute of the request is a standard Python dictionary mapping names of cookies to the values that were previously sent.

Keep in mind that this dictionary will contain entries for *all* cookies sent by the browser, even if they were set by another application on the same server. The HttpResponse section later in this chapter covers the specific rules of how a browser decides which cookies to send with a particular request and how to control that behavior.

HttpRequest.get_signed_cookie(key[, …])

If you store information in a cookie that could be used against you if it were tampered with, you can opt to sign your cookies and validate those signatures when reading the cookies back in. The signatures themselves are provided using the HttpResponse.set_signed_cookie() method described later in this chapter, but when reading them in a request, you'll need to use this method.

You can control the behavior of your cookie retrieval using a few additional arguments:

- default=RAISE_ERROR—This argument allows you to specify a default value that should be returned if the requested key was not found or was invalid. This is equivalent to passing a default value into a standard dictionary's get() method. If you don't supply a value, this method will raise a standard KeyError if the key is missing or django.core.signing.BadSignature if the signature is invalid.

- salt=''—This is a complement to the same argument in the set_signed_cookie() method. It allows you to use the same key in different aspects of your application, perhaps on multiple domains, without risk of the signature being reused from one use to another. This must match the value you provide when setting the cookie in order for the signature check to match.

- max_age=None—By default, cookie signatures also have an expiration associated with them to avoid them being reused longer than intended. If you supply a max_age that exceeds the age of a given cookie, you'll get a django.core.signing.SignatureExpired exception. By default, this won't check the expiration date when validating the signature.

HttpRequest.get_host()

Many server configurations allow a single Web application to respond to requests sent to multiple different domain names. To help with these situations, the get_host() method of the incoming request allows a view to identify the name that the Web browser used to reach the Web site.

In addition to the host name used to make the request, the value returned from this method will include a port number if the server was configured to respond on a nonstandard port.

HttpRequest.get_full_path()

In addition to the host information, the get_full_path() method returns the entire path portion of the URL; everything after the protocol and domain information. This includes the full path that was used to determine which view to use, as well as any query-string that was provided.

HttpRequest.build_absolute_uri(location=None)

This method generates an absolute URL for the provided location, if any. If no location is supplied explicitly, the request's current URL is returned, including the query-string. The exact behavior of the method if the location *is* provided depends on what value is passed in.

- If the value contains a fully-qualified URL—including the protocol—that URL is already absolute and is returned as provided.

- If the value begins with a forward slash (/), it is appended to the protocol and domain information of the current URL, then returned. This will generate an absolute URL for the provided path, without having to hard-code the server information.

- Otherwise, the value is assumed to be a path relative to the request's current URL, and the two will be joined together using Python's urlparse.urljoin() utility function.

HttpRequest.is_secure()

This simple method returns True if the request came in using the Secure Sockets Layer (SSL) protocol or False if the request was unsecured.

HttpRequest.is_ajax()

Useful for "Web 2.0" sites, this method returns True if the request has an X-Requested-With header with a value of "XMLHttpRequest". Most JavaScript libraries designed to make calls to the server will provide this header, providing a convenient way to identify them.

HttpRequest.encoding

This is a simple attribute representing the encoding to be used when accessing the GET and POST attributes described earlier. Values in those dictionaries are forced to unicode objects using this encoding, if one is set. By default, its value is None, which will use the default encoding of utf-8 when accessing values.

In most cases, this attribute can be left as is, with most input being converted properly using the default encoding. Specific applications may have different needs, so if the application expects input with a different encoding, simply set this attribute to a value that will decode those values properly.

HttpResponse

After a request is received and processed, every view is responsible for returning a response—an instance of HttpResponse. This object maps cleanly to an actual HTTP response, including headers, and is the only way of controlling what is sent back to the Web browser. Like its cousin for requests, HttpResponse lives at django.http, but several shortcuts are available to create responses more easily.

Creating a Response

Unlike the request, the author of a view has full control over how its response is created, allowing a variety of options. The standard HttpResponse class is instantiated rather simply, but accepts three arguments to customize its behavior. None of these are required; options described later in this section can set these values in other ways.

- content—This accepts text—or other content—to be used as the body of the request.

- status—This sets the HTTP status code[5] to be sent with the request.

- content_type—This controls the Content-Type header to be sent with the request. If this is supplied, make sure it also contains the charset value when appropriate.

```
>>> from django.http import HttpResponse
>>> print HttpResponse()
Content-Type: text/html; charset=utf-8
```

```
>>> print HttpResponse(content_type='application/xml; charset=utf-8')
Content-Type: application/xml; charset=utf-8
```

```
>>> print HttpResponse('content')
Content-Type: text/html; charset=utf-8

content
```

There is also a mimetype argument, provided for backwards-compatibility with older Django applications, but content_type should be used instead. It's still important to keep mimetype in mind, though, as it means that status and content_type should be specified as keyword arguments, if supplied at all.

Dictionary Access to Headers

Once a response has been created, it's simple to customize the headers that will be sent out along with its content, using standard dictionary syntax. This is quite straightforward and works just as you'd expect. The only notable variation from a standard dictionary is that all key comparisons are case-insensitive.

```
>>> from django.http import HttpResponse
>>> response = HttpResponse('test content')
>>> response['Content-Type']
'text/html; charset=utf-8'
>>> response['Content-Length']
Traceback (most recent call last):
  ...
KeyError: 'content-length'
>>> response['Content-Length'] = 12
>>> for name, value in response.items():
...     print '%s is set to %r' % (name, value)
...
Content-Length is set to '12'
Content-Type is set to 'text/html; charset=utf-8'
```

---

[5]http://prodjango.com/http-status-codes/

File-Like Access to Content

In addition to the ability to specify body content as a string when creating the response object, content can be created by many third-party libraries that know how to write to open files. Django's `HttpResponse` implements a few file protocol methods—most notably `write()`—that enable it to be treated as a write-only file for many of these libraries. This technique can be especially useful when using Django to generate binary content, such as PDF files, dynamically within views.

One important thing to note regarding file-like access to the response body is that not all file protocol methods are implemented. This means that certain libraries, such as Python's own `zipfile.ZipFile` class, which require those extra methods, will fail with an `AttributeError`, indicating which method was missing. This is by design, as HTTP responses aren't true files, so there is no predictable way to implement those methods.

HttpResponse.status_code

This attribute contains the numerical status code representing the type of response being sent to the client. As described earlier, this can be set immediately when instantiating the response object, but as a standard object attribute, it can also be set any time after the response has been created.

This should only be set to known HTTP response status codes. See the HTTP specification for details on valid status codes. This status can be set while instantiating the response, but it can also be set as a class attribute on a subclass, which is how Django configures many of its specialized responses.

HttpResponse.set_cookie(key, value=''[, …])

When looking to store values across multiple requests, cookies are the tool of choice, passing values to the Web browser through special headers, which are then sent back to the server on subsequent requests. By calling `set_cookie()` with a key and a value, the HTTP response sent to the client will contain a separate header, telling the browser what to store and when to send it back to the server.

In addition to just the key and value, `set_cookie()` can take a few extra arguments that configure when the browser should send the cookie back to the server. While a quest for readability suggests that these arguments be specified using keywords, this list uses their positional order. More details on what values are allowed for each of these options can be found in the official specification for HTTP state management.[6]

- `max_age=None`—Corresponding to the `max-age` option from the specification, this specifies the number of seconds the cookie should remain active.

- `expires=None`—Not all browsers accept and respect `max-age` as required by the official specification but instead follow an early pattern set out by Netscape. The `expires` attribute takes an exact date when the cookie should expire, rather than an offset in seconds. The specified date is in the following format: `Sun, 15-Jun-2008 12:34:56 GMT`.

- `path='/'`—This specifies a base path under which the browser should send this cookie back to the server. That is, if the path of the URL being requested begins with the value specified here, the browser will send the cookie's value along with the request.

- `domain=None`—Similar to `path`, this specifies the domain under which the cookie will be sent. If left as `None`, the cookie will be restricted to the same domain that issued it, while providing a value will allow greater flexibility.

- `secure=False`—If set to `True`, this will indicate that the cookie contains sensitive information and should only be sent to the server through a secure connection, such as SSL.

---

[6]`http://prodjango.com/cookie-spec/`

```
>>> response = HttpResponse()
>>> response.set_cookie('a', '1')
>>> response.set_cookie('b', '2', max_age=3600)
>>> response.set_cookie('c', '3', path='/test/', secure=True)
>>> print response.cookies
Set-Cookie: a=1; Path=/
Set-Cookie: b=2; Max-Age=3600; Path=/
Set-Cookie: c=3; Path=/test/; secure
```

Keep in mind that this will set the cookie in the browser only after the response has made its way across the wire. That means that the cookie's value won't be available on the request object until the browser's next request.

COOKIES AND SECURITY

Although cookies can be a tremendously useful way to maintain state across multiple HTTP requests, they're stored on a user's computer, where knowledgeable users will have access to view them and alter their contents. Cookies on their own are *not* secure, and should not be used to store sensitive data or data that controls how the user can access the site.

The typical way around this problem is to only store a reference in the cookie, which can be used to retrieve the "real" data from somewhere on the server, such as a database or a file, where users don't have access. The "Applied Techniques" section near the end of this chapter provides an alternative method of storing data securely in cookies so that their data can in fact be trusted.

HttpResponse.delete_cookie(key, path='/', domain=None)

If a cookie has already been delivered to the Web browser and is no longer needed or has become invalid, the delete_cookie() method can be used to instruct the browser to remove it. As mentioned, the path and domain provided here must match an existing cookie in order to have it deleted properly.

It does this by setting a new cookie with max-age set to 0 and expires set to Thu, 01-Jan-1970 00:00:00 GMT. This causes the browser to overwrite any existing cookie matching the same key, path and domain, then expire it immediately.

HttpResponse.cookies

In addition to being able to explicitly set and delete cookies during the response phase, you can view the cookies that will be sent to the Web browser. The cookies attribute uses Python's standard Cookie module,[7] with the attribute itself being a SimpleCookie object, which behaves much like a dictionary, with each value being a Morsel object.

Using a cookie's name as the key, you can retrieve a Morsel representing a specific cookie value, along with its associated options. This object may be used as a dictionary to reference these additional options, while its value attribute contains the value that was set for the cookie. Even deleted cookies are accessible using this dictionary, since the process involves setting a new cookie that will simply expire immediately.

---

[7]http://prodjango.com/r/cookie-module/

```
>>> len(response.cookies)
3
>>> for name, cookie in response.cookies.items():
...     print '%s: %s (path: %s)' % (name, cookie.value, cookie['path'])
...
a: 1 (path: /)
b: 2 (path: /test/)
c: 3 (path: /)
```

HttpResponse.set_signed_cookie(key, value, salt=''[, …])

This works just like set_cookie(), except that it also cryptographically signs the value before sending it out to the browser. Because cookies are stored in the browser, this ensures that the user doesn't modify the values in those cookies before visiting your site again. You still don't want to store sensitive information in your cookies, but this allows you to confidently store things like a logged-in username in a cookie, without the user being able to use it as an attack vector.

This takes all the same arguments as set_cookie(), with one addition: salt. By default, Django uses your settings.SECRET_KEY to generate a signature, which is fine in most cases, where a cookie with a particular key is only likely to be used for one purpose. In other cases, the salt argument allows you to craft a signature to whatever use you currently have.

For example, if you're serving up multiple domains with a single Django installation, you could use the domain name as the salt for your signatures, so that a user can't reuse the signature from one domain on a different domain. The different salts ensure the signatures will be different, so that a copied signature would fail the signature test when retrieving the cookie in your view.

HttpResponse.content

This attribute provides access to the string content of the response body. This can be read or written, and is particularly useful during the response phase of middleware processing.

Specialty Response Objects

Since there are several common HTTP status codes, Django provides a set of customized HttpResponse subclasses with their status_code attribute already set accordingly. Like HttpResponse itself, these all live at django.http. Some of them take a different set of arguments than the standard HttpResponse, and those differences are also listed here.

- HttpResponseRedirect—Takes a single argument, a URL that the browser will redirect to. It also sets the status_code to 302, indicating a "Found" status, where the resource is located.

- HttpResponsePermanentRedirect—Takes a single argument, a URL that the browser will redirect to. It sets the status_code to 301, indicating the resource was permanently moved to the URL specified.

- HttpResponseNotModified—Sets the status_code to 304, indicating a "Not Modified" status, to be used in response to a conditional GET, when the response hasn't changed from the conditions associated with the request.

- HttpResponseBadRequest—Sets the status_code to 400, indicating a "Bad Request" where the syntax used in the request couldn't be understood by the view.

- `HttpResponseForbidden`—Sets the `status_code` to 403, "Forbidden," where the requested resource does exist, but the requesting user doesn't have permission to access it.

- `HttpResponseNotFound`—Perhaps most common of all custom classes, this sets the `status_code` to 404, "Not Found," where the URL in the request didn't map to a known resource.

- `HttpResponseNotAllowed`—Sets the `status_code` to 405, "Not Allowed," indicating that the method used in the request isn't valid for the resource specified by the URL.

- `HttpResponseGone`—Sets the `status_code` to 410, "Gone," to indicate that the resource specified by the URL is no longer available and can't be located at any other URL.

- `HttpResponseServerError`—Sets the `status_code` to 500, "Server Error," used whenever the view encountered an unrecoverable error.

Some of these specialized responses aren't supported by Web browsers, but they're all quite useful for Web service applications, where a wider range of options are available. It often makes more sense to set these statuses on a site-wide basis, so individual views don't have to worry about managing them directly. For this, Django provides HTTP middleware.

Writing HTTP Middleware

While Django itself creates an `HttpRequest` and each view is responsible for creating an `HttpResponse`, applications commonly need certain tasks to be performed on every incoming request or outgoing response. This portion of the process, called *middleware*, can be a useful way to inject advanced processing into the flow.

Common examples of middleware processing are compressing response content, denying access to certain types of requests or those from certain hosts and logging requests and their associated responses. Although these tasks could be done in individual views, doing so would not only require a great deal of boilerplate but would also require each view to know about every piece of middleware that would be applied.

This would also mean that adding or removing HTTP processing would require touching every single view in an entire project. That's not only a maintenance issue in its own right, but it also causes additional maintenance problems if your project uses any third-party applications. After all, changing third-party code restricts your ability to upgrade it in the future without unnecessary hassle. Django solves these problems by performing middleware operations in a separate part of the request/response cycle.

Each piece of middleware is simply a Python class that defines at least one of the following methods. There are no other requirements for this class; that is, it doesn't have to subclass any provided base class, contain any particular attributes or be instantiated in any specific way. Just provide the class at an importable location and a site will be able to activate it.

There are four distinct points where middleware can hook into Django's HTTP handling, performing whatever tasks it needs along the way. Each part of the process is controlled simply by specifying a method on the middleware class. Remember, it's all just Python, so anything that's valid Python is valid in middleware as well.

MiddlewareClass.process_request(self, request)

As soon as the incoming HTTP request is made into an `HttpRequest` object, middleware has its first chance to change how things get handled. This hook occurs even before Django analyzes the URL to determine which view to use.

Being standard Python, the `process_request()` method can perform any task, but common tasks include prohibiting access to certain clients or request types, adding attributes to the request for use by context processors or returning a previously-cached response based on details of the request.

This method can change any attribute on the request, but keep in mind that any changes will affect how Django handles the request throughout the rest of the process. For example, because this method is called prior to the URL resolution, it can modify `request.path` to redirect the request to an entirely different view than would've otherwise been used. While something like this is often the desired behavior, it can possibly be an unintended side effect, so take care when modifying the request.

MiddlewareClass.process_view(self, request, view, args, kwargs)

This method is called after the URL has been mapped to a view and arguments have been extracted from it, but before the view is actually called. In addition to the request, the arguments passed to this method are as follows:

- view—The view function that will be called. This is the actual function object, not the name, regardless of whether the view was configured using a string or a callable.

- args—A tuple containing the positional arguments that will be passed to the view.

- kwargs—A dictionary containing the keyword arguments that will be passed to the view.

Now that the view's arguments have been extracted from the URL, it is possible to verify these against what the configuration was supposed to obtain. This can be quite useful during development as a way to verify that everything is configured properly. Simply set up a middleware class to print out the args and kwargs variables along with request.path. Then, if anything goes wrong with a view, the development server's console will have a handy way to identify or rule out a potential problem.

This may seem like a perfect opportunity to do some detailed logging of the view that's about to be executed as well, since the view function object is available too. While this is true, the common use of decorators on views complicates matters. Specifically, the view function passed to this method will often be a wrapper function created by the decorator, rather than the view itself.

This means that the introspection features detailed in Chapter 2 can't reliably be used to line up positional arguments with the names they were given in the function definition. There is still some good, though, as you should still be able to access the module and name of the view, as long as the decorators use the special wraps decorator described in Chapter 9.

```
class ArgumentLogMiddleware(object):
    def process_view(request, view, args, kwargs):
        print 'Calling %s.%s' % (view.__module__, view.__name__)
        print 'Arguments: %s' % (kwargs or (args,))
```

MiddlewareClass.process_response(self, request, response)

After the view has been executed, the new response object is made available for middleware to view it and make any necessary changes. This is where middleware could cache the response for future use, compress the response body for faster transmission over the wire or modify the headers and content that will be sent with the response.

It receives the original request object as well as the response object returned by the view. At this point, the request has already exhausted its usefulness to the HTTP cycle, but it can be useful if some of its attributes are used to determine what to do with the response. The response object can be—and often is—modified at this stage, before being returned by the method.

The process_response() method should always return an HttpResponse object, regardless of what's done with it beforehand. Most often, this will be the response it was given in the first place, just with some minor modifications. Sometimes, it may make more sense to return an entirely different response, such as when redirecting to a different URL.

MiddlewareClass.process_exception(self, request, exception)

If something goes wrong during any part of the request-handling process, including the middleware methods, an exception will usually be thrown. Most of these exceptions will be sent to the process_exception() to be logged or handled in a special way. The exception argument passed to this method is the exception object that was thrown, and it can be used to retrieve specific details about what went wrong.

A common task for this stage of the process is to log exceptions in a way that's specific to the site currently in use. The exception's string representation is usually sufficient for this, along with its type, though the exact usefulness of this will depend on the exception that was raised. By combining details of the original request with details of the exception, you can generate useful and readable logs.

Deciding Between Middleware and View Decorators

Chapter 4 showed how views can use decorators to perform extra work before or after the view is executed, and keen readers will notice that middleware can perform a similar function. View decorators have access to the incoming request as well as the response generated by the view. They can even access the view function and the arguments that will be passed to it, and they can wrap the view in a try block to handle any exceptions that are raised.

So what makes them different, and when should you use one over the other? That's a rather subjective topic, and there's no one answer to satisfy all cases. Each approach has advantages and disadvantages, which should help you decide which route to take for a particular application.

Differences in Scope

One of the most notable differences between middleware and view decorators is how much of the site is covered. Middleware is activated in a site's settings.py, so it covers all requests that come in on any URL. This simple fact provides a few advantages:

- Many operations—such as caching or compression—should naturally happen for every request on the site; middleware makes these tasks easy to implement.

- Future additions to the site are automatically covered by existing middleware, without having to make any special allowances for the behavior they provide.

- Third-party applications don't need any modifications in order to take advantage of middleware behavior.

Decorators, on the other hand, are applied to individual functions, which means that every view must have decorators added manually. This makes decorators a bit more time-consuming to manage, but some operations—such as access restriction or specialized cache requirements—are more appropriate for limited parts of the site, where decorators can be used to great effect.

Configuration Options

Middleware classes are referenced as strings containing the import path to the class, which doesn't allow any direct way to configure any of their features. Most middleware that accept options do so by way of custom settings that are specific to that middleware. This does provide a way to customize how the middleware works, but like middleware themselves, these settings are sitewide, by definition. There isn't any room for customizing them for individual views.

As shown in Chapter 2, decorators can be written to accept configuration options when they're applied to a function, and view decorators are no different. Each view could have a separate set of options or curry could be used to create a brand-new decorator with a set of preconfigured arguments.

Using Middleware As Decorators

Given the similarities between middleware and decorators, Django provides a utility to transform an existing middleware class into a decorator. This allows code to be reused across an entire site, using the best tool for the job in any situation.

Living at `django.utils.decorators`, the special `decorator_from_middleware()` function takes, as its only argument, a middleware class that should be applied to a single view. The return value is a perfectly functional decorator, which can be applied to any number of views.

Allowing Configuration Options

Since decorators can accept options to configure their behavior, we need a way for middleware classes to utilize this same flexibility. Providing an `__init__()` method on the middleware class that accepts additional arguments will allow a class to be written from the beginning to be used either as middleware or as a view decorator.

One thing to keep in mind is that middleware will be most commonly called without any arguments, so any additional arguments you define *must* use defaults. Failing to do so will result in a `TypeError` whenever it is used as a standard middleware and also with `decorator_from_middleware()` on its own, which doesn't accept any arguments.

```
class MinimumResponseMiddleware(object):
    """
    Makes sure a response is at least a certain size
    """

    def __init__(self, min_length=1024):
        self.min_length = min_length

    def process_response(self, request, response):
        """
        Pads the response content to be at least as
        long as the length specified in __init__()
        """
        response.content = response.content.ljust(self.min_length)
```

When used as middleware, this class will pad all responses to be at least 1,024 characters in length. In order for individual views to receive specific values for this minimum length, we can instead turn to `decorator_from_middleware_with_args()`. That will accept arguments when decorating the view and pass those arguments into the `__init__()` method of the middleware class.

Also, be aware that if a middleware class is already defined as middleware *and* as a decorator, any views that use the decorator will actually be calling the middleware twice for every request. For some, such as those that set attributes on the request object, this won't be an issue. For others—especially those that modify the outgoing response—this can cause a world of trouble.

HTTP-Related Signals

Since requests are spawned outside the control of any application code, signals are used to inform application code of the beginning and completion of all request/response cycles. Like all signals, these are simply `Signal` objects, and they live at `django.core.signals`. For more information on signals, how they work and how to use them, refer to Chapter 9.

django.core.signals.request_started

Whenever a request is received from the outside, this signal is fired without any additional parameters. It fires early in the process, even before the `HttpRequest` object has been created. Without any arguments, its uses are limited, but it does provide a way to notify applications when a request is received, before any middleware has a chance to get access to the request object.

One potential use for this would be as a way to register new listeners for other signals, which should only operate during requests coming in over HTTP. This is in contrast to situations where those other signals might get fired due to some non-HTTP event, such as a scheduled job or a command-line application.

django.core.signals.request_finished

Once the response has been generated by the view and middleware has been processed, this signal fires just prior to sending the response back to the client that sent the original request. Like `request_started`, it doesn't provide any parameters to the listener, so its use is fairly limited, but it could be used as a way to disconnect any listeners that were attached when `request_started` fired.

django.core.signals.got_request_exception

If an exception occurs any time while processing a request but it isn't handled explicitly somewhere else, Django fires the `got_request_exception` signal with just one parameter: the request object that was being processed.

This is different from the `process_exception()` method of middleware, which is only fired for errors that occur during execution of the view. Many other exceptions will fire this signal, such as problems during URL resolution or any of the other middleware methods.

Applied Techniques

By providing so many hooks into the protocol handling, Django makes possible a great variety of options for modifying HTTP traffic for an application. This is an area where each application will have its own needs, based on what type of traffic it receives and what type of interface it expects to provide. Therefore, take the following examples as more of an explanation of how to hook into Django's HTTP handling, rather than an exhaustive list of what can be done to customize this behavior.

Signing Cookies Automatically

Django's support for signed cookies is convenient, but it requires that you call separate methods for setting and retrieving cookies, in order to make sure the signature is applied and validated correctly. You can't simply access the cookies attribute on the request without losing the security benefits of signatures. By using a custom middleware, however, it's possible to do exactly that: add and verify signatures automatically, using the simple access methods normally reserved for unsigned cookies.

At a high level, there are a few tasks this middleware will be responsible for:

- Signing cookies in outgoing requests

- Verifying and removing cookies on incoming requests

- Managing the salt and expiration options for those signatures

The first two tasks can be achieved fairly simply, by inspecting the request and response to look for cookies and calling the signed variations of the cookie methods to manage the signatures. Let's start with setting response cookies.

Signing Outgoing Response Cookies

The middleware can start with the `process_response()` method, which will need to find any cookies that were set by the view and add signatures to their values.

```
class SignedCookiesMiddleware(object):
    def process_response(self, request, response):
        for (key, morsel) in response.cookies.items():
```

```
            response.set_signed_cookie(key, morsel.value,
                max_age=morsel['max-age'],
                expires=morsel['expires'],
                path=morsel['path'],
                domain=morsel['domain'],
                secure=morsel['secure']
            )
        return response
```

This approach uses all the attributes of the original cookie when setting the new one, so that it's identical except for the method that's used to set it. Using set_signed_cookie() will do all the appropriate things behind the scenes.

Deleted cookies show up in response.cookies as well, though, even though they don't have a value and don't need to be signed. These can be identified by their max-age of 0, which can be used to ignore them and only sign actual values that matter to the application.

```
class SignedCookiesMiddleware(object):
    def process_response(self, request, response):
        for (key, morsel) in response.cookies.items():
            if morsel['max-age'] == 0:
                # Deleted cookies don't need to be signed
                continue
            response.set_signed_cookie(key, morsel.value,
                max_age=morsel['max-age'],
                expires=morsel['expires'],
                path=morsel['path'],
                domain=morsel['domain'],
                secure=morsel['secure']
            )
        return response
```

Validating Incoming Request Cookies

Working with incoming requests is also fairly simple. The process_request() method is our entry point for this part of the process, and it merely has to find all the incoming cookies and use get_signed_cookie() to check the signatures and remove those signatures from the values.

```
class SignedCookiesMiddleware(object):
    def process_request(self, request):
        for key in request.COOKIES:
            request.COOKIES[key] = request.get_signed_cookie(key)
```

Reading cookies is simpler than writing them, because we don't have to deal with all the individual parameters; they're already part of the cookies themselves. This code still has one problem, though. If any signature is missing, invalid or expired, get_signed_cookie() will raise an exception, and we'll need to handle that in some way.

One option is to simply let the errors go through, hoping they'll get caught in some other code, but because your views and other middleware won't even know that this middleware is signing cookies, they aren't likely to deal with signature exceptions. Worse, if you don't have code that handles these exceptions, they'll work their way all the way out to your users, typically in the form of an HTTP 500 error, which doesn't explain the situation at all.

Instead, this middleware can handle the exceptions directly. Since only values with valid signatures can be passed to your views, an obvious approach is to simply remove any invalid cookies from the request altogether. The exceptions go away, along with the cookies that generated those exceptions. Your views will just see the valid cookies, just like they're expecting, and any invalid cookies won't exist in the request anymore. Users can clear their cookies at any time, so views that rely on cookies should always handle requests with missing cookies anyway, so this approach fits well with what views will already be doing.

Supporting this behavior requires nothing more than catching the relevant exceptions and removing those cookies responsible for raising them.

```
from django.core.signing import BadSignature, SignatureExpired

class SignedCookiesMiddleware(object):
    def process_request(self, request):
        for (key, signed_value) in request.COOKIES.items():
            try:
                request.COOKIES[key] = request.get_signed_cookie(key)
            except (BadSignature, SignatureExpired):
                # Invalid cookies should behave as if they were never sent
                del request.COOKIES[key]
```

Signing Cookies As a Decorator

So far, SignedCookiesMiddleware hasn't used any of the signature-specific options when setting and retrieving signed cookies. The defaults are often good enough for a middleware that's meant for use on the whole site. Since middleware can also be used as decorators, though, we also need to account for customizations to individual views. That's where the salt and expiration settings become useful.

As shown earlier in the chapter, decorator_from_middleware() can supply arguments to the middleware's __init__() method, so that will provide a path for customizing the salt and max_age arguments. Once accepting those arguments in __init__(), the individual hook methods can incorporate them as appropriate.

```
from django.core.signing import BadSignature, SignatureExpired

class SignedCookiesMiddleware(object):
    def __init__(self, salt='', max_age=None):
        self.salt = salt
        self.max_age = max_age

    def process_request(self, request):
        for (key, signed_value) in request.COOKIES.items():
            try:
                request.COOKIES[key] = request.get_signed_cookie(key,
                    salt=self.salt,
                    max_age=self.max_age)
            except (BadSignature, SignatureExpired):
                # Invalid cookies should behave as if they were never sent
                del request.COOKIES[key]

    def process_response(self, request, response):
        for (key, morsel) in response.cookies.items():
            if morsel['max-age'] == 0:
```

```
                # Deleted cookies don't need to be signed
                continue
        response.set_signed_cookie(key, morsel.value,
            salt=self.salt
            max_age=self.max_age or morsel['max-age'],
            expires=morsel['expires'],
            path=morsel['path'],
            domain=morsel['domain'],
            secure=morsel['secure']
        )
    return response
```

Now you can create a decorator using decorator_from_middleware_with_args() and supply salt and max_age arguments to customize that decorator's behavior for each individual view.

```
from django.utils.decorators import decorator_from_middleware_with_args
signed_cookies = decorator_from_middleware_with_args(SignedCookiesMiddleware)

@signed_cookies(salt='foo')
def foo(request, ...):
    ...
```

Now What?

The request and response cycle is the primary interface Django applications use to communicate with the outside world. Just as important is the collection of utilities available behind the scenes that allow applications to perform their most fundamental tasks.

CHAPTER 8

■ ■ ■

Backend Protocols

As a framework, Django's purpose is to provide a cohesive set of interfaces to make the most common tasks easier. Some of these tools are contained entirely within Django itself, where it's easy to maintain consistency. Many other features are—or at least, could be—provided by external software packages.

Although Django itself supports some of the most common software packages for these various features, there are many more out there, especially in corporate environments. In addition to a developer's preferences for one type of database over another, many other servers are already in use by existing applications that can't be easily converted to use something different.

Because these types of problems do come up in real life, Django provides easy ways to reference these features without worrying about what implementation actually makes it happen in the background. This same mechanism also allows you to swap out many of these lower-level features with third-party code, to support connecting to other systems or just to customize some facet of behavior.

The sections listed throughout this chapter serve something of a dual purpose. In addition to documenting Django's generic API for each of these features, each section will also describe how a new backend should be written to implement these features. This includes not only what classes and methods to declare, but also what the package structure might look like, as well as how each piece of the puzzle is expected to behave.

Database Access

Connecting to databases is one of the most fundamental requirements of a modern Web application, and there are a variety of options available. Currently, Django ships with support for some of the more popular open-source database engines, including MySQL, PostgreSQL and SQLite, and even some commercial offerings such as Oracle.

Given the unique features and SQL inconsistencies of different database systems, Django requires an extra layer between its models and the database itself, which must be written specifically for each database engine used. The supported options each ship within Django as a separate Python package containing this intermediary layer, but other databases can also be supported by providing this layer externally.

While Python provides a standardized API for accessing databases, PEP-249,[1] each database system interprets the base SQL syntax in a slightly different way and supports a different set of features on top of it, so this section will focus on the areas provided by Django for hooking into the way models access the database. This leaves to the reader the nitty-gritty details of formulating the right queries in each situation.

django.db.backends

This references the backend package's base module, from which the entirety of the database can be accessed. Accessing the database backend in this manner ensures a unified, consistent interface, regardless of which database package is being used behind the scenes.

---

[1] http://prodjango.com/pep-249/

Django does a lot of work to make this level of access unnecessary, but there's only so far it can go without overcomplicating things. When the ORM fails to offer some necessary bit of functionality—for example, updating one column based on the value of another column in pure SQL—it's always possible to go straight to the source and peek at what's really going on and adjust the standard behavior or replace it altogether.

Because this is really just an alias for a backend-specific module, the full import paths listed throughout this chapter are only valid when trying to access the database in this manner. When implementing a new backend, the package path will be specific to that backend. For instance, if a backend for connecting with IBM's DB2[2] were placed in a package named db2, this module would actually be located at db2/base.py.

DatabaseWrapper

One of the main features of a database backend is the DatabaseWrapper, the class that acts as a bridge between Django and the features of the database library itself. All database features and operations go through this class, in particular an instance of it that's made available at django.db.connection.

An instance of DatabaseWrapper is created automatically, using the DATABASE_OPTIONS setting as a dictionary of keyword arguments. There isn't any mandated set of arguments for this class, so it's essential to document what arguments the backend accepts so developers can customize it accordingly.

There are a few attributes and methods on the DatabaseWrapper class that define some of the more general aspects of the backend's behavior. Most of these are suitably defined in a base class provided to make this easier. By subclassing django.db.backends.BaseDatabaseWrapper, some sensible default behaviors can be inherited.

Though individual backends are free to override them with whatever custom behavior is appropriate, some must always be explicitly defined by a backend's DatabaseWrapper. Where that's the case, the following sections will state this requirement directly.

DatabaseWrapper.features

This object, typically an instance of a class specified as django.db.backends.DatabaseFeatures, contains attributes to indicate whether the backend supports each of a variety of database-related features Django can take advantage of. While the class could technically be named anything, because it's only ever accessed as an attribute of DatabaseWrapper, it's always best to remain consistent with Django's own naming conventions to avoid confusion.

Like DatabaseWrapper itself, Django provides a base class specifying defaults for all the available attributes on this object. Located at django.db.backends.BaseDatabaseFeatures, this can be used to greatly simplify the definition of features in a particular backend. Simply override whatever feature definitions are different for the backend in question.

This is a list of supported features and their default support status:

- allows_group_by_pk—Indicates whether GROUP BY clauses can use the primary key column. If so, Django can use this to optimize queries in these situations; defaults to False.

- can_combine_inserts_with_and_without_auto_increment_pk—When inserting multiple records in one pass, this attribute indicates whether the backend can support some inserting records that have values for auto-incrementing primary keys alongside other records that don't have values. This defaults to False, where Django will simply remove those primary key values from the data before inserting the records into the database.

- can_defer_constraint_checks—Indicates whether the database allows a record to be deleted without first nullifying any relationships that point to that record; defaults to False.

---

[2] http://prodjango.com/db2/

- `can_distinct_on_fields`—Indicates whether the database supports using the `DISTINCT ON` clause to only check uniqueness of certain fields. This defaults to `True`, so if the database doesn't support this clause, be sure to also override the `distinct_sql()` method, described in the next section, to raise an exception when fields are requested.

- `can_introspect_foreign_keys`—Indicates whether the database provides a way for Django to determine what foreign keys are in use; defaults to `True`.

- `can_return_id_from_insert`—Indicates whether the backend can provide the new auto-incremented primary key ID immediately after the record is inserted. Defaults to `False`; if set to `True`, you'll need to also supply the `return_insert_id()` function described in the next section.

- `can_use_chunked_reads`—Indicates whether the database can iterate over portions of the result set without reading it all into memory at once. Defaults to `True`; if `False`, Django will load all results into memory before passing them back to an application.

- `empty_fetchmany_value`—Specifies what value the database library returns to indicate that no more data is available, when fetching multiple rows; defaults to an empty list.

- `has_bulk_insert`—Indicates whether the backend supports inserting multiple records in a single SQL statement; defaults to `False`.

- `has_select_for_update`—Indicates whether the database supports `SELECT FOR UPDATE` queries, which locks the row while working with it; defaults to `False`.

- `has_select_for_update_nowait`—If you use `SELECT FOR UPDATE`, and another query already has a lock, some backends allow you to specify a `NOWAIT` option to fail immediately, rather than wait for the lock to be released. This attribute indicates whether the database supports this feature; defaults to `False`.

- `interprets_empty_strings_as_nulls`—Indicates whether the database treats an empty string as the same value as `NULL`; defaults to `False`.

- `needs_datetime_string_cast`—Indicates whether dates need to be converted from a string to a `datetime` object after being retrieved from the database; defaults to `True`.

- `related_fields_match_type`—Indicates whether the database requires relationship fields to be of the same type as the fields they relate to. This is used specifically for the `PositiveIntegerField` and `PositiveSmallIntegerField` types; if `True`, the actual type of the related field will be used to describe the relationship; if `False`—the default—Django will use an `IntegerField` instead.

- `supports_mixed_date_datetime_comparisons`—Indicates whether the database supports comparing a `date` to a `datetime` using a `timedelta` when finding records; defaults to `True`. If set to `True`, make sure to also supply the `date_interval_sql()` method described in the next section.

- `supports_select_related`—Indicates whether the backend allows a `QuerySet` to pull in related information in advance, to reduce the number of queries in many cases. It defaults to `True`, but can be set to `False` when working with non-relational databases, where the notion of "related" doesn't really apply in the same way.

- `supports_tablespaces`—This indicates whether the table supports tablespaces. They're not part of the SQL standard, so this defaults to `False`. If this is set to `True`, be sure to implement the `tablespace_sql()` method described in the next section.

- `update_can_self_select`—Indicates whether the database is capable of performing a SELECT subquery on a table that's currently being modified with an UPDATE query; defaults to True.

- `uses_autocommit`—Indicates whether the backend allows the database to manage auto-commit behavior directly; defaults to False.

- `uses_custom_query_class`—Indicates whether the backend supplies its own Query class, which would be used to customize how queries are performed; defaults to False.

- `uses_savepoints`—Indicates whether the database supports savepoints in addition to full transactions. Savepoints allow database queries to be rolled back on a more granular basis, without requiring the entire transaction to be undone if something goes wrong. This attribute defaults to False; setting it to True will also require implementations for the `savepoint_create_sql()`, `savepoint_commit_sql()`, and `savepoint_rollback_sql(sid)` methods described in the next section.

There are some additional attributes on this class that aren't used directly by Django, except in tests. If you try to use any of these features, Django will simply pass through the raw database errors. These attributes are only used in tests to confirm that the database should in fact raise an error for the related operation.

- `allow_sliced_subqueries`—Indicates whether the backend can perform slice operations on subqueries; defaults to True.

- `allows_primary_key_0`—Indicates whether the backend allows 0 to be used as the value of a primary key column; defaults to True.

- `has_real_datatype`—Indicates whether the database has a native datatype to represent real numbers; defaults to False.

- `ignores_nulls_in_unique_constraints`—When checking for duplicates on a table with a unique constraint spanning multiple columns, some databases will take NULL values into account and prevent duplicates, while others will ignore them. This attribute defaults to True, which indicates that the database will allow duplicate entries if the only duplicated columns contain NULL values.

- `requires_explicit_null_ordering_when_grouping`—Indicates whether the database needs an extra ORDER BY NULL clause when using a GROUP BY clause to prevent the database from trying to order the records unnecessarily; defaults to False.

- `requires_rollback_on_dirty_transaction`—If a transaction can't be completed for any reason, this attribute indicates whether the transaction needs to be rolled back before a new transaction can be started; defaults to False.

- `supports_1000_query_parameters`—Indicates whether the backend supports up to 1,000 parameters passed into the query, particularly when using the IN operator; defaults to True.

- `supports_bitwise_or`—As its name suggests, this one indicates whether the database supports the bitwise OR operation; defaults to True.

- `supports_date_lookup_using_string`—Indicates whether you can use strings instead of numbers when querying against date and datetime fields; defaults to True.

- `supports_forward_references`—If the database checks foreign key constraints at the end of the transaction, one record will be able to reference another that has yet to be added to the transaction. This is True by default, but you'll need to set it to False if the database instead checks these constraints for each record inside a transaction.

- `supports_long_model_names`—This one is more self-explanatory, indicating whether the database allows table names to be longer than you might normally expect. This defaults to True and is mostly used to test MySQL, which supports only 64 characters in a table name.

- `supports_microsecond_precision`—Indicates whether `datetime` and `time` fields support microseconds at the database level; defaults to True.

- `supports_regex_backreferencing`—Indicates whether the database's regular expression engine supports the use of grouping and backreferences of those groups; defaults to True.

- `supports_sequence_reset`—Indicates whether the database supports resetting sequences; defaults to True.

- `supports_subqueries_in_group_by`—Indicates whether the database supports selecting from a subquery while also performing aggregation using a `GROUP BY` clause; defaults to True.

- `supports_timezones`—Indicates whether you can supply `datetime` objects that have time zones when interacting with `datetime` fields in the database; defaults to True.

- `supports_unspecified_pk`—If a model uses a primary key other than the default auto-incrementing option, each instance will typically need to specify a primary key. If the database saves the instance even without a primary key, you'll need to set this to True so that Django can skip the test for that behavior.

- `test_db_allows_multiple_connections`—Indicates whether a test-only database supports multiple connections. This defaults to True because most databases do support it, but others might use things like in-memory databases for testing, which might not support multiple connections.

DatabaseWrapper.ops

This is the gateway to most of the database-specific features, primarily to handle the various differences in how each database handles certain types of SQL clauses. Each database vendor has its own set of special syntaxes that need to be supported, and defining those in the backend allows Django to operate without needing to worry about those details.

   Like the situations described previously, backends only need to write those operations that deviate from the standard. `BaseDatabaseOperations`, also living at `django.db.models.backends`, provides default behaviors for many of these operations, while others must be implemented by the backend itself. The following list explains their purposes and default behaviors.

- `autoinc_sql(table, column)`—Returns the SQL necessary to create auto-incrementing primary keys. If the database has a field to support this natively, that field will be chosen using the `creation` module described in the "Creation of New Structures" section, and this method should return None instead of any SQL statements, which is also the default behavior.

- `bulk_batch_size(fields, objs)`—When inserting records in bulk, you will find that some databases have limits that require the records to be split up into multiple batches. Given the fields to insert and the objects containing values for those fields, this method returns the number of records to insert in a single batch. The default implementation simply returns the number of objects, thus always using a single batch to insert any number of records.

- `cache_key_culling_sql()`—Returns an SQL template used for selecting a cache key to be culled. The returned template string should contain one %s placeholder, which will be the name of the cache table. It should also include a %%s reference, so that it can be replaced later with the index of the last key before the one that should be culled.

- `compiler(compiler_name)`—Returns an SQL compiler based on the given compiler name. By default, this method will import a module according to the `compiler_module` attribute on the `BaseDatabaseOperations` object and look up the given `compiler_name` within that module. The `compiler_module` is set to `"django.db.models.sql.compiler"`, but you can override it if you'd like to use your own compiler without overriding this method.

- `date_extract_sql(lookup_type, field_name)`—Returns an SQL statement that pulls out just a portion of a date so it can be compared to a filter argument. The `lookup_type` will be one of `"year"`, `"month"`, or `"day"`, while `field_name` is the name of the table column that contains the date to be checked. This has no default behavior and must be defined by the backend to avoid a `NotImplementedError`.

- `date_interval_sql(sql, connector, timedelta)`—Returns an SQL clause that will perform an operation with a `date` or `datetime` column and a `timedelta` value. The `sql` argument will contain the necessary SQL for the `date` or `datetime` column, and the `connector` will contain the operator that will be used with the `timedelta` value. This method is responsible for formatting the expression, as well as for describing the `timedelta` using the database's vocabulary.

- `date_trunc_sql(lookup_type, field_name)`—Returns an SQL statement that drops off that portion of the date that's beyond the specificity provided by `lookup_type`. The possible values are the same as those for `date_extract_sql()`, but this differs in that if `lookup_type` is `"month"`, for example, this will return a value that specifies both the month *and* the year, while `date_extract_sql()` will return the month *without* the year. Also like `date_extract_sql()`, this is no default behavior and must be implemented.

- `datetime_cast_sql()`—Returns the SQL required to force a `datetime` value into whatever format the database library uses to return a true `datetime` object in Python. The return value will be used as a Python format string, which will receive just the field name, to be referenced as `%s` in the string. By default, it simply returns `"%s"`, which will work just fine for databases that don't require any special type casting.

- `deferrable_sql()`—Returns the SQL necessary to append to a constraint definition to make that constraint initially deferred, so that it won't get checked until the end of the transaction. This will be appended immediately after the constraint definition, so if a space is required, the return value must include the space at the beginning. By default, this returns an empty string.

- `distinct_sql(fields)`—Returns an SQL clause to select unique records, optionally based on a list of field names. The default implementation returns `"DISTINCT"` when `fields` is empty, and raises `NotImplementedError` when `fields` is populated, so be sure to override this if the database does support checking for uniqueness based on a limited set of fields.

- `drop_foreignkey_sql()`—Returns the SQL fragment that will drop a foreign key reference as part of an `ALTER TABLE` statement. The name of the reference will be appended automatically afterward, so this needs to specify only the command itself. For example, the default return value is simply `"DROP CONSTRAINT"`.

- `drop_sequence_sql(table)`—Returns an SQL statement to drop the auto-incrementing sequence from the specified table. This forms something of a pair with `autoinc_sql()` because the sequence only needs to be dropped explicitly if it was created explicitly. By default, this returns `None` to indicate no action is taken.

- `end_transaction_sql(success=True)`—Returns the SQL necessary to end an open transaction. The `success` argument indicates whether the transaction was successful and can be used to determine what action to take. For example, the default implementation returns `"COMMIT;"` if `success` is set to `True` and `"ROLLBACK;"` otherwise.

- `fetch_returned_insert_id(cursor)`—Returns the ID of the last inserted record for backends that support getting that information. The default implementation calls `cursor.fetchone()[0]`.

- `field_cast_sql(db_type)`—Returns an SQL fragment for casting the specified database column type to some value that can be more accurately compared to filter arguments in a WHERE clause. The return value must be a Python format string, with the only argument being the name of the field to be cast. The default return value is `"%s"`.

- `force_no_ordering()`—Returns a list of names that can be used in an ORDER BY clause to remove all ordering from the query. By default, this returns an empty list.

- `for_update_sql(nowait=False)`—Returns an SQL clause that will request a lock when selecting data from the database. The `nowait` argument indicates whether to include the necessary clause to fail immediately if a lock is already in place, rather than waiting for that lock to be released.

- `fulltext_search_sql(field_name)`—Returns an SQL fragment for issuing a full-text search against the specified field, if supported. The string returned should also include a %s placeholder for the user-specified value to be searched against, which will be quoted automatically outside this method. If full-text search isn't supported by the database, the default behavior will suffice by raising a `NotImplementedError` with an appropriate message to indicate this.

- `last_executed_query(cursor, sql, params)`—Returns the last query that was issued to the database, exactly as it was sent. By default, this method has to reconstruct the query by replacing the placeholders in the `sql` argument with the parameters supplied by `params`, which will work correctly for all backends without any extra work. Some backends may have a faster or more convenient shortcut to retrieve the last query, so the database cursor is provided as well, as a means to use that shortcut.

- `last_insert_id(cursor, table_name, pk_name)`—Returns the ID of the row inserted by the last INSERT into the database. By default, this simply returns `cursor.lastrowid`, as specified by PEP-249, but other backends might have other ways of retrieving this value. To help access it accordingly, the method also receives the name of the table where the row was inserted and the name of the primary key column.

- `lookup_cast(lookup_type)`—Returns the SQL necessary to cast a value to a format that can be used with the specified `lookup_type`. The return value must also include a %s placeholder for the actual value to be cast, and by default it simply returns `"%s"`.

- `max_in_list_size()`—Returns the number of items that can be used in a single IN clause. The default return value, None, indicates that there's no limit on the number of those items.

- `max_name_length()`—Returns the maximum number of characters the database engine allows to be used for table and column names. This returns None by default, which indicates there's no limit.

- `no_limit_value()`—Returns the value that should be used to indicate a limit of infinity, used when specifying an offset without a limit. Some databases allow an offset to be used without a limit, and in these cases, this method should return None. By default, this raises a `NotImplementedError`, and must be implemented by a backend to allow offsets to be used without limits.

- `pk_default_value()`—Returns the value to be used when issuing an `INSERT` statement to indicate that the primary key field should use its default value—that is, increment a sequence—rather than some specified ID; defaults to `"DEFAULT"`.

- `prep_for_like_query(x)`—Returns a modified form of x, suitable for use with a `LIKE` comparison in the query's `WHERE` clause. By default, this escapes any percent signs (%), underscores (_) or double backslashes (\\) found in x with extra backslashes as appropriate.

- `prep_for_ilike_query(x)`—Just like `prep_for_like_query()`, but for case-insensitive comparisons. By default, this is an exact copy of `prep_for_like_query()`, but can be overridden if the database treats case-insensitive comparisons differently.

- `process_clob(value)`—Returns the value referenced by a CLOB column, in case the database needs some extra processing to yield the actual value. By default, it just returns the provided value.

- `query_class(DefaultQueryClass)`—If the backend provides a custom `Query` class, as indicated by `DatabaseWrapper.features.uses_custom_query_class`, this method must return a custom `Query` class based on the supplied `DefaultQueryClass`. If `uses_custom_query_class` is `False`, this method is never called, so the default behavior is to simply return `None`.

- `quote_name(name)`—Returns a rendition of the given `name` with quotes appropriate for the database engine. The name supplied might have already been quoted once, so this method should also take care to check for that and not add extra quotes in that case. Because there's no established standard for quoting names in queries, this must be implemented by the backend, and will raise a `NotImplementedError` otherwise.

- `random_function_sql()`—Returns the necessary SQL for generating a random value; defaults to `"RANDOM()"`.

- `regex_lookup(lookup_type)`—Returns the SQL for performing a regular expression match against a column. The return value should contain two `%s` placeholders, the first for the name of the column and the other for the value to be matched. The lookup type would be either `regex` or `iregex`, the difference being case-sensitivity. By default, this raises a `NotImplementedError`, which would indicate that regular expressions aren't supported by the database backend. However, for simple cases, `regex` and `iregex` can be supported using the `DatabaseWrapper.operators` dictionary described in the next section.

- `return_insert_id()`—Returns a clause that can be used at the end of an `INSERT` query to return the ID of the newly inserted record. By default, this simply returns `None`, which won't add anything to the query.

- `savepoint_create_sql(sid)`—Returns an SQL statement for creating a new savepoint. The `sid` argument is the name to give the savepoint so it can be referenced later.

- `savepoint_commit_sql(sid)`—Explicitly commits the savepoint referenced by the `sid` argument.

- `savepoint_rollback_sql(sid)`—Rolls back a portion of the transaction according to the savepoint referenced by the `sid` argument.

- `set_time_zone_sql()`—Returns an SQL template that can be used to set the time zone for the database connection. The template should accept one `%s` value, which will be replaced with the time zone to use. By default, this returns an empty string, indicating that the database doesn't support time zones.

- `sql_flush(style, tables, sequences)`—Returns the SQL necessary to remove all the data from the specified structures, while leaving the structures themselves intact. Because this is so different from one database engine to another, the default behavior raises a `NotImplementedError` and must be implemented by the backend.

- `sequence_reset_by_name_sql(style, sequences)`—Returns a list of SQL statements necessary to reset the auto-incrementing sequences named in the `sequences` list. Like `autoinc_sql()` and `drop_sequence_sql()`, this is useful only for databases that maintain independent sequences for automatic IDs, and can return an empty list if not required, which is the default behavior.

- `sequence_reset_sql(style, model_list)`—Like `sequence_reset_by_name_sql()`,—Returns a list of SQL statements necessary to reset auto-incrementing sequences, but the specified list contains Django models instead of sequence names. This also shares the same default behavior of returning an empty list.

- `start_transaction_sql()`—Returns the SQL used to enter a new transaction; defaults to `"BEGIN;"`.

- `sql_for_tablespace(tablespace, inline=False)`—Returns the SQL to declare a tablespace, or `None` if the database doesn't support them, which is the default.

- `validate_autopk_value(value)`—Validates that a given value is suitable for use as a serial ID in the database. For example, if the database doesn't allow zero as a valid ID, that value should raise a `ValueError`. By default, this simply returns the value, which indicates that it was valid.

- `value_to_db_date(value)`—Converts a `date` object to an object suitable for use with the database for `DateField` columns.

- `value_to_db_datetime(value)`—Converts a `datetime` object to a value suitable for use with `DateTimeField` columns.

- `value_to_db_time(value)`—Converts a `time` object to a value that can be used with the database for `TimeField` columns.

- `value_to_db_decimal(value)`—Converts a `Decimal` object to a value that the database can place in a `DecimalField` column.

- `year_lookup_bounds(value)`—Returns a two-item list representing the lower and upper bounds of a given year. The `value` argument is an `int` year and each of the return values is a string representing a full date and time. The first return value is the lowest date and time that is considered part of the supplied year, while the second is the highest date and time that is considered part of that same year.

- `year_lookup_bounds_for_date_feld(value)`—Also returns a 2-item list representing the upper and lower date and time boundaries for the year supplied as `value`. By default, this defers to `year_lookup_bounds()` but can be overridden in case the database can't compare a full date/time value against a `DateField`.

Comparison Operators

Many of the comparisons that can be done in a database follow a simple format, with one value being followed by some kind of operator, then followed by another value to compare it to. Because this is such a common case, and is quite simple to work with, Django uses a much simpler method for defining the operators for these types of comparisons.

Another attribute on the DatabaseWrapper object, operators, contains a dictionary mapping various lookup types to the database operators that implement them. This relies very heavily on the basic structure, because while the key for this dictionary is the lookup type, the value is the SQL fragment that should be placed *after* the name of the field being compared.

For example, consider the common case where the "exact" lookup is handled by the standard = operator, which would be handled by a dictionary like the following:

```
class DatabaseWrapper(BaseDatabaseWrapper):
    operators = {
        "exact": "= %s",
    }
```

This dictionary would then be filled out with the other operators supported by Django.

Obtaining a Cursor

Combining all of these database-specific features with Django's object-oriented database API makes available a world of possibilities, but they're all designed to cover the most common cases. Databases support a wide variety of additional functionality that's either less commonly used or extremely disparate across different implementations. Rather than try to support all these features in all databases, Django instead provides easy access straight to the database itself.

The cursor() method of DatabaseWrapper returns a database cursor straight from the third-party library used to connect with the database itself. In keeping with standard Python policy, this cursor object is compatible with PEP-249, so it might even be possible to use other database abstraction libraries with it. Because the behavior of the attributes and methods on this object are outside Django's control—often varying wildly across implementations—it's best to consult the full PEP and your database library's documentation for details on what can be done with it.

Creation of New Structures

One of the more convenient features Django's database connection provides is the ability to automatically create tables, columns, and indexes based solely on model definitions declared in Python. Along with a powerful database querying API, this is a key feature in avoiding the use of SQL code throughout an application, keeping it clean and portable.

While the SQL syntax itself is reasonably well standardized with regards to creation of data structures, the names and options available for individual field types are quite varied across different implementations. This is where Django's database backends come in, providing a mapping of Django's basic field types to the appropriate column types for that particular database.

This mapping is stored in the backend package's creation module, which must contain a DatabaseCreation class that subclasses django.db.backends.creation.BaseDatabaseCreation. This class contains an attribute named data_types, with contains a dictionary with keys that match up with the available return values from the various Field subclasses and string values that will be passed to the database as the column's definition.

The value can also be a Python format string, which will be given a dictionary of field attributes so that customized field settings can be used to determine how the column is created. For example, this is how CharField passes along the max_length attribute. While many field types have common attributes, the ones that are of most use to the column type are likely specific to each individual field. Consult the field's source code to determine what attributes are available for use in this mapping.

There are a number of basic field types available as internal column types:

- AutoField—An auto-incrementing numeric field, used for primary keys when one isn't defined explicitly in the model.

- BooleanField—A field representing just two possible values: on and off. If the database doesn't have a separate column that represents this case, it's also possible to use a single-character CharField to store "1" and "0" to simulate this behavior.

- CharField—A field containing a limited about of free-form text. Typically, this uses a variable-length string type in the database, using the extra max_length attribute to define the maximum length of a stored value.

- CommaSeparatedIntegerField—A field containing a list of integers, typically representing IDs, which are stored in a single string separated by commas. Because the list is stored as a string, this also uses a variable-length string type on the database side. Although some databases might have a more intelligent and efficient means of storing this type of data, the field's code still expects a string of numbers, so the backend should always return one.

- DateField—A standard date, without any time information associated with it. Most databases should have a date column type, so this should be easy to support. Just make sure the column type used returns a Python datetime.date upon retrieval.

- DateTimeField—A date, but with associated time information attached, excluding time zones. Again, most reasonable databases will support this easily, but make sure the Python library for it returns a datetime.datetime when retrieving from the database.

- DecimalField—A fixed-precision decimal number. This is another example of using field attributes to define the database column because the max_digits and decimal_places field attributes should control the database column equivalents.

- FileField—The name and location of a file stored elsewhere. Django doesn't support storing files as binary data in the database, so its files are referenced by a relative path and name, which is stored in the associated column. Because that's text, this again uses a standard variable-length text field, which also utilizes the max_length field attribute.

- FilePathField—The name and path of a file in a storage system. This field is similar to FileField in many respects, but this is intended to allow users to choose from existing files, while FileField exists to allow saving new files. Because the data actually being stored is essentially the same format, it works the same way, using a variable-length string specified using the max_length attribute.

- FloatField—A field containing a floating point number. It doesn't matter if the database stores the number with fixed precision internally, as long as the Python library returns a float for values stored in the column.

- IntegerField—A field containing a signed 32-bit integer.

- BigIntegerField—A field containing a signed 64-bit integer.

- IPAddressField—An Internet Protocol (IP) address, using the current IPv4[3] standard, represented in Python as a string.

- GenericIPAddressField—An IP address using either the original IPv4 standard or the newer IPv6[4] standard.

---

[3] http://prodjango.com/ipv4/
[4] http://prodjango.com/ipv6/

- `NullBooleanField`—A Boolean field that also allows `NULL` values to be stored in the database.

- `PositiveIntegerField`—A field containing an unsigned 32-bit integer.

- `PositiveSmallIntegerField`—A field containing an unsigned 8-bit integer.

- `SmallIntegerField`—A field containing a signed 8-bit integer.

- `TextField`—An unlimited-length text field, or at least the largest text field the database makes available. The `max_length` attribute has no effect on the length of this field.

- `TimeField`—A field representing the time of day, without any associated date information. The database library should return a `datetime.time` object for values in this column.

Introspection of Existing Structures

In addition to being able to create new table structures based on model information, it's also possible to use an existing table structure to generate new models. This isn't a perfect process because some model information doesn't get stored in the table's own definition, but it's a great starting point for new projects that have to work with existing databases, usually to run alongside a legacy application that's being phased out.

The backend should provide a module called `introspection.py` for this purpose, which provides a `DatabaseIntrospection` class with a number of methods for retrieving various details about the table structures. Each method receives an active database cursor; all arguments and return values of each of these methods are documented in the following list, as well as another mapping for picking the right field types based on the underlying column types.

- `get_table_list(cursor)`—Returns a list of table names that are present in the database.

- `get_table_description(cursor, table_name)`—Given the name of a specific table, found using `get_table_list()`, this returns a list of tuples, each describing a column in the table. Each tuple follows PEP-249's standard for the cursor's `description` attribute: `(name, type_code, display_size, internal_size, precision, scale, null_ok)`. The `type_code` here is an internal type used by the database to identify the column type, which will be used by the reverse mapping described at the end of this section.

- `get_relations(cursor, table_name)`—Given a table's name, this returns a dictionary detailing the relationships the table has with other tables. Each key is the column's index in the list of all columns, while the associated value is a 2-tuple. The first item is the index of the related field according to its table's columns, and the second item is the name of the associated table. If the database doesn't provide an easy way to access this information, this function can instead raise `NotImplementedError`, and relationships will just be excluded from the generated models.

- `get_key_columns(cursor, table_name)`—Given a table's name, this returns a list of columns that relate to other tables and how those references work. Each item in the list is a tuple consisting of the column name, the table it references, and the column within that referenced table.

- `get_indexes(cursor, table_name)`—Given the name of a table, this returns a dictionary of all the fields that are indexed in any way. The dictionary's keys are column names, while the values are additional dictionaries. Each value's dictionary contains two keys: `'primary_key'` and `'unique'`, each of which is either `True` or `False`. If both are `False`, the column is still indicated as indexed by virtue of being in the outer dictionary at all; it's just an ordinary index, without primary key or unique constraints. Like `get_relations()`, this can also raise `NotImplementedError` if there's no easy way to obtain this information.

In addition to the preceding methods, the introspection class also provides a dictionary called data_types_reverse, which maps the type_code values in the dictionary returned from get_table_description(). The keys are whatever values are returned with as type_code, regardless of whether that's a string, integer, or something else entirely. The values are strings containing the names of the Django fields that will support the associated column type.

DatabaseClient

Living in the database backend's client.py module, this class is responsible for calling the command-line interface (shell) for the current database specified by DATABASE_ENGINE. This is called using the manage.py dbshell command, allowing users to manage the underlying tables' structure and data manually if necessary.

The class consists of just a single method, runshell(), which takes no arguments. This method is then responsible for reading the appropriate database settings for the given backend and configuring a call to the database's shell program.

DatabaseError and IntegrityError

Pulled in from {{ backend }}.base, these classes allow exceptions to be handled easily, while still being able to swap out databases. IntegrityError should be a subclass of DatabaseError, so that applications can just check for DatabaseError if the exact type of error isn't important.

Third-party libraries that conform to PEP-249 will already have these classes available, so they can often just be assigned to the base module's namespace and work just fine. The only time they would need to be subclassed or defined directly is if the library being used doesn't behave in a way that's similar to other databases supported by Django. Remember, it's all about consistency across the entire framework.

Authentication

While the combination of a username and password is a very common authentication method, it's far from the only one available. Other methods, such as OpenID, use completely different techniques, which don't even include a username or password. Also, some systems that do use usernames and passwords may already be storing that information in a different database or structure than Django looks at by default, so some extra handling still needs to be done to verify credentials against the right data.

To address these situations, Django's authentication mechanism can be replaced with custom code, supporting whatever system needs to be used. In fact, multiple authentication schemes can be used together, with each falling back to the next if it doesn't produce a valid user account. This is all controlled by a tuple of import paths assigned to the AUTHENTICATION_BACKENDS setting. They will be tried in order from first to last, and only if all backends return None will it be considered a failure to authenticate. Each authentication backend is just a standard Python class that provides two specific methods.

get_user(user_id)

Any time a user's ID is known in advance, whether from a session variable, a database record, or somewhere else entirely, the authentication backend is responsible for converting that ID into a usable django.contrib.auth.models.User instance. What it means to be an ID could be different for different backends, so the exact type of this argument might also change depending on the backend being used. For django.contrib.auth.backends.ModelBackend, the default that ships with Django, this is the database ID where the user's information is stored. For others, it might be a username, a domain name, or something else entirely.

authenticate(**credentials)

When the user's ID isn't known, it's necessary to ask for some credentials, with which the appropriate User account can be identified and retrieved. In the default case, these credentials are a username and password, but others may use a URL or a single-use token, for example. In the real world, the backend won't accept arguments using the ** syntax, but rather it will accept just those arguments that make sense for it. However, because different backends will take different sets of credentials, there's no single method definition that will suit all cases.

PASSING INFORMATION TO CUSTOM BACKENDS

You might have noticed from the previous sections that the data passed in to an authentication backend depends very much on the backend being used. Django, by default, passes in a username and password from its login form, but other forms can supply whatever other credentials are appropriate for the form.

Storing User Information

One aspect of authentication that might not seem obvious is that all users must, for all intents and purposes, still be represented in Django as User objects in the django.contrib.auth application. This isn't strictly required by Django as a framework, but most applications—including the provided admin interface—expect users to exist in the database and will make relationships with that model.

For backends that call out to external services for authentication, this means duplicating every user in Django's database to make sure applications work correctly. On the surface, this sounds like a maintenance nightmare; not only does every existing user need to be copied, but new users need to be added and changes to user information should also be reflected in Django. If all this had to be managed by hand for all users, it would certainly be a considerable problem.

Remember, though, that the only real requirement for an authentication backend is that it receives the user's credentials and returns a User object. In between, it's all just standard Python, and the whole of Django's model API is up for grabs. Once a user has been authenticated behind the scenes, the backend can simply create a new User if one doesn't already exist. If one does exist, it can even update the existing record with any new information that's updated in the "real" user database. This way, everything can stay in sync without having to do anything special for Django. Just administer your users using whatever system you're already using, and let your authentication backend handle the rest.

Files

Web applications typically spend most of their time dealing with information in databases, but there are a number of reasons an application might need to work directly with files as well. Whether it be users uploading avatars or presentations, generating images or other static content on the fly, or even backing up log files on a regular basis, files can become a very important part of an application. As with many other things, Django provides both a single interface for working with files and an API for additional backends to provide additional functionality.

The Base File Class

Regardless of source, destination or purpose, all files in Django are represented as instances of `django.core.files.File`. This works very much like Python's own file object, but with a few additions and modifications for use on the Web and with large files. Subclasses of `File` can alter what goes on behind the scenes, but the following API is standard for all file types. The following attributes are available on all `File` objects:

- `File.closed`—A Boolean indicating whether the file has been closed. When instantiated, all `File` objects are open, and its contents can be accessed immediately. The `close()` method sets this to `True`, and the file must be reopened using `open()` before its contents can be accessed again.

- `File.DEFAULT_CHUNK_SIZE`—Typically an attribute of the file's class rather than an instance of it, this determines what size chunks should be used with the `chunks()` method.

- `File.mode`—The access mode the file was opened with; defaults to `'rb'`.

- `File.name`—The name of the file, including any given path relative to where it was opened.

- `File.size`—The size of the file's contents, in bytes.

The following methods are also available on `File` objects:

- `File.chunks(chunk_size=None)`—Iterates over the file's contents, yielding it in one or more smaller chunks to avoid filling up the server's available memory with large files. If no `chunk_size` is provided, the `DEFAULT_CHUNK_SIZE`, which defaults to 64 KB, will be used.

- `File.close()`—Closes the file so its contents become inaccessible.

- `File.flush()`—Writes any new pending contents to the actual filesystem.

- `File.multiple_chunks(chunk_size=None)`—Returns `True` if the file is big enough to require multiple calls to `chunks()` to retrieve the full contents, or `False` if it can all be read in one pass. The `chunk_size` argument works the same as in `chunks()`. Note that this will not actually read the file at this point; it determines the value based on the file's `size`.

- `File.open(mode=None)`—Reopens the file if it had been previously closed. The `mode` argument is optional and will default to whatever mode the file had used when it was last open.

- `File.read(num_bytes=None)`—Retrieves a certain number of bytes from the file. If called without a size argument, this will read the remainder of the file.

- `File.readlines()`—Retrieves the content of the file as a list of lines, as indicated by the presence of newline characters (`\r` and `\n`) in the file. These newline characters are left at the end of each line in this list.

- `File.seek(position)`—Moves the internal position of the file to the specified location. All read and write operations are relative to this position, so this allows different parts of the file to be accessed by the same code.

- `File.tell()`—Returns the position of the internal pointer, as the number of bytes from the beginning of the file.

- `File.write(content)`—Writes the specified contents to the file. This is only available if the file was opened in write mode (a mode beginning with `'w'`).

- `File.xreadlines()`—A generator version of `readlines()` yielding one line, including newline characters, at a time. In keeping with Python's own transition away from `xreadlines()`, this functionality is also provided by iterating over the `File` object itself.

Handling Uploads

When accepting files from users, things get a little bit trickier, because these files shouldn't necessarily be saved alongside the rest of your files until your code has had a chance to review them. To facilitate this, Django treats uploaded files a bit differently, using upload handlers to decide what subclass of File should be used to represent them. Each upload handler has a chance to step in during the upload and alter how Django proceeds.

Upload handlers are specified with the FILE_UPLOAD_HANDLERS setting, which takes a sequence of import paths. As uploaded files are being processed, Django calls various methods on each of these handlers in turn, so they can inspect the data as it comes in. There's no need to all these directly, as it's automatically handled by Django's request processing code, but the API for new upload handlers provides ample opportunity to customize how incoming files are managed.

- FileUploadHandler.__init__(request)—The handler is initialized every time a request comes in with files attached, and the incoming request is passed in so the handler can decide if it needs to handle the files for the request. For example, if it's designed to write details of the upload to the console of the development server, it might check if the DEBUG setting is True and if request.META['REMOTE_ADDR'] is in the INTERNAL_IPS setting. If a handler should always process every request, this doesn't need to be defined manually; the inherited default will suffice for most cases.

- FileUploadHandler.new_file(field_name, file_name, content_type, content_length, charset=None)—This is called for each file submitted in the request, with various details about the file, but none of its actual content. The field_name is the form field name that was used to upload the file, while the file_name is the name of the file itself as reported by the browser. The content_type, content_length and charset are all properties of the file's contents, but they should be taken with a grain of salt because they can't be verified without accessing the file's contents.

  While not strictly required, the primary function of this method is to set aside a place for the file's content to be stored when received_data_chunk() is called. There's no requirement on what type of storage is used, or what attribute is used for it, so nearly anything's fair game. Common examples are temporary files or StringIO objects. Also, this method provides a way to decide whether certain features should be enabled, such as automatically generated thumbnails of images, determined by the content_type.

- FileUploadHandler.receive_data_chunk(raw_data, start)—This is one of only two required methods and is called repeatedly throughout the processing of the file, each time receiving a portion of the file's contents as raw_data, with start being the offset within the file where that content was found. The amount of data called each time is based on the handler's chunk_size attribute, which defaults to 64KiB.

  Once this method has completed processing the data chunk, it can also control how other handlers deal with that data. This is determined by whether the method returns any data or not, with any data returned being passed along to the next handler in line. If it returns None, Django will simply repeat the process with the next chunk of data.

- FileUploadHandler.file_complete(file_size)—As a complement to new_file(), this method is called when Django finds the end of the file in the request. Because this is also the only time the file's total size can be known with certainty, Django gives each handler a chance to determine what to do with that information.

This is the only other required method on an upload handler and should return an UploadedFile object if the file was processed by this handler. The UploadedFile returned will be used by the associated form as the content for the field used to upload the file. If the handler didn't do anything with the file, for whatever reason, this can return None. However, be careful with this because at least one upload handler must return an UploadedFile to be used with forms.

- FileUploadHandler.upload_complete()—While file_complete() is called when each file is finished loading, upload_complete() is called once per request, after all uploaded files have been processed completely. If the handler needs to set up any temporary resources while dealing with all the files, this method is the place to clean up after itself, freeing up resources for the rest of the application.

Notice that many of the features made possible by these methods rely on one method knowing what decisions a previous method has already made, but there's no obvious way to persist this information. Since handlers are instantiated on every incoming request and process files one at a time, it's possible to simply set custom attributes on the handler object itself, which future method calls can read back to determine how to proceed.

For example, if __init__() sets self.activated to False, receive_data_chunk() can read that attribute to determine whether it should process the chunks it receives or just pass them through to the next handler in line. It's also possible for new_file() to set the same or similar attribute, so those types of decisions can be made on a per-file basis as well as per-request.

Because each handler works in isolation from the others, there isn't any standard imposed on which attributes are used or what they're used for. Instead, interaction among the various installed upload handlers is handled by raising a number of exceptions in various situations. Proper operation of an upload handler doesn't require the use of any of these, but they can greatly customize how a number of them can work together. Like FileUploadHandler, these are all available at django.core.files.uploadhander.

- StopUpload—Tells Django to stop processing all files in the upload, preventing all handlers from handling any more data than they've already processed. It also accepts a single optional argument, connection_reset, a Boolean indicating whether Django should stop without reading in the remainder of the input stream. The default value of False for this argument means that Django will read the entire request before passing control back to a form, while True will stop without reading it all in, resulting in a "Connection Reset" message shown in the user's browser.

- SkipFile—Tells the upload process to stop processing the current file, but continue on with the next one in the list. This is a much more appropriate behavior if there were a problem with a single file in the request, which wouldn't affect any other files that might be uploaded at the same time.

- StopFutureHandlers—Only valid if thrown from the new_file() method, this indicates the current upload handler will handle current file directly, and no other handlers should receive any data after it. Any handlers that process data *before* the handler that raises this exception will continue to execute in their original order, as determined by their placement within the FILE_UPLOAD_HANDLERS setting.

Storing Files

All file storage operations are handled by instances of StorageBase, which lives at django.core.files.storage, with the default storage system specified by an import path in the DEFAULT_FILE_STORAGE setting. A storage system encompasses all the necessary functions for dealing with how and where files are stored and retrieved. By using this extra layer, it's possible to swap out which storage system is used, without having to make any changes to existing code. This is especially important when moving from development to production because production servers often have specialized needs for storing and serving static files.

To facilitate this level of flexibility, Django provides an API for dealing with files that goes beyond the standard open() function and associated file object provided by Python. Earlier in this chapter, Django's File object was described, explaining what features are available for dealing with individual files. However, when looking to store, retrieve or list files, storage systems have a different set of tools available.

- Storage.delete(name)—Deletes a file from the storage system.

- Storage.exists(name)—Returns a Boolean indicating whether the specified name references a file that already exists in the storage system.

- Storage.get_valid_name(name)—Returns a version of the given name that's suitable for use with the current storage system. If it's already valid, it will be returned unchanged. One of only two methods with default implementations, this will return filenames suitable for a local filesystem, regardless of operating system.

- Storage.get_available_name(name)—Given a valid name, this returns a version of it that's actually available for new files to be written, without overwriting any existing files. Being the other method with a default behavior, this will add underscores to the end of the requested name until an available name is found.

- Storage.open(name, mode='rb', mixin=None)—Returns an open File object, through which the file's contents can be accessed. The mode accepts all the same arguments as Python's open() function, allowing for both read and write access. The optional mixin argument accepts a class to be used alongside the File subclass provided by the storage system, to enable additional features on the file returned.

- Storage.path(name)—Returns the absolute path to the file on the local filesystem, which can be used with Python's built-in open() function to access the file directly. This is provided as a convenience for the common case where files are stored on the local filesystem. For other storage systems, this will raise a NotImplementedError if there is no valid filesystem path at which the file can be accessed. Unless you're using a library that only accepts file paths instead of open file objects, you should always open files using Storage.open(), which works across all storage systems.

- Storage.save(name, content)—Saves the given content to the storage system, preferably under the given name. This name will be passed through get_valid_name() and get_available_name() before being saved, and the return value of this method will be the name that was actually used to store the content. The content argument provided to this method should be a File object, typically as a result of a file upload.

- Storage.size(name)—Returns the size, in bytes, of the file referenced by name.

- Storage.url(name)—Returns an absolute URL where the file's contents can be accessed directly by a Web browser.

- listdir(path)—Returns the contents of the directory specified by the path argument. The return value is a tuple containing two lists: the first for directories located at the path and the second for files located at that same path.

By default, Django ships with FileSystemStorage, which, as the name implies, stores files on the local filesystem. Typically this means the server's hard drive, but there are many ways to map other types of filesystems to local paths, so there are already a number of possibilities. There are even more storage options available, though, and there are plenty of ways to customize how even the existing options behave. By subclassing StorageBase, it's possible to make available a number of other options.

There are a number of things a storage system must provide, starting with most of these methods. One of those methods, get_available_name(), doesn't strictly need to be supplied by the new storage class because its default implementation is suitable for many situations; overriding it is a matter of preference, not requirement. On the other hand, the get_valid_name() method has a default behavior that's suitable for most backends, but some might have different file naming requirements and would require a new method to override it.

Two other methods, open() and save(), have still further requirements. By definition, both of these require special handling for each different storage system, but they shouldn't be overridden directly in most situations. They provide additional logic beyond what's necessary to store and retrieve files, and that logic should be maintained. Instead, they defer the interaction with the actual storage mechanism to _open() and _save(), respectively, which have a simpler set of expectations.

- Storage._open(name, mode='rb')—The name and mode arguments are the same as open(), but it no longer has the mixin logic to deal with, so _open() can focus solely on returning a File object suitable for accessing the requested file.

- Storage._save(name, content)—The arguments here are the same as save(), but the name provided here will have already gone through get_valid_name() and get_available_name(), and the content is guaranteed to be a File instance. This allows the _save() method to focus solely on committing the file's content to the storage system with the given name.

In addition to providing these methods, most custom storage systems will also need to provide a File subclass with read() and write() methods that are designed to access the underlying data in the most efficient manner. The chunks() method defers to read() internally, so there shouldn't need to be anything done there to make large files more memory-friendly for applications to work with. Keep in mind that not all filesystems allow reading or writing just part of a file, so the File subclass might also need to take additional steps to minimize both memory usage and network traffic in these situations.

Session Management

When users are casually browsing a Web site, it's often useful to track some information for them temporarily, even if there are no User accounts associated with them yet. This can range from the time they first visited the site to a shopping cart. The typical solution in these cases is a session—a server-side data store referenced by a key stored in a browser-side cookie. Django comes with built-in support for sessions, with a bit of room for configuration.

Most of the session process is constant: identifying a user without a session, assigning a new key, storing that key in a cookie, retrieving that key later on and acting like a dictionary the entire time. There are some basic settings for the name of the key and how long to use it, but to actually persist any information across multiple page views, the key is used to reference some data stored somewhere on the server, and that's where the bulk of the customization comes in.

Django uses the SESSION_ENGINE setting to identify which data store class should handle the actual data itself. Three data stores ship with Django itself, covering common tactics like files, database records, and in-memory cache, but there are other options available in different environments, and even the stock classes might require additional customization. To accommodate this, SESSION_ENGINE accepts full import paths, allowing a session data store to be placed in any Django application. This import path points to a module containing a class named SessionStore, which provides the full data store implementation.

Like most of Django's swappable backends, there's a base implementation that provides most of the features, leaving fewer details for the subclass to cover. For sessions, that base class is SessionBase, located at django.contrib.sessions.backends.base. That's what handles the session key generation, cookie management, dictionary access, and accessing to the data store only when necessary. This leaves the custom SessionStore class to implement just five methods, which combine to complete the entire process.

- `SessionStore.exists(session_key)`—Returns True if the provided session key is already present in the data store, or False if it's available for use in a new session.

- `SessionStore.load()`—Loads session data from whatever storage mechanism the data store uses, returning a dictionary representing this data. If no session data exists, this should return an empty dictionary, and some backends may require the new dictionary to be saved as well, prior to returning.

- `SessionStore.save()`—Commits the current session data to the data store, using the current session key as an identifier. This should also use the session's expiration date or age to identify when the session would become invalid.

- `SessionStore.delete(session_key)`—Removes the session data associated with the given key from the data store.

- `SessionStore.create()`—Creates a new session and returns it so external code can add new values to it. This method is responsible for creating a new data container, generating a unique session key, storing that key in the session object, and committing that empty container to the backend before returning.

Also, to help session data stores access the necessary information to do their work, Django also provides a few additional attributes that are managed by `SessionBase`.

- `session_key`—The randomly generated session key stored in the client-side cookie.

- `_session`—A dictionary containing the session data associated with the current session key.

- `get_expiry_date()`—Returns a `datetime.datetime` object representing when the session should expire.

- `get_expiry_age()`—Returns the number of seconds after which the session should expire.

By implementing just five methods on a subclass of `SessionBase`, it's possible to store session data nearly anywhere. Even though this data isn't tied to a `User` object, it's still specific to individual people browsing the site. To store temporary information that's useful for everyone, a little something else is in order.

Caching

When an application has a lot of seldom-changing information to deal with, it's often useful to cache this information on the server so it doesn't have to be generated each and every time it's accessed. This can save on memory usage on the server, processing time per request, and ultimately helps the application serve more requests in the same amount of time.

There are a number of ways to access Django's caching mechanism, depending on just how much information needs to be cached. The online documentation[5] covers the many general cases on how to set up site-wide caching and per-view caching, but the lower-level details merit a bit more explanation.

---

[5] http://prodjango.com/caching/

Specifying a Backend

Specifying a cache backend in Django works quite a bit differently than other backends discussed in this chapter. Even though there are multiple configuration options to consider, there's just one setting to control them all. This setting, CACHE_BACKEND, uses the URI syntax[6] to accept all the necessary information in a way that can be parsed reliably. It can be split up into three separate parts, each with its own requirements.

```
CACHE_BACKEND = '{{ scheme }}://{{ host }}/?{{ arguments }}'
```

- The scheme portion specifies which backend code should be used to serve out the cache. Django ships with four backends that cover most cases—db, file, locmem, and memcached[7]—which are well documented online and cover the majority of cases. For custom backends, this portion of the setting can also accept a full import path to a module that implements the protocol described in the next section.

- The host specifies where the cache should actually be stored, and its format will vary depending on the backend used. For example, db expects a single database name, file expects a full directory path, memcached expects a list of server addresses, and locmem doesn't require anything at all. The host can also include by a trailing slash, which can help readability because it makes the whole setting look more like a URI.

- Arguments are optional and can be provided to customize how caching takes place within the backend. They're provided using the query-string format, with one argument required for all backends: timeout, the number of seconds before an item should be removed from the cache. Two more arguments are also available for most backends (including all those supplied by Django except for memcached): max_entries, the total number of items that should be stored in the cache before culling old items; and cull_frequency, which controls how many items to purge from the cache when it reaches max_entries.

- One important thing to realize about cull_frequency is that its value isn't actually how often items should be removed. Instead, the value is used in a simple formula, 1 / cull_frequency, which determines how many items are affected. So, if you'd like to purge 25% of the items at a time, that's equivalent to 1/4, so you'd pass cull_frequency=4 as an argument to the cache backend, while half (1/2) of the entries would require passing cull_frequency=2. Essentially, cull_frequency is the number of times the cache must be culled to guarantee all items are purged.

Using the Cache Manually

In addition to the standard site-wide and per-view caching options, it's also quite simple to use the cache directly, storing specific values so they can be retrieved later without having to perform expensive operations for data that doesn't change often. This low-level API is available in a generic form through the cache object, living at django.core.cache. Most of the usefulness of this object comes from three methods—get(), set(), and delete()—which work mostly how you'd expect.

```
>>> cache.set('result', 2 ** 16 - 64 * 4)
>>> print cache.get('result')
65280
>>> cache.delete('result')
>>> print cache.get('result')
None
```

---

[6] http://prodjango.com/uri/
[7] http://prodjango.com/memcached/

There are a few details about these methods that bear a little more explanation, and also some additional methods that prove useful. Here is a full list of the available methods, along with their functional details.

- `CacheClass.set(key, value, timeout=None)`—This sets the specified value in the cache, using the provided key. By default, the timeout for values to expire from the cache is determined by the timeout passed into the `CACHE_BACKEND` setting, but that can be overridden by specifying a different timeout as an argument to this method.

- `CacheClass.get(key, default=None)`—This method returns the value contained in the cache for the specified key. Normally, `cache.get()` returns None if the key doesn't exist in the cache, but sometimes None is a valid value to have in the cache. In these cases, just set `default` to some value that shouldn't exist in the cache, and that will be returned instead of None.

- `CacheClass.delete(key)`—This deletes the value associated with the given key.

- `CacheClass.get_many(keys)`—Given a list of keys, it returns a corresponding list of their values. For some backends, like memcached, this can provide a speed increase over calling `cache.get()` for each individual key.

- `CacheClass.has_key(key)`—This method returns True if the specified key has a value already in the cache or False if the key wasn't set or has already expired.

- `CacheClass.add(key, value, timeout=None)`—This method only attempts to add a new key to the cache, using the specified value and timeout. If the given key already exists in the cache, this method will *not* update the cache to the new value.

A common idiom when working with cache is to first check to see if a value is already present in the cache and, if not, calculate it and store it in the cache. Then, the value can be retrieved from the cache regardless of whether it was there to begin with, making the code nice and simple. To make this a bit more Pythonic, the cache object also functions a bit like a dictionary, supporting the `in` operator as an alias for the `has_key()` method.

```
def get_complex_data(complex_data):
    if 'complex-data-key' not in cache:
        # Perform complex operations to generate the data here.
        cache.set('complex-data-key', complex_data)
    return cache.get('complex-data-key')
```

Template Loading

While Chapter 6 showed that when a view or other code requests a template to render, it just passes in a name and a relative path, the actual retrieval of templates is done by special loaders, each of which accesses templates in a different way. By supplying the import paths to one or more of these to the `TEMPLATE_LOADERS` setting, Django doesn't need to know in advance how or where you'll store your templates.

Django ships with three template loaders, representing the most common ways templates are expected to be used, loading files from the filesystem in certain configurations. When these options aren't enough, it's fairly straightforward to add your own template loader to locate and retrieve templates in whatever way is best for your environment.

This is actually one of the easiest pluggable interfaces to write because it's really just a single function. There isn't even any assumption of what that function should called, much less what module it should be in, or any class it needs to be a part of. The entry in `TEMPLATE_LOADERS` points directly at the function itself, so no other structure is necessary.

load_template_source(template_name, template_dirs=None)

While the loader can be called anything, the name Django uses for all of its template loaders is `load_template_source`, so it's generally best to stick to that convention for ease of understanding. This is also typically placed in its own module, but again, the import path has to be supplied explicitly, so just make sure its location is well-documented.

The first argument is obviously the name of the template to be loaded, which is usually just a standard filename. This doesn't have to map to an actual file, but views will typically request templates using a filename, so it's up to the template loader to convert this name to whatever reference is used for templates. That may be database records, URLs pointing to external storage systems, or anything else your site might use to store and load templates.

The second argument to `load_template_source()` is a list of directories to use when searching for the template. Within Django itself, this is typically not provided, so the default of `None` is used, indicating that the `TEMPLATE_DIRS` setting should be used instead. A loader that uses the filesystem should always follow this behavior to maintain consistency with the way other template loaders work. If the loader retrieves templates from somewhere else, this argument can simply be ignored.

What goes on inside the template loader will be quite different from one template loader to the next, varying based on how each loader locates templates. Once a template is found, the loader must return a tuple containing two values: the template's contents as a string, and a string indicating where the template was found. That second value is used to generate the `origin` argument to the new `Template` object, so that it's easy to find a template if anything goes wrong.

If the given name doesn't match any templates the loader knows about, it should raise the `TemplateDoesNotExist` exception, described in Chapter 6. This will instruct Django to move on to the next template loader in the list or to display an error if there are no more loaders to use.

load_template_source.is_usable

If the Python environment doesn't have the requirements for a template loader to operate, Django also provides a way for the loader to indicate that it shouldn't be used. This is useful if a template loader relies on a third-party library that hasn't been installed. Adding an `is_usable` attribute to the function, set to `True` or `False`, will tell Django whether the template loader can be used.

load_template(template_name, template_dirs=None)

In addition to simply loading the source code for a template, this method is responsible for returning a template capable of being rendered. By default, the source returned from `load_template_source()` is processed by Django's own template language, but this gives you a chance to replace that with something else entirely. This should still use the `load_template_source()` method internally to fetch the code for the template, so that users can separate the decision of where to find templates from how those templates should be interpreted.

The return value only needs one method to work properly: `render(context)`. This `render()` method accepts a template context and returns a string generated by the template source code. The context passed in here works a lot like a standard dictionary, but Django's contexts are actually a stack of dictionaries, so if you intend to pass this context into another template rendered, you probably need to flatten it to a single dictionary first.

```
flat_dict = {}
for d in context.dicts:
    flat_dict.update(d)
```

After this, you'll have a single dictionary with all the values in it, which is usually suitable for most template languages.

Context Processors

When a template gets rendered, it's passed a context of variables, which it uses to display information and make basic presentation decisions. If a special type of context, RequestContext, is used, which is available from django.template right alongside the standard Context, Django runs through a list of context processors, each of which gets the opportunity to add new variables to the context of the template. This is not only a great way to add common variables to every template used on the site, but it's a really easy way to supply information based on information from the incoming HttpRequest object.

The interface for a context processor is quite simple; it's nothing more than a standard Python function that takes a request as its only argument and returns a dictionary of data to be added to the template's context. It should never raise an exception, and if no new variables need to be added, based on the specified request, it should just return an empty dictionary. Here's an example context processor to add an ip_address variable that contains the requesting user's IP address.

```python
def remote_addr(request):
    return {'ip_address': request.META['REMOTE_ADDR']}
```

> ■ **Note** REMOTE_ADDR isn't reliable behind proxies and load balancers because its value will be that of the proxy, rather than the true remote IP address. If you're using these kinds of software, be sure to use the values that are appropriate for your environment.

Installing a context processor is as easy as adding a string to the CONTEXT_PROCESSORS setting list, with each entry being a full Python import path, including the name of the function on the end of it. Also, remember that context processors are only called when templates are rendered using RequestContext. Since context processors accept the incoming request as an argument, there's no way to call them without this information.

Applied Techniques

The available uses of the tools described in this chapter are many and varied, but there are a few simple examples of how they can be put to good use for some common needs. Take these with a pinch of salt and a sprig of parsley, and make them your own. Without prior knowledge of an application's working environment, any examples that can be given will, by definition, be fairly abstract, but they should serve as a good outline of how these techniques can be put to good use.

Scanning Incoming Files for Viruses

For sites that allow users to upload files to be distributed to other users, a large amount of trust is placed on the quality of those incoming files. As with any form of user input, there must be a certain level of distrust in this information because there's always someone out there who wants to do harm to your site and its users.

When looking to let users share specific types of files, it's often easy to validate using third-party libraries designed to understand those files. Sharing arbitrary files, on the other hand, opens up a world of other possibilities, many of which put your site and its users at risk. Protecting against viruses is an important part of the safety of such an application, and Django's upload handlers make this an extremely simple task.

For this example, we'll use an excellent open source virus scanning application, ClamAV,[8] which is designed for use in servers, along with pyclamd,[9] a Python library for interacting with ClamAV. Together, these provide an easy-to-use interface for scanning any incoming file before it's even passed to the rest of the application. If a virus is found, the offending file can simply be removed from the input stream immediately, before it can do any harm to anyone.

```python
import pyclamd
from django.core.files import uploadhandler
from django.conf import settings

# Set up pyclamd to access running instance of clamavd, according to settings
host = getattr(settings, 'CLAMAV_HOST', 'localhost')
port = getattr(settings, 'CLAMAV_PORT', 3310)
pyclamd.init_network_socket(host, port)

class VirusScan(uploadhandler.FileUploadHandler):
    def receive_data_chunk(self, raw_data, start):
        try:
            if pyclamd.scan_stream(raw_data):
                # A virus was found, so the file should
                # be removed from the input stream.
                raise uploadhandler.SkipFile()
        except pyclamd.ScanError:
            # Clam AV couldn't be contacted, so the file wasn't scanned.
            # Since we can't guarantee the safety of any files,
            # no other files should be processed either.
            raise uploadhander.StopUpload()

        # If everything went fine, pass the data along
        return raw_data

    def file_complete(self, file_size):
        # This doesn't store the file anywhere, so it should
        # rely on other handlers to provide a File instance.
        return None
```

Your application may have more specific requirements, like explaining to users which virus was found and that they should consider cleaning their own system before attempting to share files with others. The key to this example is how easy it is to implement this type of behavior, which might seem very difficult on the surface.

Now What?

As much as there is to learn about accessing the protocols for these various types of backends, putting them to good use requires a good deal of imagination. There's only so much a book like this can say about how and why to access or replace these lower-level interfaces, so it's up to you to determine what's best for your environment and your applications.

While this chapter discussed how to use and overhaul major portions of Django's infrastructure, sometimes all that's needed is a simple utility to replace or avoid a lot of redundant code. It's important to know the difference, and the next chapter will outline the many basic utilities provided in Django's core distribution.

---

[8] http://prodjango.com/clamav/
[9] http://prodjango.com/pyclamd/

CHAPTER 9

■ ■ ■

Common Tools

While Django aims to provide a foundation for you to build your own Web application, the framework has its own underpinnings that tie it all together. These common tools and features help everything remain consistent and easier to maintain, and those same benefits can be used by your own applications. After all, what's available in Django is available for anything that uses it.

Core Exceptions (django.core.exceptions)

While Python comes with its own set of exceptions that can be raised in various situations, Django introduces enough complexity on top of that to merit some more. Since Django serves a specialty audience, these exceptions are considerably more specialized, but they're still usable by more than just core code. Some of these exceptions have been mentioned previously because they deal more specifically with a particular Django feature, but they're also useful in other situations, as the following sections will explain.

ImproperlyConfigured

This is one of the first exceptions most new users run into because it's the one raised when an application's models aren't set up correctly, a view can't be found or a number of other common configuration mistakes occur. It's typically raised during execution of manage.py validation and helps users identify and correct whatever mistakes were discovered.

Not all applications require any particular configuration, but those that do can make good use of this exception, since most users have seen it before. Common situations where this can be useful include missing or incorrect settings, a URL configuration used without an accompanying INSTALLED_APPS entry, invalid arguments given to custom model fields, and missing a required third-party library.

The most important thing to remember is to indicate not only that something went wrong, but also how the user should go about fixing it. Typically, exceptions indicate that some bit of code ran awry, and there's little to no way of informing a user how to fix it. With an application's configuration, however, there are a finite number of acceptable ways to set it up, and this error should be used as a way to steer users in the right direction.

For example, if an application is designed to work with audio files, it might require the presence of Mutagen,[1] a well-established Python library for extracting information from such files. A simple import of this library at the top of the models.py, where it's likely to be used, could identify if the library is installed correctly, and instruct the user how to proceed if not.

---

[1] http://prodjango.com/mutagen/

```
from django.core.exceptions import ImproperlyConfigured

try:
    import mutagen
except ImportError:
    raise ImproperlyConfigured("This application requires the Mutagen library.")
```

MiddlewareNotUsed

Chapter 7 described how middleware can be used to adjust how HTTP is handled, but an interesting side effect is that not all middleware is always useful. While each project has the option of setting just those middleware that are necessary by way of the `MIDDLEWARE_CLASSES` setting, there are still differences between development and production or among the various developers' computers.

Each middleware has the ability to decide whether its environment is suitable to be used and indicate if there's a problem. Middleware classes are instantiated automatically when first needed, at the beginning of the first request, which is where this check would take place. By overriding the class's `__init__()` method, middleware can check right away whether everything's set up to work properly and react accordingly.

Specifically, this reaction is to either return without doing anything if everything looks fine or raise `MiddlewareNotUsed`. If raised, Django will always catch this exception and take it to mean that the class should be removed from the list of middleware that gets applied on every request.

This is an important distinction to make because without being able to tell Django to not use the middleware at all, it would be up to each individual method to decide whether it should execute. While that would work, it would take up valuable time and memory on every request, checking for something that could be determined just once. By taking the middleware out of the list entirely, it never consumes any additional cycles or memory at all.

MultipleObjectsReturned

When retrieving objects from the database, it's often expected that exactly one row will be returned. This is always the case whenever the query is a primary key, but slugs—and perhaps even dates—can be made unique in certain applications. Django supports this situation with a QuerySet's `get()` method, and if it matches more than one result, it can throw off the whole execution of the application.

■ **Note**   Django's `SlugField` is almost always set as `unique=True` because it's used to identify objects in a URL.

Since `get()` is expected to return exactly one record from the database, a query matching multiple records is marked by an exception, `MultipleObjectsReturned`. It's not raised for other types of queries, since multiple records are to be expected in most situations. Catching this exception can be useful in a number of ways, from displaying more useful error messages to removing unexpected duplicates.

ObjectDoesNotExist

The other side of the `get()` expectation is that one row will always be returned; that is, there must always be a row in order to succeed. If a query that expects a row to exist finds instead that no such rows are present, Django responds accordingly with `ObjectDoesNotExist`. It works in much the same way as `MultipleObjectsReturned`, differing only in the situation where it's raised.

Simply called `DoesNotExist`, this subclass avoids an extra import because the class it's used on is typically already imported when the `get()` method is called. In addition, by being called `DoesNotExist` and being an attribute of a model class, it looks like perfectly readable English: `Article.DoesNotExist`.

PermissionDenied

Most applications will have some form of permissions in place to prevent access to restricted resources; this follows the pattern of a rule with exceptions. The rule is that the user attempting to access the resource will indeed have the correct permissions, so any user that doesn't will result in an exception—this time `PermissionDenied`. This serves as a convenient way to indicate the problem and stop processing the rest of the view, since the view itself could make changes that aren't valid if the user doesn't have the correct permissions.

Django also catches this exception automatically inside its request handler, using it as an instruction to return an HTTP 403 Forbidden response instead of the usual 200 OK. This will indicate to the client that the credentials provided didn't have sufficient permission to request the resource and that the user shouldn't try again without rectifying the situation. This behavior is provided by default in Django's own admin application but can also be used in any other.

Like other exceptions, `PermissionDenied` can be either raised or caught, though the default behavior of returning a special HTTP response code is appropriate most of the time. If some other behavior is desired, it's easy enough to create a middleware that catches this exception in the `process_view()` phase, possibly redirecting users to a form where they can contact the site administrators to request permission to access the page.

```
from django.core.exceptions import PermissionDenied
from django.http import HttpResponseRedirect
from django.core.urlresolvers import reverse

class PermissionRedirectMiddleware(object):
    def __init__(self, view='request_permission', args=None, kwargs=None):
        self.view = view
        self.args = args or ()
        self.kwargs = kwargs or {}

    def process_view(self, request, view, args, kwargs):
        try:
            response = view(request, *args, **kwargs)
        except PermissionDenied:
            url = reverse(self.view, args=self.args, kwargs=self.kwargs)
            return HttpResponseRedirect(url)
```

Adding a reference to this in `MIDDLEWARE_CLASSES` or creating a decorator out of it using `decorator_from_middleware()` as described in Chapter 7 is all that's necessary to redirect users to another page when their permissions weren't valid for the original request. Even without a custom handler for this exception, though, it's quite useful to raise it in any of your own views where a user doesn't satisfy the appropriate permissions. That response will then result in whatever handling is used for all other similar situations, helping make your site as cohesive and consistent as possible.

SuspiciousOperation

While users typically obey the rules and use your site the way it's expected to be used, any reasonable developer prepares for those who don't. Django takes a number of precautions to protect against unauthorized access to things like the administration interface and provides decorators to restrict access to application views, but there are still more subtle things to take into account.

For instance, the sessions framework needs to worry about users altering the session ID in an attempt to hijack another user's session. These types of things don't fall under authentication or permissions themselves, but rather a user is attempting to circumvent these usual protections. It's important to identify when this occurs, so it can be dealt with appropriately.

To identify these across the board, Django provides a SuspiciousOperation exception that can be used any time something like this happens. In many situations, this is thrown and caught in the same application but is provided so that it's possible to reach into the application and use just the portion that raises the exception. In other cases, it's left exposed to other applications to handle in whatever way makes the most sense.

The signed cookies application from Chapter 7 is a good example of where suspicious activity can be easily identified and handled. If a cookie comes in without a valid signature, it's clear that something fishy is going on and the signature validation code raises a SuspiciousOperation to signify it. Since it's designed to work as a hands-free middleware, it also provides code to catch this exception and perform a more useful function by removing the offending cookie from the request before it reaches the view. But since it's possible for other applications to sign and validate values outside the middleware, it's useful to raise an exception that accurately identifies what's going on.

ValidationError

Models and forms can both validate data before processing them further, and when that data is invalid, Django raises a ValidationError. This can be useful any time you have data to be validated, though, even outside those contexts. If you have an app that processes JSON data, for example, you may want to provide validation different from how models and forms work, and you may also want to validate the entire object, in addition to individual fields. You can maintain consistency with Django by reusing the same ValidationError that's used in other areas.

When instantiating a ValidationError, you can pass in a few different kind of objects, typically referring to the data that's invalid. Typically, you would pass in a printable object, such as a string or something that can be coerced to a string using the __str__() method. You can also pass in a list of such objects, or a dictionary where both the keys and values are printable, which allows you to combine several errors into a single exception. When printing the ValidationError in these cases, its internal code will automatically perform the necessary coercion to ensure you get strings.

■ **Note** The special handling for lists of dictionaries is limited to only lists and dictionaries. Other types of sequences and mappings will be treated as a standard printable object, without looking into it for individual values. Also, it will only look into the first level of data, so if you nest data within a list, for example, Django will only pull values out of the outer list; any inner lists will simply be coerced to strings.

ViewDoesNotExist

When resolving URLs, it's quite possible for an incoming URL to match a pattern in the URL configuration, but not match any known views. This could be for a variety of reasons, including a truly missing view, but it's also often due to an error that causes the view not to be loaded properly. After all, Django can only identify a proper view if Python can parse it and load it as a function. When any of these situations occur, Django raises ViewDoesNotExist to indicate, as best it can, what went wrong.

There's typically no need to manually catch this error or do anything special with it, since Django handles it as best as can be reasonably expected. In development, with DEBUG=True, it displays a useful error page with details on which view was attempted and a Python error message indicating why it couldn't be loaded. In production, that level of detail is unsafe, so it falls back to a standard HTTP 500 error, notifying the administrators behind the scenes.

Text Modification (django.utils.text)

At its core, the Web is a written medium, using text to convey the vast majority of ideas. Typically, this text is supplied as a combination of templates and database content, but it often needs a bit of massaging before it can be sent to users. It might have to be capitalized for use in a title, line-wrapped for use in an email or otherwise altered.

compress_string(s)

This simple utility compresses the input string using the gzip format. This allows you transfer content in a format that browsers are able to decompress on the other end.

```
>>> from django.utils.text import compress_string
>>> compress_string('foo')
'\x1f\x8b\x08\x00s={Q\x02\xffK\xcb\xcf\x07\x00!es\x8c\x03\x00\x00\x00'
```

Clearly this example doesn't look very compressed, but that's merely an artifact of how compression works with small strings. The headers and bookkeeping necessary for the compression algorithm are enough to make the string longer in these cases. When you supply a longer string, such as a file or a rendered template, you'll see a much smaller string in the output of this function.

■ **Note** If you're using this to send content to a browser, you'll also need to send a header to tell the browser how to handle it.

```
Content-Encoding: gzip
```

---

compress_sequence(sequence)

This works much like compress_string(), but it will compress individual items in the provided sequence. Rather than simply returning a string of all the compressed content, compress_sequence() is actually a generator, yielding content piece by piece. The first item in the output will be the gzip header, followed by compressed versions of each of the input strings and finally the gzip footer.

```
>>> for x in text.compress_sequence(['foo', 'bar', 'baz']):
...     print repr(x)
...
'\x1f\x8b\x08\x00\x16={Q\x02\xff'
'J\xcb\xcf\x07\x00\x00\x00\xff\xff'
'JJ,\x02\x00\x00\x00\xff\xff'
'JJ\xac\x02\x00\x00\x00\xff\xff'
"\x03\x00\xaa'x\x1a\t\x00\x00\x00"
```

get_text_list(items, last_word='or')

There are a number of ways to present a list of items to users, each appropriate for different situations. Rather than listing each item on its own line, it's often useful to display the list in plain English as a comma-separated list, such as, "red, blue and green." This may seem like a daunting task, but get_text_list() simplifies it considerably.

Simply pass in a list of items as the first argument and an optional conjunction to be used as the second argument, and it returns a string containing the items separated by a comma and the conjunction at the end.

```
>>> from django.utils.text import get_text_list
>>> 'You can use Python %s' % get_text_list([1, 2, 3])
u'You can use Python 1, 2 or 3'
>>> get_text_list(['me', 'myself', 'I'], 'and')
u'me, myself and I'
```

javascript_quote(s, quote_double_quotes=False)

When writing strings out to JavaScript, whether in source code or in a response code in JavaScript Object Notation (JSON),[2] there are certain considerations that have to be taken into account for special characters. This function properly escapes these special characters, including Unicode characters, in a way that JavaScript can understand.

```
>>> from django.utils.text import javascript_quote
>>> javascript_quote('test\ning\0')
'test\\ning\x00'
```

normalize_newlines(text)

When an application needs to work with text content coming from unknown sources, it's quite possible that input will be generated on a combination of Windows, Apple and Unix-style systems. These different platforms have different standards for what characters they use to encode line-endings, which can cause problems when the application needs to do any text processing on them. Given input like this, normalize_newlines() looks for the common line-ending alternatives and converts them all to the Unix-style \n that Python expects.

```
>>> from django.utils.text import normalize_newlines
>>> normalize_newlines(u'Line one\nLine two\rLine three\r\nLine four')
u'Line one\nLine two\nLine three\nLine four'
```

phone2numeric(phone)

Businesses often offer phone numbers as words to make them easier to remember. If phone numbers like that are offered as input to an application, they're typically only useful as-is if they're only ever displayed directly to users. If the application ever has to use those numbers as part of an automated system or show them to employees who make calls on a regular basis, it's more useful to work with them as raw numbers instead of marketing text. By passing phone numbers through phone2numeric(), you can be sure that you'll always get a real phone number to work with.

```
>>> from django.utils.text import phone2numeric
>>> phone2numeric(u'555-CODE')
u'555-2633'
```

---

[2] http://prodjango.com/json/

recapitalize(text)

Given a string that may have already been converted to lowercase, perhaps for search or other comparison, it's usually necessary to convert it back to regular mixed case before displaying it to users. The recapitalize() function does this, capitalizing letters that follow sentence-ending punctuation, such as periods and question marks.

```
>>> from django.utils.text import recapitalize
>>> recapitalize(u'does this really work? of course it does.')
u'Does this really work? Of course it does.'
```

■ **Caution**   Although Django provides many features for international audiences, the recapitalize() function only works for basic English text. Punctuation used in other languages may not be properly identified, causing the capitalized output to be incorrect.

slugify(value)

Slugs are a certain kind of string that's suitable for use in a URL, and often are a somewhat stripped down version of the article's title. Slugs consist of lower-case letters, hyphens instead of spaces, and a lack of punctuation and other non-word characters. The slugify() function takes a text value and performs the necessary transformations to make it suitable for use as a URL slug.

```
>>> from django.utils.text import slugify
>>> slugify(u'How does it work?')
u'how-does-it-work'
```

smart_split(text)

Originally developed as a way to parse template tag arguments, smart_split() takes a string and breaks it apart at spaces, while still leaving quoted passages intact. This is a good way to parse arguments for any other application, as it allows a great deal of flexibility. It recognizes both single and double quotes, safely handles escaped quotes and also leaves the quotes intact at the beginning and end of any quoted passages it comes across.

```
>>> from django.utils.text import smart_split
>>> for arg in smart_split('arg1 arg2 arg3'):
...     print arg
arg1
arg2
arg3
>>> for arg in smart_split('arg1 "arg2\'s longer" arg3'):
...     print arg
arg1
"arg2's longer"
arg3
```

unescape_entities(text)

HTML can contain entities that make it easier to represent certain international characters and other special glyphs that are difficult to type on most English keyboards or transfer using native English character encodings. These are useful when editing HTML by hand, but if you're using a broad text encoding like UTF-8, you can send the raw characters over the wire instead of relying on the browsers to convert them after the fact. By passing your string into this function, any HTML entities will be converted to the appropriate Unicode codepoints.

```
>>> from django.utils.text import unescape_entities
>>> unescape_entities('&ldquo;Curly quotes!&rdquo;')
u'\u201cCurly quotes!\u201d'
```

unescape_string_literal(s)

When writing a string that contains apostrophes or quotation marks, you often need to escape those characters by placing a backslash before them to avoid having them accidentally used to terminate the string. Because the use of a backslash for this purpose, you also need to escape any literal backslashes you want to include in the string.

Ordinarily, Python will interpret these directly and provide you with a string that has the raw characters in it, without the extra backslashes. In some cases, such as in templates, the strings aren't processed directly by Python, but are instead passed into your code as strings with the backslashes included. You can use unescape_string_literal() to get an equivalent string to what Python would normally provide.

```
>>> from django.utils.text import unescape_string_literal
>>> unescape_string_literal("'string'")
'string'
>>> unescape_string_literal('\'string\'')
'string'
```

wrap(text, width)

This takes the specified text and inserts newline characters as necessary to make sure that no line exceeds the width provided. It makes sure not to break up words, and also leaves existing newlines characters intact. It expects all newline characters to be Unix-style, though, so it's best to run the text through normalize_newlines() first if you are not controlling the source of the text to be sure it works properly.

```
>>> from django.utils.text import wrap
>>> text = """
... This is a long section of text, destined to be broken apart.
... It is only a test.
... """
...
>>> print wrap(text, 35)
This is a long section of text,
destined to be broken apart.
It is only a test.
```

Truncating Text

Another common need is to truncate text to fit into a smaller space. Whether you're limiting the number of words or characters, and whether you need to take HTML tags into account when truncating, Django has a Truncator class that can do the job. You can instantiate it by simply passing in the text you'd like to truncate.

```
>>> from django.utils.text import Truncator
```

For the sake of this example, we have to first configure Django not to use its internationalization system. If you're using manage.py shell, this will already be done for you, but if you're just using Python outside of a project, you'll need to configure this. In a real application, you won't need to perform this step.

```
>>> from django.conf import settings
>>> settings.configure(USE_I18N=False)
```

Now we have an environment capable of working with text transformations like this.

```
>>> truncate = Truncator('This is short, but you get the idea.')
```

From there, the actual operations are provided by any of the available methods.

Truncator.chars(num, truncate='…')

This method limits the text to contain no more than the number provided, without regard to any words or sentences in the original text.

```
>>> truncate.chars(20)
u'This is short, bu...'
```

■ **Note** The resulting string is 20 characters long, *including* the ellipsis. As you'll see, the truncate argument can change how many characters are used for the end of the string, and chars() will take that into account when deciding how much of the string to leave intact. Different settings for the truncate value will change how much of the original string remains. This behavior is unique to the chars() method.

The truncate argument specifies how the resulting string should be formatted. By default, it appends three periods after it, which will function as an ellipsis. You can supply any other string and it will be appended to the truncated string instead of the periods.

```
>>> truncate.chars(20, truncate='--')
u'This is short, but--'
```

You can also control the text output with more flexibility by specifying a format string, using a placeholder named truncated_text. This allows you place the truncated text anywhere within the string.

```
>>> truncate.charts(20, truncate='> %(truncated_text)s...')
u'> This is short, ...'
```

Truncator.words(num, truncate='…', html=False)

This method limits the length of the string to a specified number of words, rather than individual characters. This is usually preferable, as it avoids breaking in the middle of a word. Because words can be of varying lengths, the resulting string is less predictable than when using chars(), though.

```
>>> truncate.words(5)
u'This is short, but you...'
>>> truncate.words(4, truncate='--')
u'This is short, but--'
```

Also notice that the truncate argument no longer alters how the string gets truncated. Your text will be reduced to the specified number of words, and the truncate argument will be applied after that.

The html argument controls whether the method should avoid counting HTML attributes as separate words, because they're separated by spaces. For normal text, the default of False is preferable, as it has less work to do, but if you're outputting a string that may have HTML tags in it, you'll want to use True instead.

```
>>> truncate = Truncator('This is <em class="word">short</em>, but you get the idea.')
>>> truncate.words(4)
u'This is <em class="word">short</em>,...'
>>> truncate.words(4, html=True)
u'This is <em class="word">short</em>, but...'
>>> truncate.words(3)
u'This is <em...'
>>> truncate.words(3, html=True)
u'This is <em class="word">short</em>,...'
```

Another advantage of using html=True is that it takes care to close tags that would otherwise be left open when the string is truncated.

```
>>> truncate = Truncator('This is short, <em>but you get the idea</em>.')
>>> truncate.words(5)
u'This is short, <em>but you...'
>>> truncate.words(5, html=True)
u'This is short, <em>but you...</em>'
```

Data Structures (django.utils.datastructures)

When working with any complex system, it's often necessary to work with data in a very specific structure. This might be a sequential list of items, a mapping of keys to values, a hierarchical tree of categories, any combination of those or something else entirely. While Django doesn't pretend to provide objects for every arrangement of data an application might need, there are a few specific things that the framework itself requires, and these are made available to all applications based on it as well.

DictWrapper

This is a good example of a data structure designed for a fairly specific purpose that might have other uses in the real world. The goal of this particular type of dictionary is to provide a way to transform values on retrieval, if the requested key matches a basic criterion.

When instantiating the dictionary, you can supply a function and a prefix string. Any time you request a key that begins with that prefix, the DictWrapper will strip off the prefix and call the supplied function on the associated value before returning it. Other than that, it works just like a standard dictionary.

```
>>> from django.utils.datastructures import DictWrapper
>>> def modify(value):
...     return 'Transformed %s' % value
>>> d = DictWrapper({'foo': 'bar'}, modify, 'transformed_')
>>> d['foo']
'bar'
>>> d['transformed_foo']
'Transformed: bar'
```

ImmutableList

The difference between a list and a tuple is typically described in terms of their contents. Lists can contain any number of objects, all of which should be of the same type, so that you can iterate over them and process each item just like all the others. Essentially, a list is a collection of values.

A tuple, on the other hand, is a whole value on its own, where each item within it has a specific meaning, indicated by its position. Any particular type of tuple would have the same number of values within it. For example, a three-dimensional point in space might be represented by a 3-item tuple, containing x, y and z coordinates. Every such point would have those same three values, and always in the same positions.

A key technical distinction between the two is that tuples are immutable. In order to change a tuple, you actually need to create a new tuple with the changed values. That immutability can be a useful safety net to ensure that the sequence doesn't change out from under you, and it's also a slight performance boost because tuples are simpler data structures. They're not intended to be used as an immutable list, though.

For those situations where you have the semantics of a list, but also want the benefits of immutability, Django provides an alternative: the ImmutableList. It's a subclass of tuple, but it also contains all the mutable methods available on lists. The only difference is that those methods each raise an AttributeError, rather than alter the value. It's a subtle distinction, but it does give you the opportunity to take advantage of tuples, while still using the semantics of a list.

MergeDict

When multiple dictionaries need to be accessed together, the typical approach is to create a new dictionary that contains all the keys and values of those dictionaries together. This works well for simple applications, but it may well be necessary to maintain the mutability of the underlying dictionaries so that changes to them are reflected in the combined dictionary. The following shows how that breaks down with standard dictionaries.

```
>>> dict_one = {'a': 1, 'b': 2, 'c': 3}
>>> dict_two = {'c': 4, 'd': 5, 'e': 6}
>>> combined = dict(dict_one, **dict_two)
>>> combined['a'], combined['c'], combined['e']
(1, 4, 6)
>>> dict_one['a'] = 42
>>> combined['a']
1
```

This illustrates a simple approach at combining dictionaries, using the fact that dict() can accept both a dictionary and keyword arguments, combining them into a new dictionary. Thanks to the ** syntax described in detail in Chapter 2, this makes it a convenient way to achieve the desired result, but the example also shows where it starts to fail.

First, it only accepts two dictionaries; adding more would require calling dict() more than once, adding a new dictionary each time. Perhaps more importantly, updates to the source dictionaries don't get reflected in the combined structure. To be clear, this is ordinarily a good thing, but in cases like request.REQUEST, which combines request.GET and request.POST, changes made to the underlying dictionaries should also be revealed in the combined output.

To facilitate all of this, Django uses its own class that acts like a dictionary in many respects, but transparently accesses multiple dictionaries behind the scenes. There's no limit to the number of dictionaries that can be accessed this way. Simply supply as many dictionaries as needed when instantiating the object, and they'll be accessed in the order they're provided. Since it stores references to the real dictionaries and accesses them instead of creating a new one, modifications to the underlying dictionaries are reflected in the composite.

```
>>> from django.utils.datastructures import MergeDict
>>> dict_one = {'a': 1, 'b': 2, 'c': 3}
>>> dict_two = {'c': 4, 'd': 5, 'e': 6}
>>> combined = MergeDict(dict_one, dict_two)
>>> combined['a'], combined['c'], combined['e']
(1, 3, 6)
>>> dict_one['a'] = 42
>>> combined['a']
42
```

Since keys are checked in the internal dictionaries in the same order they were passed in to MergeDict, combined['c'] is 3 in the second example, while it was 4 in the first one.

MultiValueDict

On another extreme, it's sometimes useful to have each key in a dictionary potentially reference more than one value. Since Web browsers send data to the server as a series of name/value pairs, without any more formal structure, it's possible for a single name to be sent multiple times, probably with a different value each time. Dictionaries are designed to map one name to only one value, so this presents a challenge.

On the surface, it seems like the solution is simple: just store a list of values under each key. Digging a bit deeper, one problem is that the vast majority of applications only use one value for each key, so always using a list would make more work for everybody. Instead, the majority case should be able to use a single key to access a single value, while still allowing all the values to be accessed for those applications that need them.

Django uses MultiValueDict to handle this case, basing its default behavior on what most other frameworks do in this situation. By default, accessing a key in a MultiValueDict returns the last value that was submitted with that name. If all the values are required, a separate getlist() method is available to return the full list, even if it only contains one item.

```
>>> from django.utils.datastructures import MultiValueDict
>>> d = MultiValueDict({'a': ['1', '2', '3'], 'b': ['4'], 'c': ['5', '6']})
>>> d['a'], d['b'], d['c']
('3', '4', '6')
>>> d.getlist('a')
['1', '2', '3']
>>> d.getlist('b')
['4']
>>> d.getlist('c')
['5', '6']
```

> ■ **Caution** This doesn't automatically coerce each value to a list. If you pass in a single item for any of the values, that value will be returned as expected, but getlist() will return the original value as it was passed in. That means getlist() will return the single item only, not a list containing a single item.

```
>>> d = MultiValueDict({'e': '7'})
>>> d['e']
'7'
>>> d.getlist('e')
'7'
```

SortedDict

One of the more obscure features of Python dictionaries is that they're technically unsorted. Inspecting a variety of dictionaries may seem to yield some patterns, but they can't be relied on, as they will differ between Python implementations. This can be quite a stumbling block at times because it's easy to accidentally rely on the implicit ordering of dictionaries, only to find it change out from under you when you least expect.

It's quite common to need a reliably ordered dictionary, so that both Python code and templates can know what to expect when they encounter a dictionary. In Django, this feature is provided by the SortedDict, which keeps track of the order its keys were added to the dictionary. The first step in utilizing this functionality is to pass in an ordered sequence of key/value pairs. This order is then preserved, as well as the order that any subsequent keys are given new values.

```
>>> from django.utils.datastructures import SortedDict
>>> d = SortedDict([('c', '1'), ('d', '3'), ('a', '2')])
>>> d.keys()
['c', 'd', 'a']
>>> d.values()
['1', '3', '2']
>>> d['b'] = '4'
>>> d.items()
[('c', '1'), ('d', '3'), ('a', '2'), ('b', '4')]
```

Functional Utilities (django.utils.functional)

Python treats functions as first-class objects. They have certain attributes and methods associated with them that are obviously different from other objects, but the core language treats them just like any other object. This handling allows for some very interesting uses of functions, such as setting attributes at run-time and assembling functions in a list, to be executed in order.

cached_property(func)

A property is one of the simplest kinds of descriptors because the common case simply calls a method when the attribute is accessed. This can be useful for ensuring that its value is always up to date if it relies on other attributes or external factors. Each time you access the attribute, the method is called and a new value is produced.

```
>>> class Foo(object):
...     @property
...     def bar(self):
...         print('Called the method!')
...         return 'baz'
...
>>> f = Foo()
>>> f.bar
Called the method!
'baz'
>>> f.bar
Called the method!
'baz'
```

Sometimes, though, you have a value that doesn't change but can be expensive to produce. You don't want to generate the value if you don't need to, but you also don't want to produce it more than once. To address this situation, you can use the @cached_property decorator. Applying this to a method will cause the method to be called the first time the attribute is accessed, but it will store the result on the object, so that every subsequent access will just get the stored value, rather than calling the method again.

```
>>> from django.utils.functional import cached_property
>>> class Foo(object):
...     @cached_property
...     def bar(self):
...         print('Called the method!')
...         return 'baz'
...
>>> f = Foo()
>>> f.bar
Called the method!
'baz'
>>> f.bar
'baz'
```

curry(func)

It's often necessary to take a function with a complex set of arguments and simplify it so that code that calls it doesn't always need to supply all the arguments. The most obvious way to do this is by providing default values wherever possible, as described in Chapter 2. In many situations, though, there isn't a sensible default at the time the function is written or the default value might not be suitable to the needs of the situation. Normally, you can just call the function with whatever argument values you need, which works just fine for most needs.

Sometimes, though, the function's arguments are determined at a different time than when it actually needs to be called. For instance, it's quite common to pass a function around so it can be used later, whether as an instance method or a callback, or even a module-level function. When using a function that accepts more arguments than will be provided later, the remaining arguments must be specified in advance.

Since Python 2.5, this functionality is provided in the standard library, by way of the functools.partial function. While being bundled with Python is convenient, it's only useful for subsequent installations, while Django supports versions of Python that have been around far longer. Instead, Django provides its own implementation at django.utils.functional.curry.

The first argument to curry is always a callable, which won't be called right away, but will be tucked away to be used later. Beyond that, all positional and keyword arguments are saved as well, and will be applied to the supplied callable when the time comes. The return value is then a new function that, when called, will execute the original callable with both the original arguments *and* any arguments that were provided in the call that came later.

```
>>> from django.utils.functional import curry
>>> def normalize_value(value, max_value, factor=1, comment='Original'):
...     """
...     Normalizes the given value according to the provided maximum,
...     scaling it according to factor.
...     """
...     return '%s (%s)' % (float(value) / max_value * factor, comment)
>>> normalize_value(3, 4)
'0.75 (Original)'
>>> normalize_value(3, 4, factor=2, comment='Double')
'1.5 (Double)'
>>> percent = curry(normalize_value, max_value=100, comment='Percent')
>>> percent(50)
'0.5 (Percent)'
>>> percent(50, factor=2, comment='Double')
'1.0 (Double)'
>>> tripled = curry(normalize_value, factor=3, comment='Triple')
>>> tripled(3, 4)
'2.25 (Triple)'
```

lazy(func, *resultclasses)

Some values can be represented differently depending on their environment. A common example is translatable text, where the internal value is typically in English, but it can be represented using a different language selected by a user. Objects with behavior like this are considered lazy, because they're not populated right away, but later, when necessary.

You can create a lazy object using this lazy() function. The primary argument it accepts is a function that can produce the eventual value. That function won't be called right away, but will simply be stored away inside a Promise object. The promise can then be passed around throughout framework code like Django, which doesn't care what the object is, until it finally reaches code that does care about the object. When attempting to access the promise, the function will be called and the value returned. In fact, the function will be called every time the object is accessed, each time with the chance to use the environment to alter the returned value.

The interesting part of this process is how the promise determines whether it's being accessed. When simply passing around an object, the object itself has no access to what code keeps a reference to it. It can, however, react when its attributes are accessed. So when your code tries to access the attributes of a promise, that becomes a cue to generate a new representation of the promised value.

The remaining arguments to the lazy() function help with this part of the process. The resultclasses you specify should contain all the different types of objects that your function can return. Each of these classes has a set of attributes and methods on it, which the promise can then listen for. When any one of them is accessed, the promise will call its stored function to return a new value, then return the attribute on that value that was originally requested.

This can be particularly difficult to understand without an example. Translations are a common example, but another useful case is when working with dates and times. Specifically, social networks will often display the date and time of a particular event in terms of how long ago the event occurred, rather than as an absolute date. Django has a utility available for calculating this immediately, but you could also use it to create a lazy object. Then, every time it's displayed, your code can calculate the time difference on demand.

Like we saw earlier, this example requires us to first configure Django not to use its internationalization system, if you're not using manage.py shell.

```
>>> from django.conf import settings
>>> settings.configure(USE_I18N=False)
```

Now the system is configured to use the timesince() function. Located in django.utils.timesince, you can simply pass in a date or datetime object and it will return a string containing a human-readable representation of the duration between now and the date you passed in.

```
>>> import datetime
>>> from django.utils.timesince import timesince
>>> then = datetime.datetime.now() - datetime.timedelta(minutes=1)
>>> since = timesince(then)
>>> since
u'1 minute'
>>> print(since)
1 minute
```

That's how it normally works, returning the duration immediately. Then you're left with a string that was only valid when the function was called. A lazy object will work like a string when it needs to, but will evaluate the function whenever it needs to yield a value.

```
>>> from django.utils.functional import lazy
>>> lazy_since = lazy(timesince, str)(then)
>>> lazy_since
<django.utils.functional.__proxy__ at 0x...>
>>> print(lazy_since)
1 minute

# Wait a few minutes...

>>> print(lazy_since)
5 minutes
```

allow_lazy(func, *resultclasses)

This decorator provides another way to work with lazy options like those described in the preceding section. Most functions operate on actual objects, without knowing anything about the deferred loading behavior of lazy objects, and will just access the object's attributes directly. If you provide a lazy object to such a function, it will immediately trigger the value, which may not be very useful if the function simply transforms the value.

```
>>> def bold(value):
...     return u'<b>%s</b>' % value
...
>>> bold(lazy_since)
```

u'10 minutes'It'd be better if the new function call could be lazy as well, and even better still if you could do that without changing the function's code. That's where allow_lazy() comes into play. You can apply this to any function, so that when you call the function, it will check to see if any of the incoming arguments are lazy. If any of them are in fact lazy objects, the wrapper will step in and return a new lazy object backed by the original function. Otherwise, the original function will immediately run on the non-lazy arguments provided.

```
>>> from django.utils.functional import allow_lazy
>>> lazy_bold = allow_lazy(bold, str)
>>> lazy_bold(lazy_since)
<django.utils.functional.__proxy__ at 0x...>
>>> lazy_bold(since)
u'<b>1 minute</b>'
>>> print lazy_bold(lazy_since)
u'<b>2 minutes</b>
```

lazy_property(fget=None, fset=None, fdel=None)

Properties are a very useful way to wrap custom behavior around simple attribute access. For example, you could use a property to generate attribute values on demand or update related information when an attribute's value is changed. One potential problem with them, though, is that they wrap specific functions when they're first added to a class. Subclasses can inherit each property's behavior, but it will always use the functions that were provided to the original decorator. The only way the subclass can override a property's behavior is to create a whole new property, completely replacing every aspect of the property.

```
>>> class Foo(object):
...     def _get_prop(self):
...         return 'foo'
...     prop = property(_get_prop)
...
>>> class Bar(Foo):
...     def _get_prop(self):
...         return 'bar'
...
>>> Foo().prop
'foo'
>>> Bar().prop
'foo'
```

In order to allow a subclass to more easily override specific property behavior, you can create your property using the lazy_property() function. This will automatically look at whichever subclass is accessing the property and use any overridden functions you've added, falling back to the original functions otherwise.

```
>>> from django.utils.functional import lazy_property
>>> class Foo(object):
...     def _get_prop(self):
...         return 'foo'
...     prop = lazy_property(_get_prop)
...
>>> class Bar(Foo):
...     def _get_prop(self):
...         return 'bar'
...
>>> Foo().prop
'foo'
>>> Bar().prop
'bar'
```

memoize(func, cache, num_args)

When working with a lot of information, it's often necessary for functions to make certain basic calculations where the only true variables—that is, values that change from one call to the next—are the arguments that are passed in. To reuse a term mentioned in Chapter 7, this behavior makes the function idempotent; given the same arguments, the result will be the same, regardless of how many times the function is called. This is, in fact, the original mathematical meaning of the term, which was borrowed for use with HTTP methods.

Idempotence provides an interesting disconnect between humans and computers. While humans can easily identify when a function is idempotent and learn to memorize the result rather than continue carrying out the function each time (remember learning your multiplication tables?), computers aren't so lucky. They'll happily churn away at the function time and time again, never realizing how much unnecessary time it takes. This can be a big problem in data-intensive applications, where a function might take a very long time to execute or be executed with the same arguments hundreds or thousands of times.

It's possible for a program to take the same shortcut that we humans learn as children, but not without a little help. Django provides this assistance by way of the memoize() function, also located at django.utils.functional. It simply takes any standard function and returns a wrapper around it that records the arguments being used and maps them to the value the function returns for those arguments. Then, when those same arguments are passed in again, it simply finds and returns the value that was previously calculated, without running the original function again.

In addition to the function to be called, memoize() takes two other arguments, used to determine how its cache of return values should be managed.

- cache—A dictionary where the values will be stored, with the key being the arguments passed in to the function. Any dictionary-like object will work here, so it's possible, for instance, to write a dictionary wrapper around Django's low-level cache—described in Chapter 8—and have multiple threads, processes or even entire machines all share the same memoization cache.

- num_args—The number of arguments that are combined to form the key in the dictionary cache. This is typically the total number of arguments the function accepts, but can be lower if there are optional arguments that don't affect the return value.

```python
>>> from django.utils.functional import memoize
>>> def median(value_list):
...     """
...     Finds the median value of a list of numbers
...     """
...     print 'Executing the function!'
...     value_list = sorted(value_list)
...     half = int(len(value_list) / 2)
...     if len(value_list) % 2:
...         # Odd number of values
...         return value_list[half]
...     else:
...         # Even number of values
...         a, b = value_list[half - 1:half + 1]
...         return float(a + b) / 2
>>> primes = (2, 3, 5, 7, 11, 13, 17)
>>> fibonacci = (0, 1, 1, 2, 3, 5, 8, 13)
>>> median(primes)
Executing the function!
7
```

```
>>> median(primes)
Executing the function!
7
>>> median = memoize(median, {}, 1)
>>> median(primes)
Executing the function!
7
>>> median(primes)
7
>>> median(fibonacci)
Executing the function!
2.5
>>> median(fibonacci)
2.5
```

NOTE ABOUT MEMOIZING ARGUMENTS

Because the function's arguments will be used in a dictionary to map to return values, they must be hashable values. Typically, this means anything immutable, but certain other types of objects may be hashable as well. For example, the median() function described in this section would throw an error if passed a list instead of a tuple. Because the contents of a list can change, they can't be used as a dictionary key.

---

partition(predicate, values)

This is a simple utility function that will split a sequence of values into two lists, depending on the result of passing each value to the predicate function. The return value is a 2-tuple, with the first item in that tuple being the False responses, while the second item contains the True responses.

```
>>> from django.utils.functional import partition
>>> partition(lambda x: x > 4, range(10))
([0, 1, 2, 3, 4], [5, 6, 7, 8, 9])
```

The predicate is expected to return True or False, but internally partition() actually takes advantage of the fact that True and False are equivalent to 1 and 0, respectively, when they're used as indexes to a sequence. That means that if you have a predicate that already returns 1 and 0, you don't need to convert it to use True and False instead.

```
>>> even, odd = parittion(lambda x: x % 2, range(10))
>>> even
[0, 2, 4, 6, 8]
>>> odd
[1, 3, 5, 7, 9]
```

wraps(func)

Chapter 2 described decorators in detail, but there's one aspect of them that can cause problems in some situations because decorators often return a wrapper around the original function. This wrapper is, in fact, an entirely different function than what was written in the source file, so it has different attributes as well. When introspecting functions, this can cause confusion if several functions are passed through the same decorator because they would all share similar properties, including their names.

```
>>> def decorator(func):
...     def wrapper(*args, **kwargs):
...         return func(*args, **kwargs)
...     return wrapper
>>> def test():
...     print 'Testing!'
>>> decorated = decorator(test)
>>> decorated.__name__
'wrapper'
```

To help ease this situation, Django includes a copy of Python's own wraps() function, which was first introduced in Python 2.5. wraps() is actually another decorator, which copies details of the original function onto the wrapper function, so it looks more like the original when everything's done. Just pass in the original function to wraps() and use it as you would any other decorator on your wrapper, and it'll do the rest.

```
>>> from django.utils.functional import wraps
>>> def decorator(func):
...     @wraps(func)
...     def wrapper(*args, **kwargs):
...         return func(*args, **kwargs)
...     return wrapper
>>> def test():
...     print 'Testing!'
>>> decorated = decorator(test)
>>> decorated.__name__
'test'
```

■ **Caution**   Unfortunately, wraps() can't make the wrapper completely identical to the original function. In particular, its function signature will always reflect that of the wrapper function, so attempting to introspect the arguments of decorated functions will likely result in some confusion. Still, for automated documentation and debugging purposes, having wraps() update the name and other information is quite useful.

Signals

An important aspect of a large application is knowing when certain things happen in other parts of the application. Even better is the ability to do something the instant that event happens. For this purpose, Django includes a signal dispatcher that allows code to broadcast the occurrence of an event, while providing a method for other code to listen for those broadcasts and react accordingly, the instant the event occurs. It identifies the type of event being broadcast by allowing code to define unique signals to dispatch.

This concept of dispatching and the code that enables it isn't unique to Django, but its implementation is customized for the needs of a Web application. This implementation is located at django.dispatch.dispatcher, though it's designed to be used through the simple Signal object, available at django.dispatch. Django uses signals in a variety of places, many of which have been documented elsewhere in this book, in the areas where they're used. The following sections discuss in more generality how signals and dispatching work, and how to register listeners for particular events.

How It Works

The basic process is fairly simple. Each step will be explained in more detail in individual sections, but the following should serve as a good overview.

First, some Python code defines a signal. As described in the next section, this is a `Signal` object that is placed in a reliable location. This object represents an event that is expected to occur at some point in time—possibly multiple times. The dispatcher doesn't use any central registration of signals; it's up to your own code to know which signal to use at any given time.

When your code triggers an event that you'd like other code to know about, your code sends some information to the signal, including a "sender" object representing where the event is coming from and any arguments that describe other details of the event. The signal itself identifies just the *type* of event; these additional arguments describe what's happening at a particular time.

The signal then looks at its list of registered listeners to see if any of them match the provided signal and sender, and calls each function it finds in turn, passing along whatever arguments the signal was given when the event was triggered. Registration of listeners can happen at any time, and the signal will update its registry when a new listener is added, so that future events will include the new listener.

Defining a Signal

A signal doesn't need to implement any kind of protocol, or even supply any attributes. They're really just vehicles to use for advertising when an event occurs; they're simply instances of `Signal`. The real key to defining a successful signal is just in making sure that it doesn't get replaced. A signal object must always be available from the same import location, and it must always be the same object. The dispatcher requires this because it uses the object as an identifier, to match the event being dispatched with the appropriate listeners that have been registered.

```
>>> from django.dispatch import Signal
>>> signal = Signal()
>>> signal
<django.dispatch.dispatcher.Signal object at 0x...>
```

Sending a Signal

Whenever you'd like to notify other code of an event occurrence, signals provide a `send()` method to send that signal to any registered listeners. This method requires a `sender`, which represents the object that was responsible for dispatching the signal, which allows listeners to respond to events coming from a particular object. Typically, Django uses a class—such as a model—as the `sender`, so that listeners can be registered prior to any instances being created, while also allowing for listeners to respond to events on all instances of that class.

In addition to a sender, `send()` also accepts any number of additional keyword arguments, which will be passed through directly to listeners. As shown in the next section, listeners must always accept all keyword arguments, regardless of what they actually use. This allows the sending code to add new information to a signal later on, without causing any problems with listeners that haven't yet been updated to use that new information. It's quite likely that the code that sends a signal will have features added to it later on, and this keyword argument support makes it easy to incorporate those features into existing signals.

Once all the listeners have been called, `send()` returns a list of the responses returned by the registered listeners. This list contains a sequence of 2-tuples, of the format (`listener, response`). Django's own signals don't typically use any return values, but they can be quite useful to support plugins that send information back to the application itself.

```
>>> from django.dispatch import Signal
>>> signal = Signal()
>>> sender = object()
>>> signal.send(sender=sender, spam='eggs')
[]
```

Capturing Return Values

Functions are often expected to return a value, and signals can take full advantage of that. When each listener is called with the signal's arguments, Django captures its return value and collects all of them together in a list. Once all the listeners have been called, the full list of return values is then returned from Signal.send(), allowing the calling code to access any information provided by the listeners. This allows signals to be used for more than just extra actions; they can also be used for data processing and related tasks.

Defining a Listener

When sent, the signal passes the sender and all appropriate arguments to each listener function that is registered with that signal. A listener is simply a Python function like any other; the only difference is the fact of having been registered as a listener for a particular signal. Since the signal simply calls the listener as a function, it can actually be any valid Python callable, many of which are described in Chapter 2. In practice, standard functions are the most common.

While listeners are allowed a great deal of flexibility, signals do make one important assumption about how they're defined: all listeners must accept any keyword arguments that are passed in. Which arguments are actually used depends entirely on how a particular listener intends to use the signal, but it *must* accept unused arguments without error. As shown previously, signals may be sent with any number of keyword arguments, and these will all be passed along to all listeners.

The value in this approach is that listeners don't need to know about everything the signal is responsible for. A listener can be attached for one purpose, expecting a specific set of arguments. Then, additional arguments can be added to the signal dispatch, and all previously defined listeners will continue to function properly. As with any other function call, if a listener expects an argument that isn't provided with the signal, Python will raise a TypeError.

```
def listener(sender, a, **kwargs):
    return a * 3
```

Registering Listeners

Once you have a signal to work with and a listener intended to work with it, connecting them is a simple call to the signal's connect() method. In addition to one required argument, there are a few options that can be specified when registering a signal, customizing how that listener should be handled when the signal is dispatched later on.

- receiver—The callable that will receive the signal and its associated arguments. This is obviously required for all registrations.

- sender—A specific object to watch for signals. Since every signal must include a sender, this allows a listener to respond to just that one sender. If omitted, the listener will be called for all senders that issue the given signal.

- weak—A Boolean indicating whether weak references should be used, a topic described in more detail in the next section. This defaults to True, using weak references by default.

- dispatch_uid—A unique string used to identify the listener on the given signal. Since modules can sometimes get imported more than once, it's possible for listeners to get registered twice, which will often cause problems. Supplying a unique string here will ensure that the listener only gets registered once, no matter how many times a module gets imported. If omitted, an ID will be generated based on the listener itself.

Forcing Strong References

While weak references are a fairly complex topic, well beyond the scope of this book,[3] signals' use of them can cause confusion in certain situations, so it's worth giving a basic overview of the problem and its solution. When an object is referenced using a weak reference, as done by Django's dispatcher, this reference alone will not keep the object from being garbage collected. It must still have a strong reference somewhere else, or Python will automatically destroy it and free the memory it occupies.

While standard references in Python are strong, the dispatcher, by default, uses weak references to maintain its list of registered listeners. This is generally preferable with signals, because it means that listener functions that belong to code no longer in use won't use up valuable time and energy by being called.

However, some situations in Python would ordinarily cause an object to be destroyed, and these situations require special attention when using signals. In particular, if a listener function is defined inside another function—perhaps to customize a function for a particular object—the listener will be destroyed when its container function finishes executing and its scope is removed.

```
>>> from django.dispatch import Signal
>>> signal = Signal()
>>> def weak_customizer():
...     def weak_handler(sender, **kwargs):
...         pass
...     signal.connect(weak_handler)
...
>>> def strong_customizer():
...     def strong_handler(sender, **kwargs):
...         pass
...     signal.connect(strong_handler, weak=False)
...
>>> weak_customizer()
>>> strong_customizer()
>>> signal.send(sender="sender")
[(<function <strong_handler> at 0x...>, None)]
```

As you can see, the default form of registering the listener allows the function to be destroyed once its customization function finishes executing. By specifying weak=False explicitly, it survives to be called when the signal is sent at a later point in time.

Now What?

The tools laid out in this chapter won't provide major new features for your applications, but they can help with many of the simpler tasks many applications need. These little things can really help tie it all together. How the application actually gets used is another issue, with some of the more interesting options described in the next chapter.

---

[3] http://prodjango.com/weak-references/

CHAPTER 10

■ ■ ■

Coordinating Applications

Writing software for a business is hard work. There is no single rule book that outlines which applications to write, how they should be written, how they should interact with each other, or how customizable they should be. The answers to all these concerns are best left to developers on each project, but the examples shown throughout this chapter and Chapter 11 may help you decide the best approach for your project.

Much of a site's functionality is outward-facing, providing features to users outside the organization. Many times, more functionality is focused inward, intended to help employees perform their daily tasks more effectively. Consider a basic real estate web site that needs to keep track of its clients and available properties. In addition to just displaying properties to the outside world, agents also need to manage those properties and the people who help the process move along.

Rather than building one large application geared toward a specific need, it's more valuable to try to pull those needs apart, having multiple applications that work together to achieve the final goal. Doing so will require a bit more work in the beginning, but as new features keep getting added, clean separation of applications will help determine what should go where and how everything should work together.

Contacts

While it may seem like everything in the real estate world revolves around property, people are still the most fundamental piece of the puzzle. For example, a given property could have an owner, a real estate agent, and several prospective buyers. These people each fill a different role in the real estate process, but the data necessary to represent them is the same, regardless of the roles they play. They can all be generalized into a "contact" that simply contains the data necessary to identify and communicate with them.

This abstraction provides us a simple model that can be used for people related to a specific property, others who haven't yet expressed interest in a property, employees within our fictional real estate office itself, and even third-party contacts like quality inspectors and value assessors. What roles each person plays can be defined later by relating them to another model, such as a property.

contacts.models.Contact

Contact information typically consists of things like a person's name, address, phone number, and email address, some of which can already be captured by Django. The User model from `django.contrib.auth` contains fields for a person's first and last names as well as an email address, so all that's left is to include some of the more real-world contact information. Relating it to User allows a single contact to contain both types of data, while also opening up the possibility of contacts who can log in later.

Because our real estate company will operate in the United States, there are some specific fields available for contact information that will need to validate data according to local customs. To provide support for regional data types, there are a variety of local flavor packages available. Each package, including the `django-localflavor-us` that we'll be using, contains a selection of fields for models and forms that are specific to that region's common data types. Our Contact model can take advantage of `PhoneNumberField` and `USStateField` in particular.

```
from django.db import models
from django.contrib.auth.models import User
from django_localflavor_us import models as us_models

class Contact(models.Model):
    user = models.OneToOneField(User)
    phone_number = us_models.PhoneNumberField()
    address = models.CharField(max_length=255)
    city = models.CharField(max_length=255)
    state = us_models.USStateField()
    zip_code = models.CharField(max_length=255)

    class Meta:
        ordering = ('user__last_name', 'user__first_name')

    def __unicode__(self):
        return self.user.get_full_name()
```

WHY NOT MODEL INHERITANCE?

Chapter 3 explained how one Django model can directly inherit from another, automatically creating a reference similar to the one used here. Because that also adds some extra ease-of-use options, you may be wondering why Contact doesn't just inherit from User directly.

Model inheritance is best suited for situations where you won't be using the base model directly because Django doesn't provide a way to add an inherited instance to existing models. In our case, that means if a User already exists in the database, we wouldn't be able to create a new Contact based on it. Since there are many other applications, including Django's admin application, that might create users directly, we need to be able to create contacts for either new or existing users without any trouble.

By using a OneToOneField explicitly, we're defining the exact same relationship that model inheritance would use, but without the different syntax that restricts us in this case. We lose a few of the syntax benefits that true inheritance provides, but those can be accommodated another way.

Because a contact is essentially just a user with some added attributes, it's useful to have all the attributes available on a single object. Otherwise, template authors would have to know not only which model a given attribute comes from, but also how to refer to the other model to retrieve those attributes. For example, given a Contact object named contact, the following list shows many of its attributes and methods:

- contact.user.username
- contact.user.get_full_name()
- contact.user.email
- contact.phone_number
- contact.address
- contact.zip_code

This introduces an unnecessary burden on template authors who shouldn't need to know what type of relationship exists between contacts and users. Model inheritance alleviates this directly by placing all attributes on the contact directly. This same behavior can be achieved here by simply using a set of properties that map various attributes to the related user object behind the scenes.

```
@property
def first_name(self):
    return self.user.first_name

@property
def last_name(self):
    return self.user.last_name

def get_full_name(self):
    return self.user.get_full_name()
```

Not all methods of User make sense on Contact. For instance, the is_anonymous() and is_authenticated() methods are best left on User. Views and templates won't be using a contact to determine authentication or permissions, so a contact will instead serve as a central location for all aspects of a person's identity information.

contacts.forms.UserEditorForm

Rather than requiring users to manage their contacts through the admin interface, it's more useful to have a separate form that can be devoted solely to contact management. This is even more important for contacts than most other models because contacts actually comprise two separate models. Django's provided ModelForm helper[1] maps one form to one model, requiring the contacts application to use two separate forms to manage a single person.

A single form could contain all the fields necessary for both models, but that wouldn't work with ModelForm because the form would have to contain all the necessary logic for populating and saving the models manually. Instead, two independent forms can be used, with a view tying them together. See the description of contacts.views.EditContact for details.

Because Django provides the User model on its own, it would seem logical to reuse whatever Django uses for managing users. Unfortunately, the forms provided for user management are designed for very different use cases than contact management. There are two forms available, both living at django.contrib.auth.forms, each with a different purpose:

- UserCreationForm—Intended for the most basic user creation possible, this form accepts only a username and two copies of the password (for verification). The fields needed for contacts— name and email—are unavailable.

- UserChangeForm—Used for the admin interface, this form contains every field available on the User model. Although this does include name and email, it also includes a host of fields intended for authentication and authorization.

Because neither of these forms really fits the use case for contact management, it makes more sense to simply create a new one for this application. ModelForm makes this easy, allowing a form to just specify those things that differ from the defaults. For contact management, that means only including fields like username, first name, last name, and email address.

```
from django import forms
from django.contrib.auth.models import User
```

---

[1]http://prodjango.com/modelform/

```
class UserEditorForm(forms.ModelForm):
    class Meta:
        model = User
        fields = ('username', 'first_name', 'last_name', 'email')
```

With that information, ModelForm can manage the rest of the form's behavior, based on details provided on the underlying model. All that's left is to supply a complementary form for managing the new contact-level details.

contacts.forms.ContactEditorForm

The form for managing contacts works very similarly to the one for users, using ModelForm to handle most of the details. The only difference is that the fields used for contacts have much more specific validation requirements than were set out in the Contact model already defined. Phone numbers, for example, are stored in the model as plain text, but they follow a specific format that can be validated by the form. These validations are already provided by the same django-localflavor-us package as used in the model. There are four classes that this ContactEditorForm can use:

- USStateField for validating a two-letter code against current states

- USStateSelect to display a list box containing all valid states

- USPhoneNumberField to validate ten-digit phone numbers, including dashes

- USZIPCodeField that validates five-digit or nine-digit ZIP codes

---

■ **Note** The USStateField also includes the US territories: American Samoa, the District of Columbia, Guam, the Northern Marianas Islands, Puerto Rico, and the U.S. Virgin Islands.

There are others as well, but those four classes will suffice for customizing the validation of a contact. The only remaining editable fields, address and city, don't have established formats that can be verified programmatically. Applying these overrides, ContactEditorForm looks like this:

```
from django import forms
from django_localflavor_us import forms as us_forms

from contacts.models import Contact

class ContactEditorForm(forms.ModelForm):
    phone_number = us_forms.USPhoneNumberField(required=False)
    state = us_forms.USStateField(widget=us_forms.USStateSelect, required=False)
    zip_code = us_forms.USZipCodeField(label="ZIP Code", required=False)

    class Meta:
        model = Contact
        exclude = ('user',)
```

Note the use of exclude here instead of fields, as was used in UserEditorForm. This tells ModelForm to use all fields in the model *except* those explicitly listed. Since the user will be provided by UserEditorForm, there's no need to include that as a separate selection here. Address and city don't need to be provided as explicit field declarations because ModelForm will use standard text fields for those automatically.

contacts.views.EditContact

Contacts are made up of two models—and thus, two forms—but the users who manage those contacts should need to deal with only one form that contains all the appropriate fields. Django's form-specific generic views don't really help us here because they're only designed for one form per view. We're combining two forms, which would require either some pretty heavy modification to UpdateView or a new class that combines two forms. Neither of these are pleasant options, so we'll go with a more practical approach with a slightly more generic view, assembling the form handling behavior manually.

The first choice to make is what arguments to accept. Since this view will render the forms in a template, it's best to accept a template name in the URL configuration, so we'll rely on Django's TemplateView, which takes care of that on its own. By simply subclassing django.views.generic.TemplateView, our new view will automatically accept a template_name argument in its configuration and provide a method for rendering the template to the response.

In order to pull up a single contact for editing, the view must also have a way of identifying which contact should be used. This identifier must be unique and should be reasonably understandable for users to look at. Since every contact relates to a user and every user has a unique username, that username will serve the purpose quite well.

```
from django.views.generic import TemplateView

class EditContact(TemplateView):
    def get(self, request, username=None):
        pass
```

Notice that the username is optional. Having an optional identifier allows this same view to be used for adding new contacts as well as editing existing ones. Both situations require essentially the same behavior: accept contact details from a user, check them for valid data and save them in the database. The only difference between adding and editing is whether a Contact object already exists.

With this goal in mind, the view must be prepared to create a new Contact object and possibly even a new User, should either of them not exist. There are four distinct situations that must be handled:

- A username is provided and both a User and a Contact exist for that username. The view should proceed to edit both existing records.

- A username is provided and a User exists, but no Contact is associated with it. A new Contact should be created and associated with the User, so that both can be edited.

- A username is provided and no User exists for it, which also means no Contact exists. Requesting a username implies an existing user, so requesting one that doesn't exist should be considered an error. In this case, this is an appropriate use of the HTTP 404 (Not Found) error code.

- No username is provided, meaning that existing users and contacts are irrelevant. New User and Contact objects should be created, ignoring any that might already exist. The form will ask for a new username to be provided.

■ **Tip** Using a 404 error code doesn't always mean you have to serve a generic "Page Not Found" page. You can supply whatever content you like to the HttpResponseNotFound class instead of the default HttpResponse class. These examples simply rely on the standard 404 error page for simplicity, but it may make more sense for your site to show a 404 page that says something like, "The contact you requested doesn't exist yet." This allows you to take advantage of a known HTTP status code, while still displaying more useful messages to your users.

These situations can be handled rather easily in a get_objects() method. It's factored out into its own method because we'll end up needing it from both the get() and post() methods.

```python
from django.shortcuts import get_object_or_404
from django.views.generic import TemplateView
from django.contrib.auth.models import User

from contacts.models import Contact

class EditContact(TemplateView):
    def get_objects(self, username):
        # Set up some default objects if none were defined.
        if username:
            user = get_object_or_404(User, username=username)
            try:
                # Return the contact directly if it already exists
                contact = user.contact
            except Contact.DoesNotExist:
                # Create a contact for the user
                contact = Contact(user=user)
        else:
            # Create both the user and an associated contact
            user = User()
            contact = Contact(user=user)

        return user, contact

    def get(self, request, username=None):
        pass
```

Once both objects are known to exist, the view can then display the forms for both of those objects, so the user can fill out the information. This is handled through the get() method.

```python
from django.shortcuts import get_object_or_404
from django.views.generic import TemplateView
from django.contrib.auth.models import User

from contacts.models import Contact
from contacts import forms

class EditContact(TemplateView):
    def get_objects(self, username):
        # Set up some default objects if none were defined.
        if username:
            user = get_object_or_404(User, username=username)
            try:
                # Return the contact directly if it already exists
                contact = user.contact
            except Contact.DoesNotExist:
                # Create a contact for the user
                contact = Contact(user=user)
        else:
```

```
            # Create both the user and an associated contact
            user = User()
            contact = Contact(user=user)

        return user, contact

    def get(self, request, username=None):
        user, contact = self.get_objects()
        return self.render_to_response({
            'username': username,
            'user_form': forms.UserEditorForm(instance=user),
            'contact_form': forms.ContactEditorForm(instance=contact),
        })
```

The view can then proceed to process the form and populate those objects with the appropriate information. It must instantiate, validate, and save each form independently of the other. This way, each form needs to know only about the data it's designed to manage, while the view can tie the two together.

If both forms were saved correctly, the view should redirect to a new URL where the edited contact information can be viewed. This is especially useful for new contacts, which wouldn't have a URL assigned to them prior to processing the form. In any other case, including when the form is first viewed—that is, no data has been submitted yet—and when the submitted data fails to validate, the view should return a rendered template that can display the appropriate form.

```
from django.core.urlresolvers import reverse
from django.http import HttpResponseRedirect
from django.shortcuts import get_object_or_404
from django.views.generic import TemplateView
from django.contrib.auth.models import User

from contacts.models import User
from contacts import forms

class EditContact(TemplateView):
    def get_objects(self, username):
        # Set up some default objects if none were defined.
        if username:
            user = get_object_or_404(User, username=username)
            try:
                # Return the contact directly if it already exists
                contact = user.contact
            except Contact.DoesNotExist:
                # Create a contact for the user
                contact = Contact(user=user)
        else:
            # Create both the user and an associated contact
            user = User()
            contact = Contact(user=user)

        return user, contact

    def get(self, request):
```

```
        user, contact = self.get_objects()
        return self.render_to_response({
            'username': user.username,
            'user_form': forms.UserEditorForm(instance=user),
            'contact_form': forms.ContactEditorForm(instance=contact),
        })

    def post(self, request):
        user, contact = self.get_objects()

        user_form = forms.UserEditorForm(request.POST, instance=user)
        contact_form = forms.ContactEditorForm(request.POST, instance=contact)
        if user_form.is_valid() and contact_form.is_valid():
            user = user_form.save()
            # Attach the user to the form before saving
            contact = contact_form.save(commit=False)
            contact.user = user
            contact.save()
            return HttpResponseRedirect(reverse('contact_detail',
                                        kwargs={'slug': user.username}))

        return self.render_to_response(self.template_name, {
                'username': user.username,
                'user_form': user_form,
                'contact_form': contact_form,
        })
```

Admin Configuration

Because this application has its own views for adding and editing contacts, there isn't much need to work with the admin interface. But since the Property model described later will both relate to Contact and make heavy use of the admin, it's a good idea to configure a basic interface for managing contacts.

```
from django.contrib import admin

from contacts import models

class ContactAdmin(admin.ModelAdmin):
    pass
admin.site.register(models.Contact, ContactAdmin)
```

It doesn't offer the convenience of editing the User and Contact models at the same time, but does offer value for related models that are managed through the admin.

URL Configuration

In addition to adding and editing contacts, this application must also supply a way to view all existing contacts and details about any specific contact. These features in turn require four distinct URL patterns to be accounted for in the contact application's URL configuration. Two of these will map to the edit_contact view described in the previous section, while two more will be mapped to Django's own generic views.

- /contacts/—The list of all existing contacts, with links to individual contact details

- /contacts/add/—An empty form where a new contact can be added

- /contacts/{username}/—A simple view of all the contact information for a given user

- /contacts/{username}/edit/—A form populated with any existing data, where that data can be changed and new data can be added

The /contacts/ portion at the beginning of these URLs isn't integral to any of the contact views themselves; it's a site-level distinction, pointing to the contacts application as a whole. Therefore, it won't be included in the URL configuration for the application, but in the configuration for the site. What remains is a set of URL patterns that can be made portable across whatever URL structure the site requires.

The first pattern, the list of all existing contacts, is quite simple on the surface. Once /contacts/ is removed from the URL, there's nothing left—rather, all that's left is an empty string. An empty string is indeed easy to match with a regular expression, but the view that we'll use for it, django.views.generic.ListView, requires some additional customization to behave properly.

To start, it requires both a queryset and a template_name, controlling where it can find the objects and how they should be displayed. For the purposes of this application, all contacts are available, without any filtering. The template name could be whatever works best according to your style; I'll call it "contacts/contact_list.html".

By showing all contacts, the list could get quite long, so it would be more useful to be able to split up the results across multiple pages, if necessary. ListView provides this as well, by way of its paginate_by argument. If provided, it supplies the maximum number of results that should be shown on a single page before spilling over to the next. The template can then control how page information and links to related pages are displayed.

```python
from django.conf.urls.defaults import *
from django.views.generic import ListView

from contacts import models

urlpatterns = patterns('',
    url(r'^$',
        ListView.as_view(queryset=models.Contact.objects.all(),
                         template_name='contacts/list.html',
                         paginate_by=25),
        name='contact_list'),
)
```

Next is the URL for adding new contacts, using the custom EditContact view. Like the contact list, the regular expression for this URL pattern is quite simple, as it doesn't contain any variables to capture. In addition to matching the add/ portion of the URL, this pattern just needs to point to the correct view and pass along a template name.

```python
from django.conf.urls.defaults import *
from django.views.generic import ListView

from contacts import models, views

urlpatterns = patterns('',
    url(r'^$',
        ListView.as_view(queryset=models.Contact.objects.all(),
                         template_name='contacts/list.html',
                         paginate_by=25),
        name='contact_list'),
```

```
url(r'^add/$', views.EditContact.as_view(
        template_name='contacts/editor_form.html',
    ), name='contact_add_form'),
)
```

The remaining URL patterns both require a username to be captured from the URL itself, which is then passed to the associated view. Usernames follow a fairly simple format, allowing letters, numbers, dashes and underscores. This can be represented by the regular expression [\w-]+, a pattern often used for recognizing textual identifiers known commonly as "slugs."

■ **Note** Slugs have their roots in the news industry, just like Django itself. A slug is the name an article is given for internal communications within a news organization, prior to going to print. Just before being printed, a proper title is given to the article, but the slug remains a way to uniquely reference a specific article, whether it's available for public viewing or not.

The first of these views to write, the basic contact detail page, will use another of Django's provided generic views, django.views.generic.DetailView, so some care has to be taken with the name of the variable the username is assigned to. The custom EditContact view calls it username, but DetailView doesn't know to look for something with that name. Instead, it allows a URL pattern to capture a slug variable, which functions the same way. Another requirement is to supply a slug_field argument that contains the name of the field to match the slug against.

Ordinarily, this slug_field argument would be the name of the field on the model where the slug value can be found. Like most generic views, though, DetailView requires a queryset argument to be given a valid QuerySet, from which an object can be retrieved. The view then adds a get() call to the QuerySet, using the slug_field/slug combination to locate a specific object.

This implementation detail is important, because it allows a URL pattern additional flexibility that wouldn't be available if the view matched the slug_field to an actual field on the model. More specifically, slug_field can contain a lookup that spans related models, which is important given the fact that contacts are made up of two different models. The URL pattern should retrieve a Contact object by querying the username of its related User object. To do this, we can set slug_field to "user__username".

```
from django.conf.urls.defaults import *
from django.views.generic import ListView, DetailView

from contacts import models, views

urlpatterns = patterns('',
    url(r'^$',
        ListView.as_view(queryset=models.Contact.objects.all(),
                        template_name='contacts/list.html',
                        paginate_by=25),
        name='contact_list'),
    url(r'^add/$', views.EditContact.as_view(
            template_name='contacts/editor_form.html',
        ), name='contact_add_form'),
    url(r'^(?P<slug>[\w-]+)/$',
        DetailView.as_view(queryset=models.Contact.objects.all(),
                        slug_field='user__username',
                        template_name='contacts/list.html'),
        name='contact_detail'),
)
```

The last URL pattern, editing an individual contact, closely follows the pattern used to add a new contact. The only difference between the two is the regular expression used to match the URL. The previous pattern didn't capture any variables from the URL, but this one will need to capture a username in order to populate the form's fields. The expression used to capture the username will use the same format as the one from the detail view, but will use the name of username instead of slug.

```python
from django.conf.urls.defaults import *
from django.views.generic import ListView, DetailView

from contacts import models, views

urlpatterns = patterns('',
    url(r'^$',
        ListView.as_view(queryset=models.Contact.objects.all(),
                         template_name='contacts/list.html',
                         paginate_by=25),
        name='contact_list'),
    url(r'^add/$', views.EditContact.as_view(
            template_name='contacts/editor_form.html',
        ), name='contact_add_form'),
    url(r'^(?P<slug>[\w-]+)/$',
        DetailView.as_view(queryset=models.Contact.objects.all(),
                           slug_field='user__username',
                           template_name='contacts/list.html'),
        name='contact_detail'),
    url(r'^(?P<username>[\w-]+)/edit/$', views.EditContact.as_view(
            template_name='contacts/editor_form.html',
        ), name='contact_edit_form'),
)
```

The only things missing from this application now are the four templates mentioned in the URL patterns. Since this book is targeted at development, rather than design, those are left as an exercise for the reader.

Real Estate Properties

The meat and potatoes of a real estate company is, of course, real estate. Individual buildings or pieces of land are typically called properties, but that term shouldn't be confused with Python's notion of properties, described in Chapter 2. This name clash is unfortunate, but not unexpected; it's quite common for entirely different groups of people to use the same terms with different meanings.

When this situation arises in general, it's often best to use whatever term is most widely understood by your audience. When meeting with real estate agents, you should be able to use "property" to refer to a piece of real estate, without any confusion or explanation. When talking to programmers, "property" might refer to a model, an object, or a built-in function.

Python's property decorator is useful for many situations, but the majority of this chapter will be focusing on other Python techniques. In light of this, the term "property" will refer to a real estate property unless otherwise specified.

properties.models.Property

The most basic item in a property management application is a `Property`. In real estate terms, a property is simply a piece of land, often with one or more buildings attached. This includes things like houses, retail stores, industrial complexes and undeveloped land. Although that covers a wide range of options, there are a number of things that are shared across the spectrum. The most basic of these shared features is that all properties have an address, which is made up of a few components:

```python
from django.db import models
from django_localflavor_us import models as us_models

class Property(models.Model):
    slug = models.SlugField()
    address = models.CharField(max_length=255)
    city = models.CharField(max_length=255)
    state = us_models.USStateField()
    zip = models.CharField(max_length=255)

    class Meta:
        verbose_name_plural = 'properties'

    def __unicode__(self):
        return u'%s, %s' % (self.address, self.city)
```

This model also includes a slug, which will be used to identify the property in a URL.

■ **Note**   This model uses just one field for the address, while many address forms use two. Two address lines are always appropriate for mailing addresses, because they allow for divisions within a building, such as apartments or office suites. Real estate is often focused on the building itself and the land it sits on, rather than how the building is divided, so one field will suffice. Condominiums are subdivisions of a building that *are* sold individually, so in markets that deal in condos, an extra address field would be necessary to uniquely identify properties within a building.

In addition to being able to locate the property, more fields can be added to describe the size of the property and the building that occupies it. There are a number of ways to contain this information, and `Property` will make use of more than one, all of which are optional. Typically, all of these would be filled before a listing is made public, but the database should support managing properties with incomplete information, so agents can populate it as information becomes available.

```python
from django.db import models
from django_localflavor_us import models as us_models

class Property(models.Model):
    slug = models.SlugField()
    address = models.CharField(max_length=255)
    city = models.CharField(max_length=255)
    state = us_models.USStateField()
    zip = models.CharField(max_length=255)
    square_feet = models.PositiveIntegerField(null=True, blank=True)
    acreage = models.FloatField(null=True, blank=True)
```

```
class Meta:
    verbose_name_plural = 'properties'

def __unicode__(self):
    return u'%s, %s' % (self.address, self.city)
```

The square_feet field refers to the available area inside the building. When designing or remodeling a building, it's necessary to break this down into individual room dimensions, but for the task of buying and selling property, the total amount works just fine on its own. The acreage field represents the total land area occupied by the property, as measured in acres—a unit equal to 43,560 square feet.

■ **Tip** If an agent *does* obtain the sizes of individual rooms within the property, those can be included as individual property features using the Feature model described in the "properties.models.Feature" section later in this chapter.

So far, most aspects of the Property model have been focused on describing the property itself, but there are also aspects of the sales process that can be included. Price is perhaps the most important aspect of a property listing, and even though it's not a physical attribute, each property can have only one price at a time, so it still makes sense to have it as a field here. The next chapter will explain how we'll keep track of past prices, but this model will just store the current price.

Another such attribute is the property's status—where in the sales process it currently is. For new entries in the database, there may not be any status at all. Perhaps some property information is being recorded for a home owner who is considering selling but hasn't yet decided to list it on the market. Once the owner decides to sell, it can be listed for public consideration and the rest of the process begins.

```
from django.db import models
from django_localflavor_us import models as us_models

class Property(models.Model):
    LISTED, PENDING, SOLD = range(3)
    STATUS_CHOICES = (
        (LISTED, 'Listed'),
        (PENDING, 'Pending Sale'),
        (SOLD, 'Sold'),
    )

    slug = models.SlugField()
    address = models.CharField(max_length=255)
    city = models.CharField(max_length=255)
    state = us_models.USStateField(max_length=2)
    zip = models.CharField(max_length=255)
    square_feet = models.PositiveIntegerField(null=True, blank=True)
    acreage = models.FloatField(null=True, blank=True)
    status = models.PositiveSmallIntegerField(choices=STATUS_CHOICES,
                                              null=True, blank=True)
    price = models.PositiveIntegerField(null=True, blank=True)

    class Meta:
        verbose_name_plural = 'properties'

    def __unicode__(self):
        return u'%s, %s' % (self.address, self.city)
```

In addition to the attributes that can be stored once on a model, there are other features of properties that may occur more than once or in many varying combinations. These amenities, such as fireplaces, basements, garages, attics and appliances, aren't part of a checklist of features that every property either does or doesn't have. This makes it difficult—if not impossible—to create a field for each feature, without having to modify the model's structure every time a new property comes along that doesn't fit with prior assumptions.

Instead, features should be stored in another model, indicating which features are present on the property and describing them in detail. Another model can step in to generalize these features into common types, so they can be browsed and searched. For instance, a user might be interested in finding all properties with a fireplace. Having a model dedicated to define a fireplace, with a related model describing individual fireplaces, helps enable this type of behavior. See the "properties.models.Feature" and "properties.models.PropertyFeature" sections later for more details on how this works.

Properties also have a number of people associated with them, such as an owner, real estate agent, architect, builder and possibly several prospective buyers. These all qualify as contacts and are stored using the Contact model already defined. For the purposes of making it as generic as possible, they will be called "interested parties," since each person has some stake in the dealings regarding the property.

```python
from django.db import models
from django_localflavor_us import models as us_models

class Property(models.Model):
    LISTED, PENDING, SOLD = range(3)
    STATUS_CHOICES = (
        (LISTED, 'Listed'),
        (PENDING, 'Pending Sale'),
        (SOLD, 'Sold'),
    )

    slug = models.SlugField()
    address = models.CharField(max_length=255)
    city = models.CharField(max_length=255)
    state = us_models.USStateField()
    zip = models.CharField(max_length=255)
    square_feet = models.PositiveIntegerField(null=True, blank=True)
    acreage = models.FloatField(null=True, blank=True)
    status = models.PositiveSmallIntegerField(choices=STATUS_CHOICES,
                                              null=True, blank=True)
    price = models.PositiveIntegerField(null=True, blank=True)

    features = models.ManyToManyField('Feature', through='PropertyFeature')
    interested_parties = models.ManyToManyField(Contact,
                                                through='InterestedParty')

    class Meta:
        verbose_name_plural = 'properties'

    def __unicode__(self):
        return u'%s, %s' % (self.address, self.city)
```

Not all properties should be listed publicly. Until a property is listed, and after it is sold, it should be hidden from the general public, available only to staff members to manage. Rather than typing a query for this every time a property is needed for public display, it's easy to create a custom manager with a method to narrow down the list.

```python
class PropertyManager(models.Manager):
    def listed(self):
        qs = super(PropertyManager, self).get_query_set()
        return qs.filter(models.Q(status=Property.LISTED) | \
                         models.Q(status=Property.PENDING))
```

This can be attached to a model through a simple assignment; any name can be used, but the convention is to call the standard manager objects, so this will do so.

```python
from django.db import models
from django_localflavor_us import models as us_models

class Property(models.Model):
    LISTED, PENDING, SOLD = range(3)
    STATUS_CHOICES = (
        (LISTED, 'Listed'),
        (PENDING, 'Pending Sale'),
        (SOLD, 'Sold'),
    )

    slug = models.SlugField()
    address = models.CharField(max_length=255)
    city = models.CharField(max_length=255)
    state = us_models.USStateField()
    zip = models.CharField(max_length=255)
    square_feet = models.PositiveIntegerField(null=True, blank=True)
    acreage = models.FloatField(null=True, blank=True)
    status = models.PositiveSmallIntegerField(choices=STATUS_CHOICES,
                                              null=True, blank=True)
    price = models.PositiveIntegerField(null=True, blank=True)
    features = models.ManyToManyField('Feature', through='PropertyFeature')
    interested_parties = models.ManyToManyField(Contact,
                                                through='InterestedParty')

    objects = PropertyManager()

    class Meta:
        verbose_name_plural = 'properties'

    def __unicode__(self):
        return u'%s, %s' % (self.address, self.city)
```

properties.models.Feature

A feature is simply something noteworthy that the property offers. It could be a common necessity, such as a basement or a laundry room, but it could also be very distinct, like a fireplace or a sun room. These features are often listed in an attempt to distinguish one property from another, since buyers often have a list of features they'd like to have.

The Feature model contains just the information necessary to define a particular type of feature. Rather than describing a specific fireplace, a Feature simply defines what a fireplace is, offering an anchor point for individual fireplaces to relate to. That way, properties can be searched by feature, using this model as a starting point.

```python
class Feature(models.Model):
    slug = models.SlugField()
    title = models.CharField(max_length=255)
    definition = models.TextField()

    def __unicode__(self):
        return self.title
```

properties.models.PropertyFeature

Instead of defining a feature at a high level, specific details are far more useful when viewing a specific property. The PropertyFeature model forms a bridge between Property and Feature, providing a way to describe the individual features of a specific property.

```python
class PropertyFeature(models.Model):
    property = models.ForeignKey(Property)
    feature = models.ForeignKey(Feature)
    description = models.TextField(blank=True)

    def __unicode__(self):
        return unicode(self.feature)
```

properties.models.InterestedParty

Contacts that have an interest in a particular property come in many varieties, from owners and buyers to real estate agents and safety inspectors. Each of these people can be connected to a specific property by way of a relationship that includes some detail about the nature of the relationship.

```python
from contacts.models import Contact

class InterestedParty(models.Model):
    BUILDER, OWNER, BUYER, AGENT, INSPECTOR = range(5)
    INTEREST_CHOICES = (
        (BUILDER, 'Builder'),
        (OWNER, 'Owner'),
        (BUYER, 'Buyer'),
        (AGENT, 'Agent'),
        (INSPECTOR, 'Inspector'),
    )

    property = models.ForeignKey(Property)
    contact = models.ForeignKey(Contact)
    interest = models.PositiveSmallIntegerField(choices=INTEREST_CHOICES)

    class Meta:
        verbose_name_plural = 'interested parties'
```

```
def __unicode__(self):
    return u'%s, %s' % (self.contact, self.get_interest_display())
```

■ **Note** These roles can overlap, such as an owner who is also the builder and the real estate agent. Some databases allow for a field to be used as a bitmask, where you can toggle individual bits to indicate which roles a contact fulfills. Since Django doesn't support creating or searching on those types of fields, we instead store just one role per row; a contact with multiple roles would simply use multiple rows to describe the situation.

Admin Configuration

Property listings are meant to be viewed by the general public, but only edited by employees of the real estate agency who have extensive training and experience in the field and can be trusted with this task. That description is the same as the intended audience for Django's built-in admin application.

With the features available from the admin, it's easy to put together interfaces for users to be able to edit and maintain all the various models in the properties application. No separate editor views are required, and only minor changes are necessary to customize the admin to work with these models in a user-friendly way.

"THE ADMIN IS NOT YOUR APP"

If you spend much time in the Django community, you'll likely run across the phrase, "The admin is not your app." The general sentiment being conveyed here is that the admin has a fairly limited focus, far more limited than most sites. It's expected to be used by trusted staff members who can work with a more rudimentary data-entry interface. When you find yourself struggling to find ways to get the admin to do what you want, chances are you need to start writing your own views and stop relying on the admin.

That doesn't mean that the admin is only ever useful during development. If a basic editing interface is suitable for staff members to work with, it can save both time and energy. With a few simple customizations, the admin can perform most of the common tasks that such editing interfaces require. The contacts application described earlier in this chapter couldn't rely on the admin because it required two forms to be combined, which is outside the scope the admin was intended for.

For properties, the admin is quite capable of generating an adequate interface. Since only staff members will need to edit property data, there's no need to create custom views that integrate with the rest of the site. More of your time can be focused on building out the public-facing aspects of the application.

The first model to set up is `Property`, but due to the workings of related models, some configurations for `PropertyFeature` and `InterestedParty` need to be in place first. These are each configured using a simple class that tells the admin to add them to the property editor as tables at the end of the page. In addition to any existing relationships, the admin should show one empty record that can be used to add a new relationship.

```
from django.contrib import admin

from properties import models

class InterestedPartyInline(admin.TabularInline):
    model = models.InterestedParty
    extra = 1
```

```
class PropertyFeatureInline(admin.TabularInline):
    model = models.PropertyFeature
    extra = 1
```

In order to customize some of the more specialized fields on the Property model's admin page, a custom ModelForm subclass is required. This allows the form to specify what widgets should be used for its state and zip fields, since they adhere to a more specific format than just a free-form text field. All the other fields can remain as they were, so they don't need to be specified on this form.

```
from django.contrib import admin
from django import forms
from django_localflavor_us import forms as us_forms

from properties import models

class InterestedPartyInline(admin.TabularInline):
    model = models.InterestedParty
    extra = 1

class PropertyFeatureInline(admin.TabularInline):
    model = models.PropertyFeature
    extra = 1

class PropertyForm(forms.ModelForm):
    state = us_forms.USStateField(widget=us_forms.USStateSelect)
    zip = us_forms.USZipCodeField(widget=forms.TextInput(attrs={'size': 10}))

    class Meta:
        model = models.Property
```

Now we can finally configure the admin interface for Property itself. The first customization is to use the PropertyForm instead of the plain ModelForm that would be used normally.

```
class PropertyAdmin(admin.ModelAdmin):
    form = PropertyForm

admin.site.register(models.Property, PropertyAdmin)
```

Within that form, not all the fields should display in a simple list from top to bottom. The full address can be displayed in a more familiar format by putting the city, state, and zip fields in a tuple so they all end up on the same line. The slug is placed next to the address, since it will be populated based on that information. The sales fields can be placed in a separate grouping, as can the fields related to size, with a heading to set each group apart.

```
class PropertyAdmin(admin.ModelAdmin):
    form = PropertyForm
    fieldsets = (
        (None, {'fields': (('address', 'slug'),
                           ('city', 'state', 'zip'))}),
        ('Sales Information', {'fields': ('status',
```

```
                                        'price')}),
        ('Size', {'fields': ('square_feet',
                                'acreage')}),
    )
```

The related models are added to a tuple called `inlines`, which controls how other models are attached to an existing admin interface. Because they were already configured in their own classes, all we need to do here is add them to the PropertyAdmin.

```
class PropertyAdmin(admin.ModelAdmin):
    form = PropertyForm
    fieldsets = (
        (None, {'fields': (('address', 'slug'),
                            ('city', 'state', 'zip'))}),
        ('Sales Information', {'fields': ('status',
                                            'price')}),
        ('Size', {'fields': ('square_feet',
                                'acreage')}),
    )
    inlines = (
        PropertyFeatureInline,
        InterestedPartyInline,
    )
```

Lastly, the declaration for generating the slug requires a dictionary assigned to the `prepopulated_fields` attribute. The key in this dictionary is the name of the SlugField to generate automatically. The associated value is a tuple of field names where the slug's value should be pulled from. All properties should be unique according to their address and ZIP, so those two fields can be combined to form a slug for the property.

```
class PropertyAdmin(admin.ModelAdmin):
    form = PropertyForm
    fieldsets = (
        (None, {'fields': (('address', 'slug'),
                            ('city', 'state', 'zip'))}),
        ('Sales Information', {'fields': ('status',
                                            'price')}),
        ('Size', {'fields': ('square_feet',
                                'acreage')}),
    )
    inlines = (
        PropertyFeatureInline,
        InterestedPartyInline,
    )
    prepopulated_fields = {'slug': ('address', 'zip')}
```

▓ **Note**   Slug fields are prepopulated using JavaScript while editing the model instance in the admin application. This is a useful convenience, saving the time and trouble of having to visit a separate field as long as the default slug is suitable. When creating objects in Python, the only way a field gets populated without an explicit value is through a function passed in as its `default` argument or through the field's `pre_save()` method.

243

With that in place, the only model left to set up is Feature. Since it's a simpler model than Property, the admin declaration is considerably simpler as well. There are three fields to arrange and a SlugField to configure.

```
class FeatureAdmin(admin.ModelAdmin):
    fieldsets = (
        (None, {
            'fields': (('title', 'slug'), 'definition'),
        }),
    )
    prepopulated_fields = {'slug': ('title',)}

admin.site.register(models.Feature, FeatureAdmin)
```

URL Configuration

Since the actual management of properties is handled by the admin interface, the only URLs to configure are for users to view property listings. These types of read-only views are best handled by Django's own generic views, configured to work with the models in question. Specifically, these URLs will use the same generic list and detail views that we used for contacts earlier in the chapter.

A view for the property listings can be set up using the ListView. This view requires a QuerySet to locate items, which is where the PropertyManager proves useful. Its listed() method narrows down the query to the items that should be displayed for the general public.

```
from django.conf.urls.defaults import *
from django.views.generic import ListView, DetailView

from properties import models

urlpatterns = patterns('',
    url(r'^$',
        ListView.as_view(queryset=models.Property.objects.listed(),
                         template_name='properties/list.html',
                         paginate_by=25),
        name='property_list'),
)
```

Although the detail view requires fewer configuration options—since it doesn't need the paginate_by argument—the regular expression gets a bit more complicated. Looking up a property in a URL is best handled by a slug, but slugs can be typically made up of any combination of letters, numbers, and basic punctuation. The slug for a property is a more specific format, starting with the street number from the address and ending with a ZIP code. The street name in the middle could still be anything, but it's always surrounded by numbers.

This simple fact helps shape the regular expression used to capture the slug from the URL. The idea here is to be as specific as reasonably possible, so that one URL pattern doesn't interfere with others that might look for similar patterns. The URL configuration for the detail view of a single Property object looks like this:

```
from django.conf.urls.defaults import *
from django.views.generic import ListView, DetailView

from properties import models

urlpatterns = patterns('',
```

```
url(r'^$',
    ListView.as_view(queryset=models.Property.objects.listed(),
                     template_name='properties/list.html',
                     paginate_by=25),
    name='property_list'),
url(r'^(?P<slug>\d+-[\w-]+-\d+)/$',
    DetailView.as_view(queryset=models.Property.objects.listed(),
                       slug_field='slug',
                       template_name='properties/detail.html'),
    name='property_detail'),
)
```

This regular expression adds explicit rules for digits at the beginning and end of the slug, separate from the middle portion by dashes. This will match property slugs just as well as the usual [\w-]+, but with an important added bonus: These URLs can now be placed at the site's root. Having a more specific regular expression allows for smaller URLs like http://example.com/123-main-st-12345/. This is a great way to keep URLs small and tidy, while not impeding on other URL configurations that might also use slugs.

Now What?

With a few applications in place and ready to work together, a basic site takes shape. The next chapter will show how to bring together all the tools you've learned so far to add significant new features to applications like these.

CHAPTER 11

■ ■ ■

Enhancing Applications

Once a site has a set of basic applications in working order, the next step is to add more advanced functionality to complement the existing behavior. This can sometimes be a matter of simply adding more applications, each providing new features for users and employees alike. Other times, there are ways of enhancing your existing applications so they grow new features directly, without a separate application that can stand on its own.

These "meta-applications" or "sub-frameworks" are built with the goal of easily integrating into an existing application, using hooks that are already provided. This book has illustrated many such hooks, and they can be used in combination to great effect. It's often possible to write a tool that performs a lot of tasks but only requires adding a single line of code to an existing application.

Adding an API

These days, most sites have an API to allow programmers to interact with the site's content and functionality without requiring a user or even a web browser. The goal is to provide data in a simple way for code to work with your data, using structured, reliable techniques. Django's class-based views provide a number of ways to customize a view's behavior, which can be quite useful for generating an API without having to write a lot of new code yourself.

Building an API requires a few decisions, but not all of them need to be made right away. Here's a small sample, showing some of the common questions that need to be answered when designing an API.

- What format should be used to transfer the data?
- What types of data should be exposed?
- How should that data be structured?
- Do users need to be authenticated to access data?
- Can users customize which data they retrieve?
- Can users modify data through the API?
- Are there separate permissions for different API endpoints?

This chapter will answer some of those questions, within the context of the real estate site outlined in Chapter 10. Better yet, you'll see an example of a simple framework that can add the necessary API features without requiring much to add directly to your apps. Reusability is key to the long-term success of features like these, so it's ideal to produce a configurable tool for such tasks.

■ **Caution** Not all of these questions will be addressed in this chapter. In particular, the examples shown throughout the chapter don't use any authentication or authorization whatsoever. Django's standard session-based authentication isn't well suited for use with an API, but you have several choices. You could simply let your web server handle authentication[1], implement a full OAuth provider[2] or use some other approach that makes sense for your site. Those decisions and associated instructions are outside the scope of this book.

Serializing Data

A good first place to start is establishing a format for your data to use. These days, the de facto standard is JSON, JavaScript Object Notation. It originated as an easy way to use data inside of a browser, because browsers natively understand JavaScript objects, but it has since come into its own as a simple, readable and reliable cross-platform data format. Python has its own tools for reading and writing it directly, as do many other programming languages.

In fact, Django even has its own tools for writing model instances using JSON and reading them back in again. Because it takes an in-memory object and converts it to a sequence of characters that can be sent over a network, this process is called *serialization*. Django's serialization tools are located in django.core.serializers. Getting a JSON serializer is fairly simple, using the get_serializer() function.

To get a serializer, just pass in the name of the serialization method you'd like to use and you'll get a class that can be used to serialize objects. Django supports three serialization formats.

- json—JavaScript Object Notation
- xml—Extensible Markup Language
- yaml—YAML Ain't a Markup Language, which is available if you have PyYAML[3] installed

```
>>> from django.core import serializers
>>> JSONSerializer = serializers.get_serializer('json')
```

The serializer class you get back from this works the same way, regardless of which format you choose. The remainder of this chapter will use JSON, but you should be able to use XML or YAML with relatively minor modifications.

Usage of the serializer is a bit different than the simpler json module provided directly with Python. Rather than using dumps() and loads() methods, Django's serializers provide serialize() and deserialize() methods to transform data to and from JSON, respectively. Also, these methods work with proper Django model instances, rather than merely with native data structures like lists and dictionaries. For now, we'll just look at the serialize() method, to get data out of your application so others can use it.

```
>>> serializer = JSONSerializer()
>>> from contacts.models import Contact
>>> serializer.serialize(Contact.objects.all())
'[{...}, {...}, {...}]'
```

---

[1]http://prodjango.com/remote-user
[2]http://prodjango.com/oauth
[3]http://prodjango.com/pyyaml

If you look at the actual output for each of the serialized contacts, you'll notice some additional information you might not have expected. Django's serialization tools are intended to produce output that can be deserialized without knowing in advance what models and instances were serialized originally. To do that, the output includes some information about the model itself, as well as the primary key of each instance. Each object will look something like this.

```json
{
    "pk": 1,
    "model": "contacts.contact",
    "fields": {
        "user": 1,
        "address": "123 Main Street",
        "city": "Los Angeles",
        "state": "CA",
        "zip_code": "90210",
        "phone_number": "123-456-7890"
    }
}
```

For an API, you'll already know what model and ID you're working with, because they'll be mapped as part of the URL. Ideally, we can get the fields dictionary out of this and send just that back and forth instead. Though not documented, Django's serializers do offer a way to override their behavior to do just that. It starts by realizing that the result of get_serializer() is actually a class, not an instance object. This allows you to create a subclass before instantiating it, yielding all the benefits of overriding individual methods on the subclass. We'll put this code in a file called serializers.py, and because we'll also be adding some more files later in this chapter, we'll create this in a package called api. In the end, we'll be able to import this code as api.serializers.

```python
from django.core import serializers

class QuerySetSerializer(serializers.get_serializer('json')):
    pass
```

Understanding how to override the serializer requires knowing a bit about how the serializers work. The serialize() method accepts a QuerySet or any iterable that yields model instances. It iterates over that and for each object it finds, it iterates over its fields, outputting values at each step. The entire process can be easily seen by looking at the methods that are called along the way.

- start_serialization()—This sets up the list to hold the objects that will be output in the stream.

- start_object(obj)—This sets up a dictionary to collect information about an individual object.

- handle_field(obj, field)—Each field gets added to the object's dictionary individually.

- handle_fk_field(obj, field)—Foreign key relationships are handled using a separate method.

- handle_m2m_field(obj, field)—Like foreign keys, many-to-many relationships are handled using their own method.

- end_object(obj)—Once all the fields have been handled, the object gets a chance to finalize the dictionary for its data. This is where the model information and primary key value are added to the fields, yielding the output shown previously.

- `get_dump_object(obj)`—Called internally within end_object(), this is responsible for defining the actual structure of each object that gets serialized.

- `end_serialization()`—Once all the objects have been processed, this method finalizes the stream.

The first customization we'll apply is to simplify the structure of the output. Because we'll use the URL to indicate what type of object we're working with and what ID it has, all we need in the serialized output is the collection of fields. As hinted at in the process we've just looked at, this is handled by the get_dump_object() method. In addition to the object it's provided, get_dump_object() also has access to the current data that's already been assembled by the field handling methods. That data is stored in the _current attribute.

The default implementation of get_dump_object() wraps the field data in a dictionary, along with the object's primary key and the path and name of its model. All we need to do in our overridden method is to return just the current field data.

```python
class QuerySetSerializer(serializers.get_serializer('json')):
    def get_dump_object(self, obj):
        return self._current
```

With just this simple method in place, you can already see an improvement in the output.

```
{
    "user"
    "address": "123 Main Street",
    "city": "Los Angeles",
    "state": "CA",
    "zip_code": "90210",
    "phone_number": "123-456-7890"
}
```

Outputting a Single Object

The example shown at the end of the previous section would be just one entry in a list, because serialize() operates exclusively on iterables. For an API, you're perhaps even more likely to be outputting a single object from a detail view, which shouldn't be wrapped in a list. Instead of a QuerySetSerializer, we need a SingleObjectSerializer. It'll still be based on QuerySetSerializer, so we can reuse all the functionality we're adding there, but with just enough modifications to handle individual objects.

The first thing to override is the serialize() method, so it can accept individual objects, but in order to reuse all the serialization behavior, it will need to call its parent method with a list instead of the single object. This is a fairly simple override.

```python
class SingleObjectSerializer(QuerySetSerializer):
    def serialize(self, obj, **options):
        # Wrap the object in a list in order to use the standard serializer
        return super(SingleObjectSerializer, self).serialize([obj], **options)
```

Unfortunately, because that wraps the object in a list and returns the output without any other changes, this will in fact still output a list in the JSON string. In order to output just the values from the one object in that list, it's necessary to strip out the list characters around it. The result is a string, so these characters can be removed using the string's strip() method.

We could place this code directly in the serialize() method, after calling the parent method but before returning the string at the end, but Django's serializers have one other point of customization that we haven't looked into yet. Once all the objects have been assembled into a format that the serializer can work with, the getvalue() method is asked to return the fully serialized output. This is a much better place to put our customizations, as it matches the intent of the original methods. Aligning your overrides with the intent of the original implementation is a good way to ensure that future changes won't break your code in unexpected ways.

```python
class SingleObjectSerializer(QuerySetSerializer):
    def serialize(self, obj, **options):
        # Wrap the object in a list in order to use the standard serializer
        return super(SingleObjectSerializer, self).serialize([obj], **options)

    def getvalue(self):
        # Strip off the outer list for just a single item
        value = super(SingleObjectSerializer, self).getvalue()
        return value.strip('[]\n')
```

And that's all we need to get a new serializer that's fully capable of handling individual objects. Now, you can serialize an object on its own and get just that object's output in return.

```python
>>> serializer = SingleObjectSerializer()
>>> from contacts.models import Contact
>>> serializer.serialize(Contact.objects.get(pk=1))
'{...}'
```

Handling Relationships

Looking at the output as it currently stands, you'll notice that the user associated with the contact is represented only by its primary key. Because Django's serializers are intended for reconstituting models one at a time, they contain only the data necessary for each individual object. For an API, it's more useful to include some details of the related object as well, preferably in a nested dictionary.

This part of the output is managed by the handle_fk_field() method, with the default implementation simply outputting the numeric ID value. We can override this to provide details of the object instead, but it requires a bit of an interesting approach because of a problem you might not expect.Django's serializers wrap more generic serializers and add on the behavior necessary to work with Django models, but that added behavior only applies to the first level of data. Any Django model that you try to serialize outside the first-level iterable will raise a TypeError indicating that it's not a serializable object.

At first blush, it may seem like the answer would be to serialize the related objects separately, then attach them to the rest of the structure. The problem on that end is that the output of the serializer is a string. If you attach that output to the self._current dictionary, it'll get serialized as a single string that just happens to contain another serialized object inside of it.

So we can't leave the object unserialized, and we also can't fully serialize it. Thankfully, Django offers a path between the two by way of yet another serializer that's not normally documented. The 'python' serializer can take Django objects and produce native Python lists and dictionaries, rather than strings. These lists and dictionaries can be used anywhere in a serializable structure and will produce what you would expect.

We need two serializers now: one for outputting the overall structure, including related objects, and another for outputting the string as JSON or whichever other format you prefer. The Python serializer will do the bulk of the work, and we can build a more useful serializer by combining that with the basic JSON serializer. Here's how our existing implementation would look.

```
class DataSerializer(serializers.get_serializer('python')):
    def get_dump_object(self, obj):
        return self._current

class QuerySetSerializer(DataSerializer, serializers.get_serializer('json')):
    pass  # Behavior is now inherited from DataSerializer
```

Notice that get_dump_object() moves into the new DataSerializer, because it doesn't actually have anything to do with JSON output. Its sole purpose is to define the structure of the output, which is applicable to any of the output formats. That's also where the overridden handle_fk_field() belongs. It has three tasks to perform.

- Retrieve the related object

- Transform it into a native Python structure

- Add it to the main object's data dictionary

The first and third points are straightforward, but it's that middle one that looks a little tricky. We can't just call self.serialize() because each serializer maintains state throughout the process, by way of the _current attribute. We'll need to instantiate a new serializer instead, but we also need to make sure to always use DataSerializer instead of accidentally getting an instance of the JSON serializer. That's the only way to be sure that it outputs native Python objects, rather than strings.

```
class DataSerializer(serializers.get_serializer('python')):
    def get_dump_object(self, obj):
        return self._current

    def handle_fk_field(self, obj, field):
        # Include content from the related object
        related_obj = getattr(obj, field.name)
        value = DataSerializer().serialize([related_obj])
        self._current[field.name] = value[0]
```

The only other interesting thing to note about this new method is that it wraps the related object in a list before serializing it. Django's serializers only operate on iterables, so when processing a single object, you'll always need to wrap it in an iterable, such as a list. In the case of the Python serializer, the output is also a list, so when assigning it back to self._current, we need to only get the first item out of that list.

With that in place, the serialized output of a typical contact looks something like the following.

```
{
    "user": {
        "username": "admin",
        "first_name": "Admin",
        "last_name": "User",
        "is_active": true,
        "is_superuser": true,
        "is_staff": true,
        "last_login": "2013-07-17T12:00:00.000Z",
        "groups": [],
        "user_permissions": [],
        "password": "pbkdf2_sha256$10000$...",
        "email": "admin@example.com",
        "date_joined": "2012-12-04T17:46:00.000Z"
    },
```

```
        "address": "123 Main Street",
        "city": "Los Angeles",
        "state": "CA",
        "zip_code": "90210",
        "phone_number": "123-456-7890"
}
```

With just those few extra lines of code in one method, we now have the ability to nest objects within others, and because it utilizes DataSerializer, they can be nested as many levels deep as you'd like. But there's a lot of information in a User object, most of which doesn't really need to be included in the API, and some of it—such as the password hash—should never be revealed.

Controlling Output Fields

Django once again accommodates this situation, this time by offering a fields argument to the serialize() method. Simply pass in a list of field names, and only those fields will be processed by the handle_*_field() methods. For example, we could simplify the output of our Contact model by excluding the user from it entirely.

```
SingleObjectSerializer().serialize(Contact.objects.get(pk=1), fields=[
    'phone_number',
    'address',
    'city',
    'state',
    'zip_code',
])
```

With this in place, the output certainly gets simpler.

```
{
    "address": "123 Main Street",
    "city": "Los Angeles",
    "state": "CA",
    "zip_code": "90210",
    "phone_number": "123-456-7890"
}
```

Of course, removing the user from the output doesn't really help at all. What we really need to do is limit the fields on the user object, not the contact. Unfortunately, this is another situation where the intent of Django's serializers hampers us a little bit. Just like we had to intercept the serialization of the user object in handle_fk_field(), that's also where we'd have to supply the fields argument to its call to the serialize() method. But specifying the fields there would require overriding the method each time we want to do it, and special-casing each model we want to handle.

A more general solution would be to create a registry of models and their associated fields. The handle_fk_field() method could then check this registry for each object it receives, using the field list it finds or falling back to a standard serialization if the model wasn't registered. Setting up the registry is pretty simple, as is the function to register the model and field list combinations.

```
field_registry = {}
def serialize_fields(model, fields):
    field_registry[model] = set(fields)
```

■ **Note**   Fields can be passed in as any iterable, but are explicitly placed into a set internally. The order of the fields doesn't matter for the serialization process, and a set can be a bit smaller and faster because it doesn't worry about ordering. Also, later in this chapter we'll be able to take advantage of a specific behavior of sets to make parts of the implementation a bit easier to work with.

With this in place, we can import it wherever we need to specify the field list for a model, and simply call it once with the appropriate mapping that will need to be used later. The code to use this registry won't actually go in handle_fk_field() though, because that would only apply it for related objects, not the outer-most objects themselves. In order to make a more consistent usage pattern, it would be ideal if you could specify the fields in the registry and use those registered fields for every object you serialize, whether it was a relationship or not.

To support this more general use case, the code for reading the field registry can go in the serialize() method instead. It's the primary entry point for the main objects and related objects alike, so it's a great place to provide this extra behavior.

The first task it needs to do is determine the model being used. Because you can pass in either a QuerySet or a standard iterable, there are two ways to get the model of the objects that were passed in. The most straightforward approach takes advantage of the fact that QuerySets are iterable as well, so you can always just get the first item.

```python
class DataSerializer(serializers.get_serializer('python')):
    def serialize(self, queryset, **options):
        model = queryset[0].__class__

        return super(DataSerializer, self).serialize(queryset, **options)

    # Other methods previously described
```

This certainly works for both cases, but it will make an extra query for each QuerySet passed in, because fetching the first record is actually a different operation from iterating over all of the results. Sure, we need to do this anyway for non-QuerySet inputs, but QuerySets have a bit of extra information that we can use instead. Each QuerySet also has a model attribute on it, which already contains the model that was used to query the records, so if that attribute is present, we can just use that instead.

```python
class DataSerializer(serializers.get_serializer('python')):
    def serialize(self, queryset, **options):
        if hasattr(queryset, 'model'):
            model = queryset.model
        else:
            model = queryset[0].__class__

        return super(DataSerializer, self).serialize(queryset, **options)

    # Other methods previously described
```

And because this isn't checking specifically for a QuerySet object, but rather just checks to see if the model attribute exists, it will also work correctly if you happen to have some other iterable that yields models, as long as the iterable also has a model attribute on it.

With the model in hand, it's easy to perform a lookup in the field list registry, but it's important that we do so only if the fields argument itself wasn't provided. Global registries like this should always be easy to override when necessary for specific cases. If provided, the fields argument will be present in the options dictionary, and that's also where we'd put the field list we found from the registry. So adding this part of the process gets pretty simple as well.

```
class DataSerializer(serializers.get_serializer('python')):
    def serialize(self, queryset, **options):
        if hasattr(queryset, 'model'):
            model = queryset.model
        else:
            model = queryset[0].__class__

        if options.get('fields') is None and model in field_registry:
            options['fields'] = field_registry[model]

        return super(DataSerializer, self).serialize(queryset, **options)

    # Other methods previously described
```

■ **Note**　The second if block can look very strange at a glance, but it can't simply check to see if 'fields' exists in the options dictionary. In some cases, a None could be passed in explicitly, which should behave the same as if the argument was omitted entirely. To account for this, we use get(), which falls back to None if not found, then we check for None manually in order to make sure we're catching all the right cases. In particular, supplying an empty list should still override any registered fields, so we can't just use a Boolean not.

Now serialize() will automatically inject a field list for any model it already knows about, unless overridden by a custom fields argument. This means that you'll have to make sure to register your field lists before trying to serialize anything, but as you'll see later in this chapter, that's easily done in your URL configuration. Also note that if the model hasn't been assigned a field list and you didn't specify one yourself, this update will simply leave the fields argument unspecified, falling back to the default behavior we saw previously.

With all this in place, we can easily customize the field lists for our Contact and User models. We don't need to customize Contact specifically, because we want to include all of its fields, but it's included here as well, for demonstration purposes. Besides, explicit is better than implicit, and specifying everything here helps document the output of your API.

```
from api import serialize_fields
from contacts.models import Contact
from django.contrib.auth.models import User

serialize_fields(Contact, [
    'phone_number',
    'address',
    'city',
    'state',
    'zip_code',
    'user',
])
serialize_fields(User, [
    'username',
    'first_name',
    'last_name',
    'email',
])
```

Interestingly, these field lists mostly match the fields that were already provided to the forms we created in Chapter 10. Forms also keep a list of their own fields, so we can actually rewrite these registrations using the form field names instead, which helps us avoid repeating ourselves. This lets the forms be primarily responsible for what fields are useful to end-users, with the API simply following suit. The only change we'll need to make is to add the Contact model's user attribute back in, because that was handled differently in the form scenarios.

```
from api import serialize_fields
from contacts.models import Contact
from django.contrib.auth.models import User
from contacts.forms import ContactEditorForm, UserEditorForm

serialize_fields(Contact, ContactEditorForm.base_fields.keys() + ['user'])
serialize_fields(User, UserEditorForm.base_fields.keys())
```

And now, when we go to serialize a Contact object using the SingleObjectSerializer with these new changes in place, it finally looks like you would expect.

```
{
    "user": {
        "username": "admin",
        "first_name": "Admin",
        "last_name": "User",
        "email": "admin@example.com"
    },
    "address": "123 Main Street",
    "city": "Los Angeles",
    "state": "CA",
    "zip_code": "90210",
    "phone_number": "123-456-7890"
}
```

Many-to-Many Relationships

So far, the API will output just about everything you might need, with the major missing feature being many-to-many relationships. The handle_fk_field() method will only handle simple foreign keys that point to a single object per record, while many-to-many relationships would result in a list of related objects that all need to be serialized and inserted into the JSON string.

As outlined earlier in this chapter, serializers also have a handle_m2m_field() method, which we can use to customize how they behave with regard to these more complex relationships. Technically, these relationships are already handled slightly, but only in the same way as foreign keys were originally. Each related object will simply yield its primary key value and nothing else. We'll need to apply some of the same steps that were done for foreign keys in order to get more information from these relationships.

The first change from our foreign key handling is that the attribute that references related objects isn't an object or QuerySet itself; it's a QuerySet manager. That means it's not iterable on its own, and thus can't be serialized directly, so we'll have to call its all() method to get a QuerySet to work with. Then, rather than wrapping it in a list, we can just pass it through the standard serialize() method on its own.

```
class DataSerializer(serializers.get_serializer('python')):
    # Other methods previously described

    def handle_m2m_field(self, obj, field):
        # Include content from all related objects
        related_objs = getattr(obj, field.name).all()
        values = DataSerializer().serialize(related_objs)
        self._current[field.name] = values
```

With this in place, here's what a contact would look like if we add the 'groups' field to registry for the User object.

```
{
    "user": {
        "username": "admin",
        "first_name": "Admin",
        "last_name": "User",
        "email": "admin@example.com",
        "groups": [
            {
                "name": "Agents",
                "permission_set": [...]
            },
            {
                "name": "Buyers",
                "permission_set": [...]
            },
            {
                "name": "Sellers",
                "permission_set": [...]
            }
        ]
    },
    "address": "123 Main Street",
    "city": "Los Angeles",
    "state": "CA",
    "zip_code": "90210",
    "phone_number": "123-456-7890"
}
```

Of course, the permissions don't make much sense in this context, so you'd want to remove those from the User object's field list, but other than that, it looks like another pretty simple solution that will get us on our way. Unfortunately, many-to-many relationships in Django have one other feature that makes things considerably more complicated for us.

When you specify a many-to-many relationship, you can optionally specify a "through" model, which can contain some additional information about the relationship. This information isn't attached to either model directly, but is instead truly part of the relationship between the two. The simple approach we just applied for handle_m2m_field() completely ignores this feature, so none of that extra information will ever be included in our output.

Remember from Chapter 10 that our Property model is related to Feature and Contact by way of many-to-many relationships, and each of them used the through argument to include some extra information fields. Here's what you'd see if you tried to serialize a Property object with the code we have in place at the moment.

```
{
    "status": 2,
    "address": "123 Main St.",
    "city": "Anywhere",
    "state": "CA",
    "zip": "90909",
    "features": [
        {
            "slug": "shed",
            "title": "Shed",
            "definition": "Small outdoor storage building"
        },
        {
            "slug": "porch",
            "title": "Porch",
            "definition": "Outdoor entryway"
        }
    ],
    "price": 130000,
    "acreage": 0.25,
    "square_feet": 1248
}
```

As you can see, the features listed only include information about the generate types of features being mentioned. The definition simply explains what a shed and porch are in general terms, but there's nothing specific about the features on this particular property. Those details are only present in the PropertyFeature relationship table, which is currently being ignored. Let's take a look at what we're hoping to do with this in order to better understand how to get there. The fields we're looking for are stored in an intermediate PropertyFeature model, but we want to have them included as if they were directly on the Feature model. That requires both the Feature instance and the PropertyFeature instance, with their attributes merged into a single dictionary.

Getting the Appropriate Fields

The first problem we run into is that the PropertyFeature model has more fields on it than we really want to include. It includes two ForeignKey fields that relate to Property and Feature, which are really only there to support the relationship and don't add any useful information that we couldn't have gotten with the simple approach shown earlier. We don't want to include those, or its automatic primary key either. Everything else is useful information, but we'll need a way to identify which fields are useful and which ones aren't.

To get this information, we'll start with a helper method that can look through the fields in the PropertyFeature model and organize them according to their purpose. There are four types of fields, each of which can be identified by different things that we can introspect in code.

- The auto-incrementing primary key will be an instance of AutoField. This field doesn't do anything useful for us, so once it's found, it can be safely ignored.

- One foreign key points to the main model we're working with. In this case, it's the one that points to the Property model. This can be identified as an instance of ForeignKey, with the value of its rel.to attribute matching the class of the object that was passed in. We'll call this the source field. There's also a foreign key that points to the related model, which is Feature in this example. This can be identified as an instance of ForeignKey, with the value of its rel.to attribute matching the rel.to attribute on the ManyToMany field that was passed into handle_m2m_field(). Let's call this one the target field.

- Lastly, any other fields that don't fall into the other three categories contain information about the relationship itself, and these are the ones we're working to gather. We'll call these the extra fields.

With these rules in place, a new get_through_fields() method is rather straightforward. It just has to look through all the fields on the relationship model and identify each one according to those rules, returning the ones we need to work with in handle_m2m_field().

```python
from django.db.models import AutoField, ForeignKey

class DataSerializer(serializers.get_serializer('python')):
    # Other methods previously described

    def get_through_fields(self, obj, field):
        extra = set()

        for f in field.rel.through._meta.fields:
            if isinstance(f, AutoField):
                # Nothing to do with AutoFields, so just ignore it
                continue

            if isinstance(f, ForeignKey):
                # The source will refer to the model of our primary object
                if f.rel.to == obj.__class__:
                    source = f.name
                    continue

                # The target will be the same as on the ManyToManyField
                if f.rel.to == field.rel.to:
                    target = f.name
                    continue

            # Otherwise this is a standard field
            extra.add(f.name)

        return source, target, extra
```

Getting Information About the Relationship

Now that we have the fields we need, the meat of the process is about finding each relationship individually and pulling the appropriate information out of it. We'll build up this new version of handle_m2m_field() a few lines at a time, so it's a bit easier to see all the pieces come together along the way.

First, we need to retrieve all the field information applicable to this task. The previous section set the stage for getting information from the relationship model, but we'll also need the list of fields to include in the serialized output. We're not serializing PropertyFeature using the standard process, so it can't use the field registry the same way other models do. Besides, we'll be returning all the data from Feature and PropertyFeature together in the structure referenced by Feature, so it's better if we allow the configuration to specify all the fields for both models when specifying Feature. For example, to pull in just the title of the feature and its description for the current property, we could register them both in a single line.

```python
api.serialize_fields(Feature, ['title', 'description'])
```

The title field will come from the Feature model, while description comes from PropertyFeature instead, but this allows that implementation detail to be better hidden from view. Calling get_through_fields() is easy enough, and retrieving the registered field list is the same as it was in handle_fk_field(), with one minor exception. If there's no field list already registered, we can just use the extra fields returned from our call to get_through_fields(). We have to make sure to specify something by default, because otherwise the automatic primary key and those two extra foreign keys would be serialized as well, even though they're not useful here.

```python
class DataSerializer(serializers.get_serializer('python')):
    # Other methods previously described

    def handle_m2m_field(self, obj, field):
        source, target, extra_fields = self.get_through_fields(obj, field)
        fields = field_registry.get(field.rel.to, extra_fields)
```

Next, we prepare to iterate over all the relationships for the current object. This works a bit differently than it might seem, because the simple way to access many-to-many relationships doesn't return any of the extra relationship information. To get that, we need to query the relationship model directly, filtering for only the results where the source refers to the object that was passed into handle_m2m_field(). While we're at it, we can also set up a list to store the data retrieved from these relationships.

```python
class DataSerializer(serializers.get_serializer('python')):
    # Other methods previously described

    def handle_m2m_field(self, obj, field):
        source, target, extra_fields = self.get_through_fields(obj, field)
        fields = field_registry.get(field.rel.to, extra_fields)

        # Find all the relationships for the object passed into this method
        relationships = field.rel.through._default_manager.filter(**{source: obj})

        objects = []
```

Now we're in position to start iterating through the relationships and pull the necessary information out of each one. The first step is to actually serialize the related model according to the field list we found earlier. This will add the title data from the Feature model, for example.

```python
class DataSerializer(serializers.get_serializer('python')):
    # Other methods previously described

    def handle_m2m_field(self, obj, field):
        source, target, extra_fields = self.get_through_fields(obj, field)
        fields = field_registry.get(field.rel.to, extra_fields)

        # Find all the relationships for the object passed into this method
        relationships = field.rel.through._default_manager.filter(**{source: obj})

        objects = []
        for relation in relationships.select_related():
            # Serialize the related object first
            related_obj = getattr(relation, target)
            data = DataSerializer().serialize([related_obj])[0]
```

Notice here that we need to wrap the object in a list to serialize it, then grab the first item out of the resulting list. We created a SingleObjectSerializer earlier, but that's only designed to work with JSON output as a more public interface. We're only doing this in one method, so it's not really worth creating another single-object variation that's designed to work with native Python data structures.

The source and target fields have already proven useful, and we now have a data dictionary that contains some of what we need. In order to get the rest of the information from the relationship model, we look at the extra fields. We don't necessarily want all of them, though. We need to get only the ones that were also included in the field list registry. This is where it becomes really useful that we have both of them stored as sets. We can perform a simple intersection operation using to the & operator to get only the fields that are in both places. For each one we find, we just add it to the data dictionary alongside the other values.

```python
class DataSerializer(serializers.get_serializer('python')):
    # Other methods previously described

    def handle_m2m_field(self, obj, field):
        source, target, extra_fields = self.get_through_fields(obj, field)
        fields = field_registry.get(field.rel.to, extra_fields)

        # Find all the relationships for the object passed into this method
        relationships = field.rel.through._default_manager.filter(**{source: obj})

        objects = []
        for relation in relationships.select_related():
            # Serialize the related object first
            related_obj = getattr(relation, target)
            data = DataSerializer().serialize([related_obj])[0]

            # Then add in the relationship data, but only
            # those that were specified in the field list
            for f in fields & extra_fields:
                data[f] = getattr(relation, f)
```

Now all that's left is to add all this data to the list of objects and add that whole collection to the dictionary the serializer is using to keep track of the current object.

```python
class DataSerializer(serializers.get_serializer('python')):
    # Other methods previously described

    def handle_m2m_field(self, obj, field):
        source, target, extra_fields = self.get_through_fields(obj, field)
        fields = field_registry.get(field.rel.to, extra_fields)

        # Find all the relationships for the object passed into this method
        relationships = field.rel.through._default_manager.filter(**{source: obj})

        objects = []
        for relation in relationships.select_related():
            # Serialize the related object first
            related_obj = getattr(relation, target)
            data = DataSerializer().serialize([related_obj])[0]
```

```
            # Then add in the relationship data, but only
            # those that were specified in the field list
            for f in fields & extra_fields:
                data[f] = getattr(relation, f)

            objects.append(data)
        self._current[field.name] = objects
```

Now, when we serialize that same Property object we looked at earlier, you can see that it has information from both Feature and PropertyFeature included in a single dictionary, making it a much more useful representation of the data in our system.

```
{
    "status": 2,
    "address": "123 Main St.",
    "city": "Anywhere",
    "state": "CA",
    "zip": "90909",
    "features": [
        {
            "title": "Shed",
            "description": "Small woodshed near the back fence"
        },
        {
            "title": "Porch",
            "description": "Beautiful wrap-around porch facing north and east"
        }
    ],
    "price": 130000,
    "acreage": 0.25,
    "square_feet": 1248
}
```

Retrieving Data

With our data structure in place, the next logical step is to retrieve data from the database and present it appropriately. This is a job for views, and we can get a lot of mileage out of class-based views in particular. Internally, class-based views are made up of several mix-ins, which are combined as necessary to build up more useful classes. We'll start by creating a mix-in of our own, called ResourceView. This code will go inside the api package in a new file called views.py, alongside the serialization code from the previous sections.

ResourceView

As with most class-based views, most of the work here is about allowing its behavior to be customized for each individual use case. Because the purpose of a ResourceView will be to serialize one or more objects, we can give it the ability to accept a serializer that can be used to perform that step. For good measure, we'll also make it a little easier to use by adding in its own serialize() method, so you don't have to worry about accessing the serializer directly.

```
from django.views.generic import View

class ResourceView(View):
    serializer = None

    def serialize(self, value):
        return self.serializer.serialize(value)
```

Notice that `serializer` is set to the standard JSON serializer by default. We have different serializers for QuerySets and individual objects, and at this point, there's no way to know which one to use. Rather than flip a coin to decide which use will be more common, it's better to just leave it undefined for now and require it to be specified in subclasses or individual URL configurations.

One thing that's missing from the `serialize()` call right now is the ability to specify the output fields. A fair amount of our serialization code is designed to support that feature, so `ResourceView` should expose that behavior to individual URLs for customization. Using None as a default value here will automatically serialize all available fields on whatever model is provided.

```
from django.views.generic import View

class ResourceView(View):
    serializer = None
    fields = None

    def get_fields(self):
        return self.fields

    def serialize(self, value):
        return self.serializer.serialize(value, fields=self.get_fields())
```

We use a `get_fields()` method here instead of just raw attribute access because mix-ins are intended to be subclassed in ways we might not expect. In a later section of this chapter, you'll see a subclass that needs to change how the fields are retrieved by adding a fallback to use if `fields` wasn't specified. We could consider using a `property` in the subclass instead of a method, but that causes its own set of problems if a future subclass of that needs to override that behavior yet again, particularly if it wants to build on the behavior of its parent class. In general, methods are a much more straightforward way to handle subclassing behavior, so they work very well for mix-in classes like this.

ResourceListView

Now we can start working on a real view that's actually useful on its own. Because `ResourceView` is just a mix-in that provides a couple new options and methods, we can combine it with virtually any other Django view we'd like to use. For the most basic case, we can use Django's own `ListView` to provide a collection of objects and simply serialize them on the way out instead of rendering a template.

Because `ListView` is based on `TemplateView`, it already contains a method intended to render a given `context` dictionary into an `HttpResponse` by way of rendering a template. We're not rendering a template, but we do need to return an `HttpResponse`, and the context already gives us everything we need to do so. This allows us to use a custom `render_to_response()` to use a JSON serializer in place of a template renderer to get the right results.

To start, we'll need to specify the serializer we want to use, as the default `ResourceView` doesn't have one assigned to it.

```
from django.views.generic import View, ListView

from api import serializers

# ResourceView is defined here

class ResourceListView(ResourceView, ListView):
    serializer = serializers.QuerySetSerializer()
```

Next, we can override the render_to_response() method. This will need to perform three steps:

- Get the lists of objects out of the provided context
- Serialize those objects into a JSON string
- Return an appropriate HttpResponse

The first two steps are easy to do, given the features we already have in place. The last step can't be just a standard HttpResponse though. We'll need to customize its Content-Type to indicate to the HTTP client that the content consists of a JSON value. The value we need is application/json, and it can be set using the content_type argument of HttpResponse. All these steps combine into a pretty short function.

```
from django.http import HttpResponse
from django.views.generic import View, ListView

from api import serializers

# ResourceView is defined here

class ResourceListView(ResourceView, ListView):
    serializer = serializers.QuerySetSerializer()

    def render_to_response(self, context):
        return HttpResponse(self.serialize(context['object_list']),
            content_type='application/json')
```

Believe it or not, that's all it takes to offer up a list of JSON objects through your new API. All the options available to ListView are available here as well, with the only difference being that the output will be JSON instead of HTML. Here's what an associated URL configuration might look like, so you can see how the various serialization features combine to make this happen.

```
from django.conf.urls import *
from django.contrib.auth.models import User, Group

from api.serializers import serialize_fields
from api.views import ResourceListView
from contacts.models import Contact
from contacts import forms

serialize_fields(Contact, forms.ContactEditorForm.base_fields.keys() + ['user'])
serialize_fields(User, forms.UserEditorForm.base_fields.keys())
serialize_fields(Group, ['name'])
```

```
urlpatterns = patterns('',
    url(r'^$',
        ResourceListView.as_view(
            queryset=Contact.objects.all(),
        ), name='contact_list_api'),
)
```

ResourceDetailView

Next up, we need to provide a detail view for our models, and it works the same as the previous section described. In fact, there are only three differences:

- We need to subclass DetailView instead of ListView.
- We use the SingleObjectSerializer instead of QuerySetSerializer.
- The context variable we need is named 'object' instead of 'object_list'.

With those three changes in place, here's ResourceListView and ResourceDetailView together in the api package's views.py file.

```
from django.http import HttpResponse
from django.views.generic import View, ListView, DetailView

from api import serializers

# ResourceView is defined here

class ResourceListView(ResourceView, ListView):
    serializer = serializers.QuerySetSerializer()

    def render_to_response(self, context):
        return HttpResponse(self.serialize(context['object_list']),
            content_type='application/json')

class ResourceDetailView(ResourceView, DetailView):
    serializer = serializers.SingleObjectSerializer()

    def render_to_response(self, context):
        return HttpResponse(self.serialize(context['object']),
            content_type='application/json')
```

And for good measure, here's the continuation of the URL configuration from the previous section, extended to include a reference to ResourceDetailView as well.

```
from django.conf.urls import *
from django.contrib.auth.models import User, Group

from api.serializers import serialize_fields
from api.views import ResourceListView, ResourceDetailView
from contacts.models import Contact
from contacts import forms
```

```
serialize_fields(Contact, forms.ContactEditorForm.base_fields.keys() + ['user'])
serialize_fields(User, forms.UserEditorForm.base_fields.keys())
serialize_fields(Group, ['name'])

urlpatterns = patterns('',
    url(r'^$',
        ResourceListView.as_view(
            queryset=Contact.objects.all(),
        ), name='contact_list_api'),
    url(r'^(?P<slug>[\w-]+)/$',
        ResourceDetailView.as_view(
            queryset=Contact.objects.all(),
            slug_field='user__username',
        ), name='contact_detail_api'),
)
```

Now What?

The API shown in this chapter is just the beginning, providing anonymous read-only access to a few models. You could extend this in many different directions, adding things like authentication, authorization of external applications, and even updating data through the API using Django's forms.

The tools and techniques discussed in this book go well beyond the official Django documentation, but there's still a lot left unexplored. There are plenty of other innovative ways to use Django and Python.

As you work your way through your own applications, be sure to consider giving back to the Django community. The framework is available because others decided to distribute it freely; by doing the same, you can help even more people uncover more possibilities.

Index

■ D, E

■ F, G

■ H

Druck: KN Digital Printforce GmbH · Schockenriedstraße 37 · 70565 Stuttgart